Fifth Edition

Race and Ethnicity in the United States

Richard T. Schaefer
DePaul University

PEARSON

Prentice
Hall

Upper Saddle River, NJ 07458

Library of Congress Cataloging-in-Publication Data

Schaefer, Richard T.
  Race and ethnicity in the United States / Richard T. Schaefer. — 5th ed.
    p. cm.
  Includes bibliographical references and indexes.
  ISBN 0-13-603034-3 (alk. paper)
  1. Minorities—United States.   2. Prejudices—United States.   3. United States—Ethnic
relations.   4. United States—Race relations.   I. Title.
E184.A1S25 2008
305.800973—dc22   2008025734

Editorial Director: Leah Jewell
Director of Marketing: Brandy Dawson
AVP, Publisher: Nancy Roberts
Editorial Assistant: Nart Varoqua
Editorial Project Manager: Vanessa
  Gennarelli
Director of Marketing: Brandy Dawson
Senior Marketing Manager: Kelly May
**Composition/Full-Service Project
  Management:** TexTech International Pvt. Ltd./
  Shylaja Gattupalli
Production Liaison: Cheryl Keenan
Operations Specialist: Christina Amato
Assistant Marketing Manager: Jessica
  Muraviov

Manager, Rights and Permissions:
  Zina Arabia
Manager, Visual Research: Beth Brenzel
**Manager, Cover Visual Research and
  Permissions:** Karen Sanatar
Image Permission Coordinator:
  Joanne Dippel
Photo Researcher: Kathy Ringrose
Cover Art Director: Jayne Conte
Cover Design: Margaret Kensalaar
Cover Photo: Ryan McVay/Photodisc/
  Getty Images
Supplements Editor: Mayda Bosco
Printer, Binder, and Cover Printer:
  R.R. Donnelley & Sons

This book was set in 10/12 Adobe Garamond.

For permission to use copyrighted material, grateful acknowledgment is made to the copyright
holders listed on page 247, which is considered an extension of this copyright page.

Pearson Education Ltd., London
Pearson Education Singapore, Pte. Ltd
Pearson Education Canada, Inc.
Pearson Education–Japan
Pearson Education Australia PTY, Limited

Pearson Education North Asia, Ltd., Hong Kong
Pearson Educación de Mexico, S.A. de C.V.
Pearson Education Malaysia, Pte. Ltd.
Pearson Education Upper Saddle River,
  New Jersey

10 9 8 7 6 5 4 3 2 1

ISBN-13: 978-0-13-603034-8
ISBN-10:   0-13-603034-3

To my brother, Doug, a teacher of college students
for over forty years

Contents

Preface

"Minorities Majority" read first-page newspaper headlines in Fall 2007, when the Census Bureau released their annual population estimates. Now in 300 counties, Latinos, African Americans, Asian Americans, Native American tribal members, and others outnumber Whites who are not Hispanic. However, do these groups wield the power in all these counties? In any of these counties? By 2008, the minority population—that is, other than non-Hispanic single-race whites—now exceeds 102 million. More than one in every three Americans is a minority. In four states, Hawaii, New Mexico, California, and Texas—and the District of Columbia—minorities make up a majority of the population.

Does the United States' becoming more diverse signify a significant advancement in the quality of life of people of color relative to gains made by White Americans? These are the real questions, and rarely are they asked and almost never answered. Some people who have not followed these trends seemed stunned that several years ago, Orange County, surf n' sun capital of southern California and home of Disneyland, became a minority majority. Although these events may not signify a major shift in social inequality among groups, they do underscore the importance of being familiar with the nature of race and ethnicity in the United States.

Race and ethnicity are an important part of the national agenda. Race is not a static phenomenon, and although it has always been a part of the social reality, specific issues may change over time; but they continue to play out against a backdrop of discrimination that is rooted in the social structure and changing population composition, as influenced by immigration patterns and reproduction patterns.

We continue to be reminded about the importance of the social construction of many aspects of racial and ethnic relations. What constitutes a race in terms of identity? What meaning do race and ethnicity have amid the growing number of interracial marriages and marriages across cultural boundaries? Beyond the spectrum of race and ethnicity, we see the socially constructed meaning attached to all religions as members debate who is the "true" keeper of the faith. The very issue of national identity is also a part of the agenda. The public and politicians alike ask, "How many immigrants can we accept?" and "How much should be done to make up for past discrimination?" We are also witnessing the emergence of race, ethnicity, and national identity as global issues.

Changes in the Fifth Edition

As with all previous editions, every line, every source, and every number have been rechecked for their currency. We pride ourselves on providing the most current information possible to document the patterns in intergroup relations in the United States

Relevant scholarly findings in a variety of disciplines, including economics, anthropology, and communication sciences, have been incorporated. The feature "Listen to Our Voices" appears in every chapter. Three of these selections have been updated as indicated in bold:

Listen to Our Voices

- Problem of the Color Line, W. E. B. Du Bois (Chapter 1)
- Gangsters, Gooks, Geishas, and Geeks, Helen Zia (Chapter 2)
- Of Race and Risk, Patricia J. Williams (Chapter 3)
- **The Wall that Keeps Illegal Workers In, Douglas S. Massey (Chapter 4)**
- **I Was Born in Tirana, Harallamb Terba (Chapter 5)**
- **From Kawasaki to Chicago, Miku Ishii (Chapter 6)**

This edition includes three new selections, indicated in bold, in the "Research Focus" feature that highlights the relevant research on a topic touched upon in each of the first five chapters.

Research Focus

- Measuring Multiculturalism (Chapter 1)
- **Few of My Best Friends Are ... (Chapter 2)**
- Discrimination in Job Seeking (Chapter 3)
- **Assimilation May Be Hazardous to Your Health (Chapter 4)**
- **Immigrants: Yesterday and Today (Chapter 5)**

The Internet Resource Directory at the conclusion of the book that offers current, relevant Internet sites has been expanded with over a hundred new entries.

A new feature in all chapters is "Ask Yourself" that ties selected images in the book to the reader's own experiences. For example, in Chapter 2, an image shows a youthful member of a hate group. The "Ask Yourself" features read "Suppose you encounter a person whose prejudices is obvious. Will you say or do anything? What if it is a friend who speaks despairingly of all members of some ethnic or religious group? Will you speak out? When do you speak out?"

The fifth edition includes the following additions and changes:

Chapter 1

- New key terms—"resegregation" and "matrix of domination"
- The growing complexity of race in the United States is reflected in a new section on multiracial identity.
- A new U.S. map showing majority minority states
- The intersection of race, gender, class, and other social factors receives attention from the beginning with the presentation of Patricia Collins' matrix of domination accompanied by Figure 1.9 designed by the author of this textbook to facilitate understanding for the reader.

Chapter 2

- New key term—"color-blind racism"
- In an effort to bring the concept of "social distance" to today's audience, this is a new extended coverage on what recent data about interracial friendships tell us about friendship patterns today that cross ethnic and racial boundaries.
- Prejudice persists even if it is more subtle as described in the new section on "Color-Blind Racism"
- Figure 2.3 is new and gives the 2007 national survey data on how Latinos, Asian Americans, and African Americans view race in the United States.
- Trying to emphasize a more activist role for the reader, a new section entitled "Ways to Fight Hate" has been added.
- New Research Focus—"Few of My Best Friends Are ..."

Chapter 3

- New key term—"wealth"
- A new section on wealth inequality has been added to the presentation on income disparity among racial and ethnic minorities.
- Thought-provoking cartoon has been added related to Katrina—"I'm beginning to wonder if the water will ever recede."

Chapter 4

- New key terms—"chain immigration" and "mixed status"
- Both global immigration and the special role that women play in immigration received extended coverage with new sections for both of these important topics.
- Figure 4.2 features U.S. map showing foreign-born data

- New Research Focus—"Assimilation May Be Hazardous to Your Health"
- New Listen to Our Voices—"The Wall that Keeps Illegal Workers In," by Douglas S. Massey
- Two provocative cartoons—one shows shoppers in a grocery store commenting "It says this orange juice is made with fruit picked entirely by American workers. It's 43 dollars" while the other shows American Indians building a wall at Plymouth Block blocking the pilgrims with one of the Europeans saying "They say they're building a wall because too many of us enter illegally and won't learn their language or assimilate into their culture."

Chapter 5

- New key terms—"White privilege" and "blended identity"
- The growing diversity of the religious landscape is reflected in the new section on Islam in the United States
- New sections on Irish Americans and Polish Americans supplement the revised, update sect on Italian Americans
- New section entitled "Islam in the United States"
- New Figure 5.1 comparing immigration patterns over time of Poles, Irish, and Italians
- New Figure 5.4 featuring a U.S. map "People Who Speak English Less than " 'Very Well' "
- New Figure 5.8 illustrating Blended Identity of Muslim Americans
- New Research Focus—Immigrants: Yesterday and Today
- New Listen to Our Voices—"I Was Born in Tirana," by Harallamb Terba

Chapter 6

- New key term—"acting White"
- New Section title of "Melting Pot and Kaleidoscope"
- New Table 6.1 listing the top ten states in terms of population concentration for six different racial and ethnic groups
- A section on "acting White" has been added to complement the presentation of the model minority stereotype
- New Listen to Our Voices—"From Kawasaki to Chicago," by Miku Ishii

In addition, tables, figures, maps, and political cartoons have been updated.

Features to Aid Students

Several features are included in the text to facilitate student learning. A chapter outline appears at the beginning of each chapter and is followed by "Highlights," a short section alerting students to important issues and topics to be addressed. To help students review, each chapter ends with a summary

conclusion. The key terms are highlighted in bold when they are first introduced in the text and are listed with page numbers at the end of each chapter.
The Intergroup Relations Continuum first presented in Chapter 1 is repeated
again in Chapter 5 to reinforce major concepts while addressing the unique
social circumstances of individual racial and ethnic groups.

In addition, there is an end-of-book glossary with full definitions referenced
to page numbers. This edition includes both "Review Questions" and "Critical
Thinking Questions." The Review Questions are intended to remind the reader
of major points, whereas the Critical Thinking Questions encourage students to
think more deeply about some of the major issues raised in the chapter.
Updated Internet exercises allow students to do some critical thinking and
research on the Web. An Internet Resource Directory has been expanded to
allow access to the latest electronic sources. An extensive illustration program,
which includes maps and political cartoons, expands the text discussion, and
provokes thought.

Ancillary Materials

The ancillary materials that accompany this textbook have been carefully created to enhance the topics being discussed.

Instructor's Manual with Tests (ISBN 013603036X)   This carefully prepared
manual includes chapter overviews, key term identification exercises, discussion questions, topics for class discussion, audiovisual resources, and test
questions in both multiple-choice and essay format.

TestGEN-EQ (ISBN 0136030386)   This computerized software allows instructors
to create their own personalized examinations, to edit any or all of the existing
test questions, and to add new questions. Other special features of this program
include random generation of test questions, creation of alternate versions of the
same test, a scrambling question sequence, and test preview before printing.

MySocKit (ISBN 0136030378)   MySocKit is an electronic supplement that offers
book-specific learning objectives, chapter summaries, flashcards, and practice
tests as well as video clips, and activities to aid student learning and comprehen-
sion. Also included in MySocKit are Research Navigator™ and Web links giving
you access to powerful and reliable research material.

ABC News/Prentice Hall Video Library for Race and Ethnic Relations
(ISBN 0131791079)   Selected video segments from award-winning ABC News
programs such as *Nightline, ABC World News Tonight,* and *20/20* accompany
topics are featured in the text. An Instructor's Guide is also available. Please
contact your Prentice Hall representative for more details.

Pearson's Guide to Research Navigator™ Sociology (ISBN 0205633404)
The easiest way to do research! This guide focuses on using **Research**

Navigator™—Prentice Hall's own gateway to databases including the Search-by-Subject™ Archive, ContentSelect™ Academic Journal Database powered by EBSCO, The *Financial Times*, and the "Best of the Web" Link Library. It also includes extensive appendices on documenting online sources and on avoiding plagiarism. This supplement—which includes an access code to the Research Navigator™ Web site—is available free when packaged with *Race and Ethnicity in the United States, fifth edition.*

The brochure "10 Ways to Fight Hate" (ISBN 0130281468) produced by the Southern Poverty Law Center, the leading hate-crime and crime-watch organization in the United States, walks students through ten steps that they can take on their own campus or in their own neighborhood to fight hate every day. It comes free when packaged with *Race and Ethnicity in the United States, fifth edition.*

Acknowledgments

The fifth edition benefited from the thoughtful reaction of my students in classes. My faculty colleague Kiljoong Kim of DePaul University provided data analysis of the General Social Survey and Census Bureau data sets. Suzanne Hammond, a student at DePaul, assisted with special tasks related to the preparation of the manuscript.

The fifth edition was improved by the suggestions of:

E. M. Beck	University of Georgia
Deborah Brunson	University of North Carolina, Wilmington
Jac D. Bulk	University of Wisconsin, La Crosse
Ada Shu-Ju Cheng	DePaul University
Roberta Rosenberg Farber	Yeshiva University
Celestino Fernandez	University of Arizona
Black Hawk Hancock	DePaul University
S. Homes Hogue	Mississippi State University
Tomas R. Jimenez	University of California, San Diego
Karen Leonard	University of California, Irvine
Susan Lobo	University of Arizona
Ron Loewe	Mississippi State University
Jackquice Smith-Mahdi	Washburn University
Karyn McKinney Marvasti	Pennsylvania State University, Altoona
Efren N. Padilla	California State University, Hayward
Monique Payne	DePaul University
Kristen M. Wallingford	Davidson College
Carol Ward	Brigham Young University
William Wei	University of Colorado, Boulder
Diane L. Wolf	University of California, Davis
Earl Wright II	Texas Southern University

I would also like to thank my editors, Vanessa Gennarelli and Nancy Roberts, for assisting with this edition. Publisher Nancy Roberts has been a true colleague in this endeavor for several editions. Production Liaison Cheryl Keenan was particularly responsive to developing an effective appearance to the book.

The truly exciting challenge of writing and researching has always been for me an enriching experience, mostly because of the supportive home I share with my wife, Sandy. She knows so well my appreciation and gratitude, now as in the past and in the future.

Richard T. Schaefer
schaeferrt@aol.com
www.schaefersociology.net

About the Author

Richard T. Schaefer grew up in Chicago at a time when neighborhoods were going through transitions in ethnic and racial composition. He found himself increasingly intrigued by what was happening, how people were reacting, and how these changes were affecting neighborhoods and people's jobs. In high school, he took a course in sociology. His interest in social issues caused him to gravitate to more sociology courses at Northwestern University, where he eventually received a B.A. in sociology.

"Originally as an undergraduate I thought I would go on to law school and become a lawyer. But after taking a few sociology courses, I found myself wanting to learn more about what sociologists studied and was fascinated by the kinds of questions they raised," Dr. Schaefer says. "Perhaps the most fascinating and, to me, relevant to the 1960s was the intersection of race, gender, and social class." This interest led him to obtain his M.A. and Ph.D. in sociology from the University of Chicago. Dr. Schaefer's continuing interest in race relations led him to write his master's thesis on the membership of the Ku Klux Klan and his doctoral thesis on racial prejudice and race relations in Great Britain.

Dr. Schaefer went on to become a professor of sociology. He has taught sociology and courses on multiculturalism for thirty years. He has been invited to give special presentations to students and faculty on racial and ethnic diversity in Illinois, Indiana, Missouri, North Carolina, Ohio, and Texas.

Dr. Schaefer is the author of *Racial and Ethnic Groups,* eleventh edition (Prentice Hall, 2007). Dr. Schaefer is the general editor of the three-volume *Encyclopedia of Race, Ethnicity, and Society* (2008). He is also the author of the eleventh edition of *Sociology* (2007), the eighth edition of *Sociology: A Brief Introduction* (2009), and the fourth edition of *Sociology Matters* (2009). Schaefer coauthored with William Zellner, the eighth edition of *Extraordinary Groups* (2008). His articles and book reviews have appeared in many journals, including *American Journal of Sociology, Phylon: A Review of Race and Culture, Contemporary Sociology, Sociology and Social Research, Sociological Quarterly,* and *Teaching Sociology.* He served as president of the Midwest Sociological Society from 1994 to 1995. In recognition of his achievements in undergraduate teaching, he was named Vincent de Paul Professor of Sociology in 2004.

1 Understanding Race and Ethnicity

CHAPTER OUTLINE

——————————————⟨ HIGHLIGHTS ⟩——————————————

M inority groups are subordinated in terms of power and privilege to the majority, or dominant, group. A minority is defined not by being outnumbered but by five characteristics: unequal treatment, distinguishing physical or cultural traits, involuntary membership, awareness of subordination, and in-group marriage. Subordinate groups are classified in terms of race, ethnicity, religion, and gender. The social importance of race is derived from a process of racial formation; any biological significance is relatively unimportant to society. The theoretical perspectives of functionalism, conflict theory, and labeling offer insights into the sociology of intergroup relations.

Immigration, annexation, and colonialism are processes that may create subordinate groups. Other processes such as extermination and expulsion may remove the presence of a subordinate group. Significant for racial and ethnic oppression in the United States today is the distinction between assimilation and pluralism. Assimilation demands subordinate-group conformity to the dominant group, and pluralism implies mutual respect between diverse groups.

Minority women are also more likely to be poor, which creates what sociologists have termed the matrix of domination. Although dominant groups seek to define the social landscape, groups who experience unequal treatment have in the past resisted power and continue to do so today and seek significant social change.

Walking into the room together are the son of a German immigrant from Texas, a Mormon, an African American, a Baptist preacher, a White woman, a Latino, a Roman Catholic, and the White son of a North Carolina textile mill worker. Sounds like the beginning of a joke, but actually, it was the gathering in New Hampshire in 2008 at a televised debate of all the candidates for the

Democrat and Republican contenders for president in 2008. Was this a transforming moment or a well overdue moment for a diverse country?

Race and ethnicity is exceedingly complex in the United States. Consider the millions of people identifying themselves as biracial or multiracial. Witness the furor over radio host Don Imus's comments about Black female college basketball players that led to his firing only to be rehired to a multimillion dollar contract months later. We have a landscape in metropolitan Los Angeles, which marks Chinatown, Koreatown, Little Ethiopia, Historic Filipinotown, Little Saigon, Saigon Town, and Thai Town.

Natural disasters have not been traditionally seen as relevant to race and ethnicity, but so they emerged. We had Hurricane Katrina along the Gulf Coast in 2005 and the vivid news images that showed disproportionately African American residents of New Orleans seemingly left behind. As years passed, their relocation still seemed to be slow in coming. Then, in 2007, wildfires spread across southern California and again, the response seemed to some to come faster to the rich enclaves of Malibu than the poorer areas populated by Latinos and American Indians (Lopez 2007).

Who would have expected the hangman's noose to reemerge in the twenty-first century? In 2006, an uproar began when Black students at a high school in Jena, Louisiana, said they should be allowed to sit under what was traditionally known as the "White tree" in the courtyard. School officials said of course, but the next day, nooses hung from the tree. The White boys responsible were suspended, but no hate crime charges were filed. In the stormy aftermath, fights broke out including one where Black students beat up a White youth who was treated at a hospital, released, and attended a school event that evening. The Black juveniles were charged as adults for attempted murder.

Although racial and ethnic minorities do not dominate the decision-making process in the United States, the growing diversity of the nation is impossible to deny virtually anywhere in the nation. In 2008, Piyush "Bobby" Jindal, the son of immigrants from India, was sworn in as governor of Louisiana at the age of 36. Here, he is shown addressing the National Press Club in Washington DC.

Was this justice? In response to massive demonstrations drawing protesters from across the nation, the charges were reduced. But the use of the noose was not limited to youth. The next fall, an African American college professor found a noose on the doorknob of her office door. In 2008, at a time when Tiger Woods dominated professional golf tournaments, a commentator on the Golf Channel jokingly suggested young players faced with the challenge should "lynch him in a back alley." Woods, who personally knew the commentator, said he took no offence, but many did when *Golfweek* magazine displayed a noose on its cover to discuss the event. In response, the publisher fired the editor, and the Golf Channel suspended its on-the-air reporter. Action was taken, but how is it that these events still unfold in the first place? (Kupper Jr. 2008).

What is the welcome mat like for immigrants in the United States? There is no single response to the complexity of immigration in days past or today. Hazelton, Pennsylvania, impatient over federal inaction, adopted ordinances in 2006 to bar illegal immigrants from working or renting homes. Shortly after, 100 other communities adopted similar measures, but in 2007, a federal judge struck down the actions as interfering with federal jurisdiction in such matters. At the very same time, Fort Wayne, Indiana, was welcoming another 300 people from the Darfur region of Sudan. The first Darfur families arrived in the late 1990s attracted by jobs, an extensive web of charities, and volunteer church groups. They occasionally encounter stares when women wear a Muslim headdress while at factory jobs and when eating with their hands, as is their tradition, at buffet restaurants, but mostly they have found peace and a welcoming spirit (Preston 2007c; Saulny 2007).

Racial and ethnic tensions are not limited to the real world but are also alive and well in the virtual world. Hate groups, anti-Jewish organizations, and even the Ku Klux Klan thrive on Web sites. Such fringe groups, enjoying their First Amendment rights, spread their message in many languages globally via the Internet, whereas the creation of such hate sites are banned in Canada, Europe, and elsewhere. Facebook has emerged as a significant way in which people interact, but it also is a means to learn about others by their online profile. By 2007, colleges and universities cited Facebook as the major source of prospective students (or their parents) requesting roommate changes even before getting campus because of the race, religion, or sexual orientation of their intended roommate (Collura 2007; Working 2007).

The United States is a very diverse nation, as shown in Table 1.1. In 2006, about 19 percent of the population were members of racial minorities and about another 15 percent were Hispanic. These percentages represent one out of three people in the United States, without counting White ethnic groups. As shown in Figure 1.1, between 2006 and 2100 the population in the United States is expected to increase from 34 percent Black, Hispanic, Asian, and Native American to 60 percent. Although the composition of the population is changing, the problems of prejudice, discrimination, and mistrust remain.

Table 1.1 Racial and Ethnic Groups in the United States, 2006

Classification	Number in Thousands	Percentage of Total Population
Racial Groups		
Whites (non-Hispanic)	198,744	66.3
Blacks/African Americans	37,051	12.4
Native Americans, Alaskan Native	2,369	0.8
Asian Americans	13,100	4.4
Chinese	3,090	1.0
Filipinos	2,328	0.8
Asian Indians	2,482	0.8
Vietnamese	1,476	0.5
Koreans	1,335	0.4
Japanese	830	0.3
Pacific Islanders and other Asian Americans	1,559	.5
Ethnic Groups		
White ancestry (single or mixed, non-Hispanic)		
Germans	50,764	17.0
Irish	35,976	12.0
English	28,339	9.4
Italians	17,829	6.0
Scottish and Scotch-Irish	11,400	3.8
Poles	10,025	3.3
French	9,651	3.2
Jews	6,452	2.2
Hispanics (or Latinos)	44,252	14.8
Mexican Americans	28,339	9.5
Puerto Ricans	3,988	1.3
Cubans	1,520	.5
Salvadorans	1,300	0.4
Dominicans	1,100	.4
Other Hispanics	8,005	2.7
TOTAL (ALL GROUPS)	299,398	

Note: Percentages do not total 100 percent, and subheads do not add up to figures in major heads because of overlap between groups (e.g., Polish American Jews or people of mixed ancestry, such as Irish and Italian). White ancestry is for 2000 and percentages based on 2000 total population.

Source: Author estimates and based on Bureau of the Census 2006 American Community Survey, Tables DP-1 and R0203 accessible at http://factfinder.census.gov; Sheskin and Dashefsky 2006.

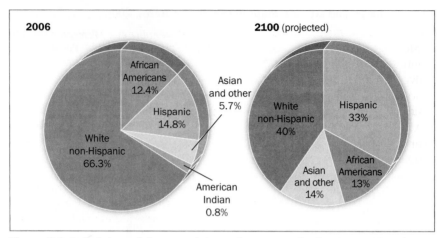

Figure 1.1 Population of the United States by Race and Ethnicity, 2006 and 2100 (Projected)

According to projections by the Census Bureau, the proportion of residents of the United States who are White and non-Hispanic will decrease significantly by the year 2050. By contrast, there will be a striking rise in the proportion of both Hispanic Americans and Asian Americans.

Source: Author's analysis based on American Community Survey 2006 and Bureau of the Census 2004.

What Is a Subordinate Group?

Identifying a subordinate group or a minority in a society seems to be a simple task. In the United States, the groups readily identified as minorities—Blacks and Native Americans, for example—are outnumbered by non-Blacks and non–Native Americans. However, minority status is not necessarily the result of being outnumbered. A social minority need not be a mathematical one. A **minority group** is a subordinate group whose members have significantly less control or power over their own lives than do the members of a dominant or majority group. In sociology, *minority* means the same as *subordinate,* and *dominant* is used interchangeably with majority.

Confronted with evidence that a particular minority in the United States is subordinate to the majority, some people respond, "Why not? After all, this is a democracy, so the majority rules." However, the subordination of a minority involves more than its inability to rule over society. A member of a subordinate or minority group experiences a narrowing of life's opportunities—for success, education, wealth, the pursuit of happiness—that goes beyond any personal shortcoming he or she may have. A minority group does not share in proportion to its numbers what a given society, such as the United States, defines as valuable.

Being superior in numbers does not guarantee a group control over its destiny and ensure majority status. In 1920, the majority of people in Mississippi and South Carolina were African Americans. Yet African Americans did not have as much control over their lives as Whites, let alone control of the states of Mississippi and South Carolina. Throughout the United States today are counties or neighborhoods in which the majority of people are African American, Native American, or Hispanic, but White Americans are the dominant force. Nationally, 50.7 percent of the population is female, but males still dominate positions of authority and wealth well beyond their numbers.

A minority or subordinate group has five characteristics: unequal treatment, distinguishing physical or cultural traits, involuntary membership, awareness of subordination, and in-group marriage (Wagley and Harris 1958):

1. Members of a minority experience unequal treatment and have less power over their lives than members of a dominant group have over theirs. Prejudice, discrimination, segregation, and even extermination create this social inequality.

2. Members of a minority group share physical or cultural characteristics that distinguish them from the dominant group, such as skin color or language. Each society has its own arbitrary standard for determining which characteristics are most important in defining dominant and minority groups.

3. Membership in a dominant or minority group is not voluntary: People are born into the group. A person does not choose to be African American or White.

4. Minority-group members have a strong sense of group solidarity. William Graham Sumner, writing in 1906, noted that people make distinctions between members of their own group (the in-group) and everyone else (the out-group). When a group is the object of long-term prejudice and discrimination, the feeling of "us versus them" often becomes intense.

5. Members of a minority generally marry others from the same group. A member of a dominant group often is unwilling to join a supposedly inferior minority by marrying one of its members. In addition, the minority group's sense of solidarity encourages marriage within the group and discourages marriage to outsiders.

Although "minority" is not about numbers, there is no denying that the majority is diminishing in size relative to the growing diversity of racial and ethnic groups. In Figure 1.2, we see that more and more states have close to a majority of non-Whites or Latinos and that several states have already reached that point today.

Types of Subordinate Groups

There are four types of minority or subordinate groups. All four, except where noted, have the five properties previously outlined. The four criteria for classifying minority groups are race, ethnicity, religion, and gender.

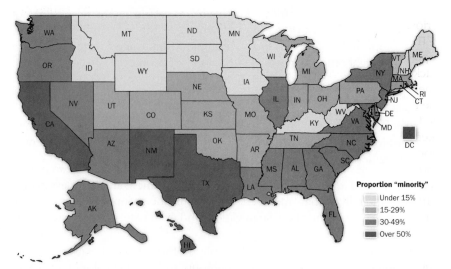

Figure 1.2 Race and Ethnic Presence by State (Projected)
According to projections by the Census Bureau, the proportion of residents of the United States who are White and non-Hispanic will decrease significantly by the year 2050. By contrast, there will be a striking rise in the proportion of both Hispanic Americans and Asian Americans.
Source: 2004 data released by the Bureau of the Census 2005b.

Racial Groups

The term **racial group** is reserved for minorities and the corresponding majorities that are socially set apart because of obvious physical differences. Notice the two crucial words in the definition: *obvious* and *physical*. What is obvious? Hair color? Shape of an earlobe? Presence of body hair? To whom are these differences obvious, and why? Each society defines what it finds obvious.

In the United States, skin color is one obvious difference. On a cold winter day when one has clothing covering all but one's head, however, skin color may be less obvious than hair color. Yet people in the United States have learned informally that skin color is important and hair color is unimportant. We need to say more than that. In the United States, people have traditionally classified and classify themselves as either Black or White. There is no in-between state except for people readily identified as Native Americans or Asian Americans. Later in this chapter, we will explore this issue more deeply and see how such assumptions have very complex implications.

Other societies use skin color as a standard but may have a more elaborate system of classification. In Brazil, where hostility between races is less than in the United States, numerous categories identify people on the basis of skin color. In the United States, a person is Black or White. In Brazil, a variety of terms, such as cafuso, mazombo, preto, and escuro, are applied to describe various combinations of skin color, facial features, and hair texture.

The designation of a racial group emphasizes physical differences as opposed to cultural distinctions. In the United States, minority races include Blacks, Native Americans (or American Indians), Japanese Americans, Chinese Americans, Arab Americans, Filipinos, Hawaiians, and other Asian peoples. The issue of race and racial differences has been an important one, not only in the United States but also throughout the entire sphere of European influence. Later in this chapter, we will examine race and its significance more closely. We should not forget that Whites are a race too. As we will consider in Chapter 5, who is White has been subject to change over time as certain European groups were felt historically not to deserve being considered White, but over time, partly to compete against a growing Black population, the "Whiting" of some European Americans has occurred.

Some racial groups may also have unique cultural traditions, as we can readily see in the many Chinatowns throughout the United States. For racial groups, however, the physical distinctiveness and not the cultural differences generally proves to be the barrier to acceptance by the host society. For example, Chinese Americans who are faithful Protestants and know the names of all the members of the Baseball Hall of Fame may be bearers of American culture. Yet these Chinese Americans are still part of a minority because they are seen as physically different.

Ethnic Groups

Ethnic minority groups are differentiated from the dominant group on the basis of cultural differences, such as language, attitudes toward marriage and parenting, and food habits. **Ethnic groups** are groups set apart from others because of their national origin or distinctive cultural patterns.

Ethnic groups in the United States include a grouping that we call Hispanics or Latinos, which includes Mexican Americans, Puerto Ricans, Cubans, and other Latin Americans in the United States. Hispanics can be either Black or White, as in the case of a dark-skinned Puerto Rican who may be taken as Black in central Texas but be viewed as a Puerto Rican in New York City. The ethnic group category also includes White ethnics, such as Irish Americans, Polish Americans, and Norwegian Americans.

The cultural traits that make groups distinctive usually originate from their homelands or, for Jews, from a long history of being segregated and prohibited from becoming a part of the host society. Once in the United States, an immigrant group may maintain distinctive cultural practices through associations, clubs, and worship. Ethnic enclaves such as a Little Haiti or a Greektown in urban areas also perpetuate cultural distinctiveness.

Ethnicity continues to be important, as recent events in Bosnia and other parts of Eastern Europe have demonstrated. Almost a century ago, African

LISTEN TO OUR VOICES

Problem of the Color Line

W. E. B. Du Bois

In the metropolis of the modern world, in this the closing year of the nineteenth century, there has been assembled a congress of men and women of African blood, to deliberate solemnly upon the present situation and outlook of the darker races of mankind. The problem of the twentieth century is the problem of the color line, the question as to how far differences of race—which show themselves chiefly in the color of the skin and the texture of the hair—will hereafter be made the basis of denying to over half the world the right of sharing to their utmost ability the opportunities and privileges of modern civilization . . .

To be sure, the darker races are today the least advanced in culture according to European standards. This has not, however, always been the case in the past, and certainly the world's history, both ancient and modern, has given many instances of no despicable ability and capacity among the blackest races of men.

In any case, the modern world must remember that in this age when the ends of the world are being brought so near together, the millions of black men in Africa, America, and Islands of the Sea, not to speak of the brown and yellow myriads elsewhere, are bound to have a great influence upon the world in the future, by reason of sheer numbers and physical contact. If now the world of culture bends itself towards giving Negroes and other dark men the largest and broadest opportunity for education and self-development, then this contact and influence is bound to have a beneficial effect upon the world and hasten human progress. But if, by reason of carelessness, prejudice, greed and injustice, the black world is to be exploited and ravished and degraded, the results must be deplorable, if not fatal—not simply to them, but to the high ideals of justice, freedom and culture which a thousand years of Christian civilization have held before Europe. . . .

Let the world take no backward step in that slow but sure progress which has successively refused to let the spirit of class, of caste, of privilege, or of birth, debar from life, liberty, and the pursuit of happiness a striving human soul.

Let not color or race be a feature of distinction between white and black men, regardless of worth or ability. . . .

Thus we appeal with boldness and confidence to the Great Powers of the civilized world, trusting in the wide spirit of humanity, and the deep sense of justice of our age, for a generous recognition of the righteousness of our cause.

Source: From W. E. B. Du Bois 1900 [1969a], *ABC of Color,* pp. 20–21, 23. Copyright 1969 by International Publishers.

American sociologist W. E. B. Du Bois, addressing in 1900 an audience at a world antislavery convention in London, called attention to the overwhelming importance of the color line throughout the world. In "Listen to Our Voices," we read the remarks of Du Bois, the first Black person to receive a doctorate from Harvard, who later helped to organize the National Association for the Advancement of Colored People (NAACP). Du Bois's observances give us a historic perspective on the struggle for equality. We can look ahead, knowing how far we have come and speculating on how much further we have to go.

Religious Groups

Association with a religion other than the dominant faith is the third basis for minority-group status. In the United States, Protestants, as a group, outnumber members of all other religions. Roman Catholics form the largest minority religion. Chapter 5 focuses on the increasing Judeo-Christian-Islamic diversity of the United States. For people who are not a part of the Christian tradition, such as followers of Islam, allegiance to the faith often is misunderstood and stigmatizes people. This stigmatization became especially widespread and legitimated by government action in the aftermath of the attacks of September 11, 2001.

Religious minorities include groups such as the Church of Jesus Christ of Latter-day Saints (the Mormons), Jehovah's Witnesses, Amish, Muslims, and Buddhists. Cults or sects associated with practices such as animal sacrifice, doomsday prophecy, demon worship, or the use of snakes in a ritualistic fashion would also constitute minorities. Jews are excluded from this category and placed among ethnic groups. Culture is a more important defining trait for Jewish people worldwide than is religious dogma. Jewish Americans share a cultural tradition that goes beyond theology. In this sense, it is appropriate to view them as an ethnic group rather than as members of a religious faith.

Gender Groups

Gender is another attribute that creates dominant and subordinate groups. Males are the social majority; females, although numerous, are relegated to the position of the social minority, a subordinate status. Women are considered a minority even though they do not exhibit all the characteristics outlined earlier (e.g., there is little in-group marriage). Women encounter prejudice and discrimination and are physically distinguishable. Group membership is involuntary, and many women have developed a sense of sisterhood. Women who are members of racial and ethnic minorities face a special challenge to achieving equality. They suffer from greater inequality because they belong to two separate minority groups: a racial or ethnic group plus a subordinate gender group. We will explore this aspect of domination–subordination later in this chapter.

SECRET ASIAN MAN by Tak Toyoshima

Given the diversity in the nation, it is not always self-evident how people view themselves in terms of ethnic and racial background as the cartoonist Tak Toyoshima humorously points out.

Source: Secret Asian Man (c) Tak Toyoshima, distributed by UFS, Inc.

Other Subordinate Groups

This book focuses on groups that meet a set of criteria for subordinate status. People encounter prejudice or are excluded from full participation in society for many reasons. Racial, ethnic, religious, and gender barriers are the main ones, but there are others. Age, disability status, and sexual orientation are among some other factors that are used to subordinate groups of people.

Does Race Matter?

We see people around us—some of whom may look quite different from us. Do these differences matter? The simple answer is no, but because so many people have for so long acted as if difference in physical characteristics as well as geographic origin and shared culture do matter, distinct groups have been created in people's minds. Race has many meanings for many people. Often, these meanings are inaccurate and based on theories discarded by scientists generations ago. As we will see, race is a socially constructed concept (Young 2003).

Biological Meaning

The way the term *race* has been used by some people to apply to human beings lacks any scientific meaning. We cannot identify distinctive physical characteristics for groups of human beings the same way that scientists distinguish one animal species from another. The idea of **biological race** is based on the mistaken notion of a genetically isolated human group.

Absence of Pure Races   Even among past proponents who believed that sharp, scientific divisions exist among humans, there were endless debates over what the races of the world were. Given people's frequent migration, exploration, and invasions, pure genetic types have not existed for some time, if they ever did. There are no mutually exclusive races. Skin color among African Americans varies tremendously, as it does among White Americans. There is even an overlapping of dark-skinned Whites and light-skinned African Americans. If we grouped people by genetic resistance to malaria and by fingerprint patterns, Norwegians and many African groups would be of the same race. If we grouped people by some digestive capacities, some Africans, Asians, and southern Europeans would be of one group and West Africans and northern Europeans of another (Leehotz 1995; Shanklin 1994).

Biologically there are no pure, distinct races. For example, blood type cannot distinguish racial groups with any accuracy. Furthermore, applying pure racial types to humans is problematic because of interbreeding. Contemporary studies of DNA on a global basis have determined that 85 percent of human genetic variation is within "local populations" such as within the French or within Afghan people. Another 5 to 9 percent is between local populations thought to be similar in public opinion like the Koreans and Chinese. The remaining 6 to 9 percent of total human variation is what we think of today as constituting races and accounts for skin color, hair form, nose shape, and so forth (Lewontin 2005).

Research as a part of the Human Genome Project mapping human DNA has only served to confirm genetic diversity with differences within traditionally regarded racial groups (e.g., Black Africans) much greater than that between groups (e.g., between Black Africans and Europeans). Research has also been conducted to determine whether personality characteristics such as temperament and nervous habits are inherited among minority groups. Not surprisingly, the question of whether races have different innate levels of intelligence has led to the most explosive controversy (Bamshad and Olson 2003).

Intelligence Tests   Typically, intelligence is measured as an **intelligence quotient (IQ),** the ratio of a person's mental age to his or her chronological age, multiplied by 100, where 100 represents average intelligence and higher scores represent greater intelligence. It should be noted that there is little consensus over just what intelligence is, other than as defined by such IQ tests.

Intelligence tests are adjusted for a person's age, so that 10-year-olds take a very different test from someone 20 years old. Although research shows that certain learning strategies can improve a person's IQ, generally IQ remains stable as one ages.

A great deal of debate continues over the accuracy of these tests. Are they biased toward people who come to the tests with knowledge similar to that of the test writers? Consider the following two questions used on standard tests.

1. Runner: marathon (A) envoy: embassy, (B) oarsman: regatta, (C) martyr: massacre, (D) referee: tournament.

2. Your mother sends you to a store to get a loaf of bread. The store is closed. What should you do? (A) return home, (B) go to the next store, (C) wait until it opens, (D) ask a stranger for advice.

Both correct answers are B. But is a lower-class youth likely to know, in the first question, what a regatta is? Skeptics argue that such test questions do not truly measure intellectual potential. Inner-city youths often have been shown to respond with A to the second question because that may be the only store with which the family has credit. Youths in rural areas, where the next store may be miles away, are also unlikely to respond with the designated correct answer. The issue of culture bias in tests remains an unresolved concern. The most recent research shows that differences in intelligence scores between Blacks and Whites are almost eliminated when adjustments are made for social and economic characteristics (Brooks-Gunn, Klebanov, and Duncan 1996; Herrnstein and Murray 1994, 30; Kagan 1971; Young 2003).

The second issue, trying to associate these results with certain subpopulations such as races, also has a long history. In the past, a few have contended that Whites have more intelligence on average than Blacks. All researchers agree that within-group differences are greater than any speculated differences between groups. The range of intelligence among, for example, Korean Americans is much greater than any average difference between them as a group and Japanese Americans.

The third issue relates to the subpopulations themselves. If Blacks or Whites are not mutually exclusive biologically, how can there be measurable differences? Many Whites and most Blacks have mixed ancestry that complicates any supposed inheritance of intelligence issue. Both groups reflect a rich heritage of very dissimilar populations, from Swedes to Slovaks and Zulus to Tutus.

In 1994, an 845-page book unleashed a new national debate on the issue of IQ. This research effort of psychologist Richard J. Herrnstein and social scientist Charles Murray (1994), published in *The Bell Curve,* concluded that 60 percent of IQ is inheritable and that racial groups offer a convenient means to generalize about any differences in intelligence. Unlike most other proponents of the race–IQ link, the authors offered policy suggestions that include ending welfare to discourage births among low-IQ poor women and changing

❓Ask Yourself

Who are we in terms of race or ethnicity? Do you ever ask someone "What are you?" or "Where are you from?" because you are uncomfortable with not knowing? Concepts of race and ethnicity in the United States are socially constructed and, although most of the time we think we correctly identify people around us, sometimes we cannot.

immigration laws so that the IQ pool in the United States is not diminished. Herrnstein and Murray even made generalizations about IQ levels among Asians and Hispanics in the United States, groups subject to even more intermarriage. It is not possible to generalize about absolute differences between groups, such as Latinos versus Whites, when almost half of Latinos in the United States marry non-Hispanics.

More than a decade later, the mere mention of "the bell curve" still signals to many the belief in a racial hierarchy with Whites toward the top and Blacks near the bottom. The research present then and repeated today points to the difficulty in definitions: What is intelligence, and what constitutes a racial group, given generations, if not centuries, of intermarriage? How can we speak of definitive inherited racial differences if there has been intermarriage between people of every color? Furthermore, as people on both sides of the debate have noted, regardless of the findings, we would still want to strive to maximize the talents of each individual. All research shows that the differences within a group are much greater than any alleged differences between group averages.

All these issues and controversial research have led to the basic question of what difference it would make if there were significant differences. No researcher believes that race can be used to predict one's intelligence. Also, there is a general agreement that certain intervention strategies can improve scholastic achievement and even intelligence, as defined by standard tests. Should we mount efforts to upgrade the abilities of those alleged to be below average? These debates tend to contribute to a sense of hopelessness among some policy makers who think that biology is destiny, rather than causing them to rethink the issue or expand positive intervention efforts.

Why does such IQ research reemerge if the data are subject to different interpretations? The argument that "we" are superior to "them" is very appealing to the dominant group. It justifies receiving opportunities that are denied to others. For example, the authors of *The Bell Curve* argue that intelligence significantly determines the poverty problem in the United States. We can anticipate that the debate over IQ and the allegations of significant group differences will continue. Policy makers need to acknowledge the difficulty in treating race as a biologically significant characteristic.

Social Construction of Race

If race does not distinguish humans from one another biologically, why does it seem to be so important? It is important because of the social meaning people have attached to it. The 1950 (UNESCO) Statement on Race maintains that "for all practical social purposes 'race' is not so much a biological phenomenon as a social myth" (Montagu 1972, 118). Adolf Hitler expressed concern over the "Jewish race" and translated this concern into Nazi death camps. Winston Churchill spoke proudly of the "British race" and used that pride to spur a nation to fight. Evidently, race was a useful political tool for two very different leaders in the 1930s and 1940s.

Race is a social construction, and this process benefits the oppressor, who defines who is privileged and who is not. The acceptance of race in a society as a legitimate category allows racial hierarchies to emerge to the benefit of the dominant "races." For example, inner-city drive-by shootings have come to be seen as a race-specific problem worthy of local officials cleaning up troubled neighborhoods. Yet, schoolyard shoot-outs are viewed as a societal concern and placed on the national agenda.

People could speculate that if human groups have obvious physical differences, then they could have corresponding mental or personality differences. No one disagrees that people differ in temperament, potential to learn, and sense of humor. In its social sense, race implies that groups that differ physically also bear distinctive emotional and mental abilities or disabilities. These beliefs are based on the notion that humankind can be divided into distinct groups. We have already seen the difficulties associated with pigeonholing people into racial categories. Despite these difficulties, belief in the inheritance of behavior patterns and in an association between physical and cultural traits is widespread. It is called **racism** when this belief is coupled with the feeling that certain groups or races are inherently superior to others. Racism is a doctrine of racial supremacy, stating that one race is superior to another (Bash 2001; Bonilla-Silva 1996).

We questioned the biological significance of race in the previous section. In modern complex industrial societies, we find little adaptive utility in the presence or absence of prominent chins, epicanthic folds of the eyelids, or the comparative amount of melanin in the skin. What is important is not that people are genetically different but that they approach one another with dissimilar perspectives. It is in the social setting that race is decisive. Race is significant because people have given it significance.

Race definitions are crystallized through what Michael Omi and Howard Winant (1994) called racial formation. **Racial formation** is a sociohistorical process by which racial categories are created, inhibited, transformed, and destroyed. Those in power define groups of people in a certain way that depends on a racist social structure. The Native Americans and the creation of the reservation system for Native Americans in the late 1800s is an example of this racial formation. The federal American Indian policy combined previously distinctive tribes into a single group. No one escapes the extent and frequency to which we are subjected to racial formation.

In the southern United States, the social construction of race was known as the "one-drop rule." This tradition stipulated that if a person had even a single drop of "Black blood," that person was defined and viewed as Black. Today children of biracial or multiracial marriages try to build their own identities in a country that seems intent on placing them in some single, traditional category—a topic we will return to later in this chapter.

With rising immigration from Latin America in the latter part of the twentieth century, the fluid nature of racial formation is evident. As if it happened in one day, people in the United States have spoken about the Latin Americanization of the United States or that bi-racial order of Black and White was now replaced with a tri-racial order. It is this social context of the changing nature of diversity that we look at to understand how scholars have sought to generalize about intergroup relations in the United States and elsewhere.

Sociology and the Study of Race and Ethnicity

Before proceeding further with our study of racial and ethnic groups, let us consider several sociological perspectives that provide insight into dominant–subordinate relationships. **Sociology** is the systematic study of social behavior and human groups and, therefore, is aptly suited to enlarge our understanding of intergroup relations. There is a long, valuable history of the study of race relations in sociology. Admittedly, it has not always been progressive; indeed, at times it has reflected the prejudices of society. In some instances, scholars who are members of racial, ethnic, and religious minorities, as well as women, have not been permitted to make the kind of contributions they are capable of making to the field.

Stratification by Class and Gender

All societies are characterized by members having unequal amounts of wealth, prestige, or power. Sociologists observe that entire groups may be assigned less or more of what a society values. The hierarchy that emerges is called stratification. **Stratification** is the structured ranking of entire groups of people that perpetuates unequal rewards and power in a society.

Much discussion of stratification identifies the **class,** or social ranking, of people who share similar wealth, according to sociologist Max Weber's classic definition. Mobility from one class to another is not easy. Movement into classes of greater wealth may be particularly difficult for subordinate-group members faced with lifelong prejudice and discrimination (Banton 2007; Gerth and Mills 1958).

🔅 Ask Yourself

Celebración or tokenism? In 2006, the Milwaukee Brewers baseball team debuted a new member of their famous sausage race. A 9-foot-high chorizo with goatee, sombrero, and bandana joined the four-team mascots of hot dog, a Polish sausage, a bratwurst, and an Italian sausage. Although still relatively small, Wisconsin's Hispanic population has tripled over the last fifteen years, so the team wanted to acknowledge its growing Latino fan base. Is this a genuine tribute or just another example of tokenism with no meaningful social significance?

Recall that the first property of subordinate-group standing is unequal treatment by the dominant group in the form of prejudice, discrimination, and segregation. Stratification is intertwined with the subordination of racial, ethnic, religious, and gender groups. Race has implications for the way people are treated; so does class. One also has to add the effects of race and class together. For example, being poor and Black is not the same as being either one by itself. A wealthy Mexican American is not the same as an affluent Anglo American or as Mexican Americans as a group.

Public discussion of issues such as housing or public assistance often is disguised as discussion of class issues, when in fact the issues are based primarily on race. Similarly, some topics such as the poorest of poor or the working poor are addressed in terms of race when the class component should be explicit. Nonetheless, the link between race and class in society is abundantly clear (Winant 2004).

Another stratification factor that we need to consider is gender. How different is the situation for women as contrasted with men? Returning again to the first property of minority groups—unequal treatment and less control—treatment of women is not equal to that received by men. Whether the issue is jobs or poverty, education or crime, the experience of women typically is more difficult. In addition, the situation faced by women in areas such as health care and welfare raises different concerns than it does for men. Just as we need to consider the role of social class to understand race and ethnicity better, we also need to consider the role of gender. Later in this chapter we will consider how these different social dimensions intersect.

Theoretical Perspectives

Sociologists view society in different ways. Some see the world basically as a stable and ongoing entity. The endurance of a Chinatown, the general sameness of male–female roles over time, and other aspects of intergroup relations impress them. Some sociologists see society as composed of many groups in conflict, competing for scarce resources. Within this conflict, some people or even entire groups may be labeled or stigmatized in a way that blocks their access to what a society values. We will examine three theoretical perspectives that are widely used by sociologists today: the functionalist, conflict, and labeling perspectives.

Functionalist Perspective   In the view of a functionalist, a society is like a living organism in which each part contributes to the survival of the whole. The **functionalist perspective** emphasizes how the parts of society are structured to maintain its stability. According to this approach, if an aspect of social life does not contribute to a society's stability or survival, it will not be passed on from one generation to the next.

It seems reasonable to assume that bigotry between races offers no such positive function, and so we ask, why does it persist? Although agreeing that racial hostility is hardly to be admired, the functionalist would point out that it serves some positive functions from the perspective of the racists. We can identify five functions that racial beliefs have for the dominant group:

1. Racist ideologies provide a moral justification for maintaining a society that routinely deprives a group of its rights and privileges.
2. Racist beliefs discourage subordinate people from attempting to question their lowly status; to do so is to question the very foundation of the society.
3. Racial ideologies not only justify existing practices but also serve as a rallying point for social movements, as seen in the rise of the Nazi party.
4. Racist myths encourage support for the existing order. Some argue that if there were any major societal change, the subordinate group would suffer even greater poverty, and the dominant group would suffer lower living standards (Nash 1962).

5. Racist beliefs relieve the dominant group of the responsibility to address the economic and educational problems faced by subordinate groups.

As a result, racial ideology grows when a value system (e.g., that underlying a colonial empire or slavery) is being threatened.

There are also definite dysfunctions caused by prejudice and discrimination. **Dysfunctions** are elements of society that may disrupt a social system or decrease its stability. There are six ways in which racism is dysfunctional to a society, including to its dominant group:

1. A society that practices discrimination fails to use the resources of all individuals. Discrimination limits the search for talent and leadership to the dominant group.
2. Discrimination aggravates social problems such as poverty, delinquency, and crime and places the financial burden of alleviating these problems on the dominant group.
3. Society must invest a good deal of time and money to defend the barriers that prevent the full participation of all members.
4. Racial prejudice and discrimination undercut goodwill and friendly diplomatic relations between nations. They also negatively affect efforts to increase global trade.
5. Social change is inhibited because change may assist a subordinate group.
6. Discrimination promotes disrespect for law enforcement and for the peaceful settlement of disputes.

That racism has costs for the dominant group as well as for the subordinate group reminds us that intergroup conflict is exceedingly complex (Bowser and Hunt 1996; Feagin, Vera, and Batur 2000; Rose 1951).

Conflict Perspective   In contrast to the functionalists' emphasis on stability, conflict sociologists see the social world as being in continual struggle. The **conflict perspective** assumes that the social structure is best understood in terms of conflict or tension between competing groups. Specifically, society is a struggle between the privileged (the dominant group) and the exploited (the subordinate groups). Such conflicts need not be physically violent and may take the form of immigration restrictions, real estate practices, or disputes over cuts in the federal budget.

The conflict model often is selected today when one is examining race and ethnicity, because it readily accounts for the presence of tension between competing groups. According to the conflict perspective, competition takes place between groups with unequal amounts of economic and political power. The minorities are exploited or, at best, ignored by the dominant group. The conflict perspective is viewed as more radical and activist than functionalism because conflict theorists emphasize social change and the redistribution of resources. Functionalists are not necessarily in favor of inequality; rather, their approach helps us to understand why such systems persist.

Those who follow the conflict approach to race and ethnicity have remarked repeatedly that the subordinate group is criticized for its low status. That the dominant group is responsible for subordination is often ignored. William Ryan (1976) calls this an instance of **blaming the victim:** portraying the problems of racial and ethnic minorities as their fault rather than recognizing society's responsibility.

The recognition that many in society fault the weak rather than embrace the need for restructuring society is not new. Gunnar Myrdal, a Swedish social economist of international reputation, headed a project that produced the classic 1944 work on Blacks in the United States, *The American Dilemma.* Myrdal concluded that the plight of the subordinate group is the responsibility of the dominant majority. It is not a Black problem but a White problem. Similarly, we can use the same approach and note that it is not a Hispanic problem or a Haitian refugee problem but a White problem. Myrdal and others since then have reminded the public and policy makers alike that the ultimate responsibility for society's problems must rest with those who possess the most authority and the most economic resources (Hochschild 1995; Southern 1987).

Labeling Approach   Related to the conflict perspective and its concern over blaming the victim is labeling theory. **Labeling theory,** a concept introduced by sociologist Howard Becker, is an attempt to explain why certain people are viewed as deviant and others engaging in the same behavior are not. Students of crime and deviance have relied heavily on labeling theory. According to labeling theory, a youth who misbehaves may be considered and treated as a delinquent if she or he comes from the "wrong kind of family." Another youth, from a middle-class family, who commits the same sort of misbehavior might be given another chance before being punished.

The labeling perspective directs our attention to the role negative stereotypes play in race and ethnicity. The image that prejudiced people maintain of a group toward which they hold ill feelings is called a stereotype. **Stereotypes** are unreliable generalizations about all members of a group that do not take individual differences into account. The warrior image of Native American (America Indian) people is perpetuated by the frequent use of tribal names or even terms such as "Indians" and "Redskins" as sports team mascots. In Chapter 2, we will review some of the research on the stereotyping of minorities. This labeling is not limited to racial and ethnic groups, however. For instance, age can be used to exclude a person from an activity in which he or she is qualified to engage. Groups are subjected to stereotypes and discrimination in such a way that their treatment resembles that of social minorities. Social prejudice exists toward ex-convicts, gamblers, alcoholics, lesbians, gays, prostitutes, people with AIDS, and people with disabilities, to name a few.

The labeling approach points out that stereotypes, when applied by people in power, can have very negative consequences for people or groups identified falsely. A crucial aspect of the relationship between dominant and subordinate groups is the prerogative of the dominant group to define society's values. U.S. sociologist William I. Thomas (1923), an early critic of racial and gender discrimination, saw that the "definition of the situation" could mold the personality of the individual. In other words, Thomas observed that people respond not only to the objective features of a situation (or person) but also to the meaning these features have for them. So, for example, a lone walker seeing a young Black man walking toward him may perceive the situation differently than if the oncoming person is an older woman. In this manner, we can create false images or stereotypes that become real in their social consequences.

In certain situations, we may respond to negative stereotypes and act on them, with the result that false definitions become accurate. This is known as a **self-fulfilling prophecy.** A person or group described as having particular characteristics begins to display the very traits attributed to him or her. Thus, a child who is praised for being a natural comic may focus on learning to become funny to gain approval and attention.

Self-fulfilling prophecies can be devastating for minority groups (Figure 1.3). Such groups often find that they are allowed to hold only low-paying jobs with

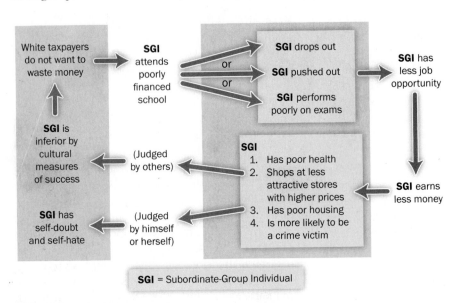

SGI = Subordinate-Group Individual

Figure 1.3 Self-Fulfilling Prophecy
The self-validating effects of dominant-group definitions are shown in this figure. The subordinate-group individual (SGI) attends a poorly financed school and is left unequipped to perform jobs that offer high status and pay. He or she then gets a low-paying job and must settle for a standard of living far short of society's standards. Because the person shares these societal standards, he or she may begin to feel self-doubt and self-hatred.

little prestige or opportunity for advancement. The rationale of the dominant society is that these minority people lack the ability to perform in more important and lucrative positions. Training to become scientists, executives, or physicians is denied to many subordinate-group individuals (SGI), who are then locked into society's inferior jobs. As a result, the false definition becomes real. The subordinate group has become inferior because it was defined at the start as inferior and was, therefore, prevented from achieving the levels attained by the majority.

Because of this vicious circle, a talented subordinate-group person may come to see the worlds of entertainment and professional sports as his or her only hope for achieving wealth and fame. Thus, it is no accident that successive waves of Irish, Jewish, Italian, African American, and Hispanic performers and athletes have made their mark on culture in the United States. Unfortunately, these very successes may convince the dominant group that its original stereotypes were valid—that these are the only areas of society in which subordinate-group members can excel. Furthermore, athletics and the arts are highly competitive areas. For every LeBron James and Jennifer Lopez who makes it, many, many more will end up disappointed.

The Creation of Subordinate-Group Status

Three situations are likely to lead to the formation of a subordinate-group–dominant-group relationship. A subordinate group emerges through migration, annexation, and colonialism.

Migration

People who emigrate to a new country often find themselves a minority in that new country. Cultural or physical traits or religious affiliation may set the immigrant apart from the dominant group. Immigration from Europe, Asia, and Latin America has been a powerful force in shaping the fabric of life in the United States. **Migration** is the general term used to describe any transfer of population. **Emigration** (by emigrants) describes leaving a country to settle in another; **immigration** (by immigrants) denotes coming into the new country. From Vietnam's perspective, the "boat people" were emigrants from Vietnam to the United States, but in the United States they were counted among this nation's immigrants.

Although people may migrate because they want to, leaving the home country is not always voluntary. Conflict or war has displaced people throughout human history. In the twentieth century, we saw huge population movements caused by two world wars; revolutions in Spain, Hungary, and Cuba; the partition of British India; conflicts in Southeast Asia, Korea, and Central America; and the confrontation between Arabs and Israelis.

In all types of movement, even the movement of a U.S. family from Ohio to Florida, two sets of forces operate: push factors and pull factors. Push factors discourage a person from remaining where he or she lives. Religious persecution and economic factors such as dissatisfaction with employment opportunities are possible push factors. Pull factors, such as a better standard of living, friends and relatives who have already emigrated, and a promised job, attract an immigrant to a particular country.

Although generally we think of migration as a voluntary process, much of the population transfer that has occurred in the world has been involuntary. The forced movement of people into another society guarantees a subordinate role. Involuntary migration is no longer common; although enslavement has a long history, all industrialized societies today prohibit such practices. Of course, many contemporary societies, including the United States, bear the legacy of slavery.

Migration has taken on new significance in the twenty-first century partly due to globalization. **Globalization** refers to the worldwide integration of government policies, cultures, social movements, and financial markets through trade and the exchange of ideas. The increased movement of people and money across borders has made the distinction between temporary and permanent migration less meaningful. Although migration has always been fluid, in today's global economy, people are connected across societies culturally and economically like they have never been before. Even after they have relocated, people maintain global linkages to their former country and with a global economy (Richmond 2002).

Annexation

Nations, particularly during wars or as a result of war, incorporate or attach land. This new land is contiguous to the nation, as in the German annexation of Austria and Czechoslovakia in 1938 and 1939 and in the U.S. Louisiana Purchase of 1803. The Treaty of Guadalupe Hidalgo that ended the Mexican-American War in 1848 gave the United States California, Utah, Nevada, most of New Mexico, and parts of Arizona, Wyoming, and Colorado. The indigenous peoples in some of this huge territory were dominant in their society one day, only to become minority-group members the next.

When annexation occurs, the dominant power generally suppresses the language and culture of the minority. Such was the practice of Russia with the Ukrainians and Poles and of Prussia with the Poles. Minorities try to maintain their cultural integrity despite annexation. Poles inhabited an area divided into territories ruled by three countries but maintained their own culture across political boundaries.

Colonialism

Colonialism has been the most common way for one group of people to dominate another. **Colonialism** is the maintenance of political, social, economic,

Colonialism in India and elsewhere established for generations a hierarchical relationship between Europeans and much of the rest of the world. Pictured here is a British officer being fanned and pampered by two Indian attendants.

and cultural dominance over people by a foreign power for an extended period (Bell 1991). Colonialism is rule by outsiders but, unlike annexation, does not involve actual incorporation into the dominant people's nation. The long-standing control that was exercised by the British Empire over much of North America, parts of Africa, and India is an example of colonial domination.

Societies gain power over a foreign land through military strength, sophisticated political organization, and investment capital. The extent of power may also vary according to the dominant group's scope of settlement in the colonial land. Relations between the colonial nation and the colonized people are similar to those between a dominant group and exploited subordinate groups. The colonial subjects generally are limited to menial jobs and the wages from their labor. The natural resources of their land benefit the members of the ruling class.

By the 1980s, colonialism, in the sense of political rule, had become largely a phenomenon of the past, yet industrial countries of North America and Europe still dominated the world economically and politically. Drawing on the conflict perspective, sociologist Immanuel Wallerstein (1974) views the global economic system of today as much like the height of colonial days. Wallerstein has advanced the **world systems theory,** which views the global economic system as divided between nations that control wealth and those that provide natural resources and labor. The limited economic resources available in developing nations exacerbate many of the ethnic, racial, and religious conflicts noted at the beginning of this chapter. In addition, the presence of massive inequality between nations only serves to encourage immigration generally and, more specifically, the movement of many of the most skilled from developing nations to the industrial nations.

A significant exception to the end of foreign political rule is Puerto Rico, whose territorial or commonwealth status with the United States is basically that of a colony. The nearly 4 million people on the island are U.S. citizens but are unable to vote in presidential elections unless they migrate to the mainland. In 1998, 50 percent of Puerto Ricans on the island voted for options favoring continuation of commonwealth status, 47 percent favored statehood, and less than 3 percent voted for independence. Despite their poor showing, proindependence forces are very vocal and enjoy the sympathies of others concerned about the cultural and economic dominance of the U.S. mainland (Navarro 1998; Saad 1998).

Colonialism is domination by outsiders. Relations between the colonizer and the colony are similar to those between the dominant and subordinate peoples within the same country. This distinctive pattern of oppression is called **internal colonialism.** Among other cases, it has been applied to the plight of Blacks in the United States and Mexican Indians in Mexico, who are colonial peoples in their own country. Internal colonialism covers more than simple economic oppression. Nationalist movements in African colonies struggled to achieve political and economic independence from Europeans. Similarly, some African Americans also call themselves nationalists in trying to gain more autonomy over their lives (Blauner 1969, 1972).

The Consequences of Subordinate-Group Status

There are several consequences for a group with subordinate status. These differ in their degree of harshness, ranging from physical annihilation to absorption into the dominant group. In this section, we will examine six consequences of subordinate-group status: extermination, expulsion, secession, segregation, fusion, and assimilation. Figure 1.4 illustrates how these consequences can be defined.

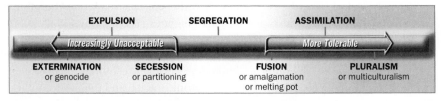

Figure 1.4 Intergroup Relations Continuum
The social consequences of being in a subordinate group can be viewed along a continuum ranging from extermination to forms of mutual acceptance such as pluralism.

Extermination

The most extreme way of dealing with a subordinate group is to eliminate it. Today, the term **genocide** is used to describe the deliberate, systematic killing of an entire people or nation. This term is often used in reference to the Holocaust, Nazi Germany's extermination of 12 million European Jews and other ethnic minorities during World War II. The term **ethnic cleansing** refers to the forced deportation of people accompanied by systematic violence. The term was introduced in 1992 to the world's vocabulary as ethnic Serbs instituted a policy intended to "cleanse"—eliminate—Muslims from parts of Bosnia. More recently, a genocidal war between the Hutu and Tutsi people in Rwanda left 300,000 school-age children orphaned (Chirot and Edwards 2003; Naimark 2004).

However, genocide also appropriately describes White policies toward Native Americans in the nineteenth century. In 1800, the American Indian population in the United States was about 600,000; by 1850, it had been reduced to 250,000 through warfare with the U.S. Army, disease, and forced relocation to inhospitable environments.

In 2008, the Australian government offically apologized for past treatment to its native people, the Aboriginal population. Not only did this involve brutality and neglect but a quarter of their children, the so-called "lost generation," were taken from their families until the policy was finally abandoned in 1969 (Johnston 2008).

Expulsion

Dominant groups may choose to force a specific subordinate group to leave certain areas or even vacate a country. Expulsion, therefore, is another extreme consequence of minority-group status. European colonial powers in North America and eventually the U.S. government itself drove almost all Native Americans out of their tribal lands into unfamiliar territory.

More recently, Vietnam, in 1979, expelled nearly 1 million ethnic Chinese from the country, partly as a result of centuries of hostility between the two Asian neighbors. These "boat people" were abruptly eliminated as a minority within Vietnamese society. This expulsion meant that they were uprooted and became a new minority group in many nations, including Australia, France, the United States, and Canada. Thus, expulsion may remove a minority group from one society; however, the expelled people merely go to another nation, where they are again a minority group.

Secession

A group ceases to be a subordinate group when it secedes to form a new nation or moves to an already established nation, where it becomes dominant. After Great Britain withdrew from Palestine, Jewish people achieved a dominant position in 1948, attracting Jews from throughout the world to the new state of Israel. Similarly, Pakistan was created in 1947 when India was partitioned. The predominantly Muslim areas in the north became Pakistan, making India predominantly Hindu. Throughout this century, minorities have repudiated dominant customs. In this spirit, the Estonian, Latvian, Lithuanian, and Armenian peoples, not content to be merely tolerated by the majority, all seceded to form independent states after the demise of the Soviet Union in 1991. In 1999, ethnic Albanians fought bitterly for their cultural and political recognition in the Kosovo region of Yugoslavia.

Some African Americans have called for secession. Suggestions dating back to the early 1700s supported the return of Blacks to Africa as a solution to racial problems. The settlement target of the American Colonization Society was Liberia, but proposals were also advanced to establish settlements in other areas. Territorial separatism and the emigrationist ideology were recurrent and interrelated themes among African Americans from the late nineteenth century well into the 1980s. The Black Muslims, or Nation of Islam, once expressed the desire for complete separation in their own state or territory within the present borders of the United States. Although a secession of Blacks from the United States has not taken place, it has been proposed.

Segregation

Segregation is the physical separation of two groups in residence, workplace, and social functions. Generally, the dominant group imposes segregation on a subordinate group. Segregation is rarely complete, however; intergroup contact inevitably occurs even in the most segregated societies.

Sociologists Douglas Massey and Nancy Denton (1993) wrote *American Apartheid,* which described segregation in U.S. cities on the basis of 1990 data. The title of their book was meant to indicate that neighborhoods in the United States resembled the segregation of the rigid government-imposed racial segregation that prevailed for so long in the Republic of South Africa.

Analyzing the 2000 census results shows little change despite growing racial and ethnic diversity in the nation. Sociologists measure racial segregation using a segregation index or index of dissimilarity. The index ranges from 0 to 100, giving the percentage of a group that would have to move to achieve even residential patterns. For example, Atlanta has an index of 65.6 for Black–White segregation, which means that about 66 percent of either Blacks or Whites would have to move so that each small neighborhood (or census tract) would have the same racial balance as the metropolitan area as a whole. In Figure 1.5, we give the index values for the most and the least segregated metropolitan areas among the fifty largest in the nation with respect to the Black–White racial divide.

Overall, the least segregated metropolitan areas tend to be those with the smallest African American populations. For Latinos, the separation patterns are

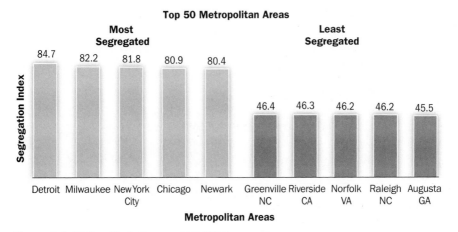

Figure 1.5 White–Black Segregation, 2000

Source: From *Ethnic Diversity Grows, Neighborhood Integration Lags Behind.* Reprinted by permission of John Logan, Brown University, http://www.s4.brown.edu. (Also see Lewis Mumford Center 2001).

similar, with the highest patterns of isolation occurring in the cities with the larger number of Hispanics (Figure 1.6). There has been little change in overall levels of racial and ethnic segregation from 1990 to 2000. Similarly, Asian–White segregation remains high and showed little change during the 1990s (Lewis Mumford Center 2001; Logan, Stults, and Farley 2004).

This focus on metropolitan areas should not cause us to ignore the continuing legally sanctioned segregation of Native Americans on reservations. Although the majority of our nation's first inhabitants live outside these tribal areas, the reservations play a prominent role in the identity of Native Americans. Although it is easier to maintain tribal identity on the reservation, economic and educational opportunities are more limited in these areas that are segregated from the rest of society.

The social consequences of residential segregation are significant. Given the elevated rates of poverty experienced by racial and ethnic minorities, their patterns of segregation mean that the consequences of poverty (dismal job opportunities, poor health care facilities, delinquency, and crime) are much more likely to be experienced by even the middle-class Blacks, Latinos, and tribal people than it is by middle-class Whites. Race, rather than class, explains the persistence of segregation (Adelman and Gocker 2007; Massey 2004).

A particularly troubling pattern has been the emergence of resegregation. **Resegregation** is the physical separation of racial and ethnic groups reappearing after a period of relative integration. Resegregation has occurred in both neighborhoods and schools after a transitional period of desegregation. For example, in 1954, there was only one in 100,000 Black students who attended a majority White school in the South. Thanks to the Civil Rights

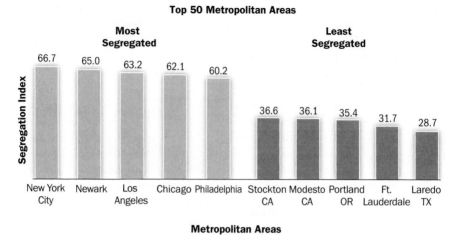

Figure 1.6 White–Latino Segregation, 2000

Source: From *Ethnic Diversity Grows, Neighborhood Integration Lags Behind.* Reprinted by permission of John Logan, Brown University, http://www.s4.brown.edu. (Also see Lewis Mumford Center 2001).

Movement and a series of civil rights measures, by 1968, this was up to 23 percent and then 47 percent by 1988. But after White households relocated or alternatives reemerged through private schools and home schooling, the proportion had dropped back to 27 percent in 2004. The latest analysis shows continuing if not increasing racial isolation (Orfield 2007; Orfield and Lee 2007; Rich 2008).

Given segregation patterns, many Whites in the United States have limited contact with people of other racial and ethnic backgrounds. In one study of 100 affluent powerful White men looking at their experiences past and present, it was clear they had lived in a "white bubble"—neighborhoods, schools, elite colleges, and workplaces overwhelmingly White. The continuing pattern of segregation in the United States means our diverse population grows up in very different nations (Bonilla-Silva and Embrick 2007; Feagin and O'Brien 2003).

Fusion

Fusion occurs when a minority and a majority group combine to form a new group. This combining can be expressed as A + B + C → D where A, B, and C represent the groups present in a society, and D signifies the result, an ethnocultural-racial group sharing some of the characteristics of each initial group. Mexican people are an example of fusion, originating as they do out of the mixing of the Spanish and indigenous Indian cultures. Theoretically, fusion does not entail intermarriage, but it is very similar to **amalgamation,** or the process by which a dominant group and a subordinate group combine through intermarriage into a new people. In everyday speech, the words fusion and amalgamation are rarely used, but the concept is expressed in the notion of a human **melting pot,** in which diverse racial or ethnic groups form a new creation, a new cultural entity (Newman 1973).

The analogy of the cauldron, the "melting pot," was first used to describe the United States by the French observer Crèvecoeur in 1782. The phrase dates back to the Middle Ages, when alchemists attempted to change less-valuable metals into gold and silver. Similarly, the idea of the human melting pot implied that the new group would represent only the best qualities and attributes of the different cultures contributing to it. The belief in the United States as a melting pot became widespread in the early twentieth century. This belief suggested that the United States had an almost divine mission to destroy artificial divisions and create a single kind of human. However, the dominant group had indicated its unwillingness to welcome such groups as Native Americans, Blacks, Hispanics, Jews, Asians, and Irish Roman Catholics into the melting pot. It is a mistake to think of the United States as an ethnic mixing bowl. Although there are superficial signs of fusion, as in a cuisine that includes sauerkraut and spaghetti, most contributions of subordinate groups are ignored (Gleason 1980).

Marriage patterns indicate the resistance to fusion. People are unwilling, in varying degrees, to marry outside their own ethnic, religious, and racial groups, and indeed through the 1960s, there were many states where it was illegal to cross racial boundaries. Surveys today show that 20 to 50 percent of various White ethnic groups report single ancestry. When White ethnics do cross boundaries, they tend to marry within their religion and social class. For example, Italians are more likely to marry Irish, who are also Catholic, than they are to marry Protestant Swedes.

Although it may seem that interracial matches are everywhere, there is only modest evidence of a fusion of races in the United States. Racial intermarriage has been increasing, and the number of interracial couples immigrating to the United States has also grown. In 1980, there were 167,000 Black–White couples, but by 2006, there were 403,000. That is still less than one out of every 100 marriages involving a White and Black person.

Among couples in which at least one member is Hispanic, marriages with a non-Hispanic partner account for 37 percent. Taken together, all interracial and Hispanic–non-Hispanic couples account for 7.5 percent of married couples today (Bureau of the Census 2007a, Table 59).

Assimilation

Assimilation is the process by which a subordinate individual or group takes on the characteristics of the dominant group and is eventually accepted as part of that group. Assimilation is a majority ideology in which A + B + C → A. The majority (A) dominates in such a way that the minorities (B and C) become

Faced with new laws restricting rights of noncitizens, people representing countries from around the world participate in naturalization ceremonies in New York City, in 2006, aboard the *USS Intrepid*. About 18,000 new citizens took the oath during the July 4th week.

indistinguishable from the dominant group. Assimilation dictates conformity to the dominant group, regardless of how many racial, ethnic, or religious groups are involved (Newman 1973, 53).

To be complete, assimilation must entail an active effort by the minority-group individual to shed all distinguishing actions and beliefs and the unqualified acceptance of that individual by the dominant society. In the United States, dominant White society encourages assimilation. The assimilation perspective tends to devalue alien culture and to treasure the dominant. For example, assimilation assumes that whatever is admirable among Blacks was adapted from Whites and that whatever is bad is inherently Black. The assimilation solution to Black–White conflict has been typically defined as the development of a consensus around White American values.

Assimilation is very difficult. The person must forsake his or her cultural tradition to become part of a different, often antagonistic culture. Members of the subordinate group who choose not to assimilate look on those who do as deserters.

Assimilation does not occur at the same pace for all groups or for all individuals in the same group. Typically, assimilation is not a process completed by the first generation. Assimilation tends to take longer under the following conditions:

- The differences between the minority and the majority are large.
- The majority is not receptive or the minority retains its own culture.
- The minority group arrives over a short period of time.

- The minority-group residents are concentrated rather than dispersed.
- The arrival is recent, and the homeland is accessible.

Assimilation is not a smooth process (Warner and Srole 1945).

Assimilation is viewed by many as unfair or even dictatorial. However, members of the dominant group see it as reasonable that people shed their distinctive cultural traditions. In public discussions today, assimilation is the ideology of the dominant group in forcing people how to act. Consequently, the social institutions in the United States, such as the educational system, economy, government, religion, and medicine, all push toward assimilation, with occasional references to the pluralist approach.

The Pluralist Perspective

Thus far, we have concentrated on how subordinate groups cease to exist (removal) or take on the characteristics of the dominant group (assimilation). The alternative to these relationships between the majority and the minority is pluralism. **Pluralism** implies that various groups in a society have mutual respect for one another's culture, a respect that allows minorities to express their own culture without suffering prejudice or hostility. Whereas the assimilationist or integrationist seeks the elimination of ethnic boundaries, the pluralist believes in maintaining many of them.

There are limits to cultural freedom. A Romanian immigrant to the United States cannot expect to avoid learning English and still move up the occupational ladder. To survive, a society must have a consensus among its members on basic ideals, values, and beliefs. Nevertheless, there is still plenty of room for variety. Earlier, fusion was described as A + B + C → D and assimilation as A + B + C → A. Using this same scheme, we can think of pluralism as A + B + C → A + B + C, where groups coexist in one society (Manning 1995; Newman 1973; Simpson 1995).

In the United States, cultural pluralism is more an ideal than a reality. Although there are vestiges of cultural pluralism—in the various ethnic neighborhoods in major cities, for instance—the rule has been for subordinate groups to assimilate. Yet as the minority becomes the numerical majority, the ability to live out one's identity becomes a bit easier. African Americans, Hispanics, and Asian Americans already outnumber Whites in ten of the eleven largest cities with San Diego having a slight majority of White non-Hispanic (Figure 1.7). The trend is toward even greater diversity. Nonetheless, the cost of cultural integrity throughout the nation's history has been high. The various Native American tribes have succeeded to a large extent in maintaining their heritage, but the price has been bare subsistence on federal reservations.

In the United States, there is a reemergence of ethnic identification by groups that had previously expressed little interest in their heritage. Groups that make up the dominant majority are also reasserting their ethnic heritages.

Figure 1.7 Race and Ethnicity, 15 Largest Cities, 2005
Source: Author analysis based on American Community Survey 2006 and U.S. Bureau of the Census 2001.

Various nationality groups are rekindling interest in almost forgotten languages, customs, festivals, and traditions. In some instances, this expression of the past has taken the form of a protest against exclusion from the dominant society. For example, Chinese youths chastise their elders for forgetting the old ways and accepting White American influence and control.

The most visible expression of pluralism surrounds language use. As of 2006, nearly one of every five people (19.1 percent) over the age of 5 speaks a native language other than English at home. Later, in Chapters 4 and 5, we will consider how language-use figures into issues relating to immigration and education (Bureau of the Census 2007b: Table R1601).

Facilitating a diverse and changing society emerges in just about every aspect of society. Yet another nod to pluralism, not nearly so obvious as language to the general population, has been the changes within the funeral industry. Where Christian and Jewish funeral practices have dominated,

Let's play Scrabble! This is not your typical board game. In order to preserve their language among young people, residents of the Lake Traverse Reservation of the Sisseton Wahpeton Oyate hold Scrabble tournaments where only Dakotah language words are permitted.

funeral homes are now retraining to accommodate a variety of practices. Latinos often expect 24-hour viewing of their deceased while Muslims may wish to participate in washing the deceased before burial in a grave pointing to Mecca. Hindu and Buddhist requests to participate in cremation are now being respected (Brulliard 2006).

Biracial and Multiracial Identity—Who Am I?

People are now more willing to accept and advance identities that do not neatly fit into mutually exclusive categories. Hence, increasing numbers of people are identifying themselves as biracial or multiracial or, at the very least, explicitly viewing themselves as reflecting a diverse racial and ethnic identity. This is especially true among younger people, which is not too surprising given that 94 percent of the people born since 1977 approve of interracial dating compared to 84 percent for baby boomers (those born between 1946 and 1964) and only 65 percent born before 1946 (Brunsma 2006; Lewis 2007).

When Tiger Woods first appeared on *The Oprah Winfrey Show,* he was asked whether it bothered him, the only child of a Black American father and a Thai mother, to be called an African American. He replied, "It does. Growing up, I came up with this name: I'm a Cabalinasian" (White 1997, 34). This is a self-crafted acronym to reflect that Tiger Woods is one-eighth Caucasian, one-fourth Black, one-eighth American Indian, one-fourth Thai, and one-fourth Chinese. Soon after he achieved professional stardom, another golfer was strongly criticized for making racist remarks based on seeing Woods only as African American. If Tiger Woods was not so famous, would most people, upon meeting him, see him as anything but an African American? Probably not. Tiger Woods's problem is really the challenge to a diverse society that continues to try to place people in a few socially constructed racial and ethnic boxes.

The diversity of the United States today has made it more difficult for many people to place themselves on the racial and ethnic landscape. It reminds us that racial formation continues to take place. Obviously, the racial and ethnic landscape, as we have seen, is constructed not naturally but socially and, therefore, is subject to change and different interpretations. Although our focus is on the United States, almost every nation faces the same problems.

The United States tracks people by race and ethnicity for myriad reasons, ranging from attempting to improve the status of oppressed groups to diversifying classrooms. But how can we measure the growing number of people whose ancestry is mixed by anyone's definition? In "Research Focus" we consider how the U.S. Census Bureau dealt with this issue.

Besides the increasing respect for biracial identity and multiracial identity, group names undergo change as well. Within little more than a generation during the twentieth century, labels that were applied to subordinate groups changed from Negroes to Blacks to African Americans, from American Indians to Native Americans or Native Peoples. However, more Native Americans prefer the use of their tribal name, such as *Seminole,* instead of a collective label. The old 1950s statistical term of "people with a Spanish surname" has long been discarded, yet there is disagreement over a new term: *Latino* or *Hispanic*. Like Native Americans, Hispanic Americans avoid such global terms and prefer their native names, such as *Puerto Ricans* or *Cubans*. People of Mexican ancestry indicate preferences for a variety of names, such as *Mexican American, Chicano,* or simply *Mexican*.

In the United States and other multiracial, multiethnic societies, panethnicity has emerged. **Panethnicity** is the development of solidarity between ethnic subgroups. The coalition of tribal groups as Native Americans or American Indians to confront outside forces, notably the federal government, is one example of panethnicity. Hispanics or Latinos and Asian Americans are other examples of panethnicity. Although it is rarely recognized by dominant society, the very term Black or African American represents the descendants of many different ethnic or tribal groups, such as Akamba, Fulani, Hausa, Malinke, and Yoruba (Lopez and Espiritu 1990).

Is panethnicity a convenient label for "outsiders" or a term that reflects a mutual identity? Certainly, many people outside the group are unable or unwilling to recognize ethnic differences and prefer umbrella terms such as Asian Americans. For some small groups, combining with others is emerging as a useful way to make them heard, but there is always a fear that their own

RESEARCH FOCUS

Measuring Multiculturalism

Approaching Census 2000, a movement was spawned by people who were frustrated by government questionnaires that forced them to indicate only one race. Take the case of Stacey Davis in New Orleans. The young woman's mother is Thai and her father is Creole, a blend of Black, French, and German. People seeing Stacey confuse her for a Latina, Filipina, or Hawaiian. Officially, she has been "White" all her life because she looked White. Congress was lobbied by groups such as Project RACE (Reclassify All Children Equally) for a category "biracial" or "multiracial" that one could select on census forms instead of a specific race. Race is only one of six questions asked of every person in the United States on census day every ten years. After various trial runs with different wordings on the race question, Census 2000 for the first time gave people the option to check off one or more racial groups. "Biracial" or "multiracial" was not an option because pretests showed very few people would use it. This meant that the government recognized in Census 2000 different social constructions of racial identity—that is, a person could be Asian American and White.

Most people did select one racial category in Census 2000. Overall, about 7 million people, or 2.4 percent of the total population, selected two or more racial groups. This was a smaller proportion than many had anticipated. In fact, not even the majority of mixed-race couples identified their children with more than one racial classification. As shown in Figure 1.8, White and American Indian were the most common multiple identity, with about a million people selecting that response. As a group, American Indians were most likely to select a second category and Whites least likely. Race is socially defined.

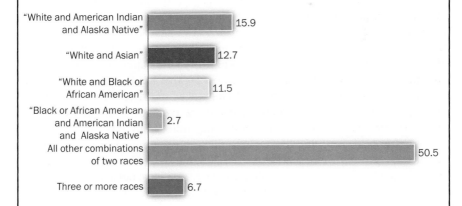

Figure 1.8 Multiple Race Choices in Census 2000
This figure shows the percentage distribution of the 6.8 million people who chose two or more races out of 281.4 million total population.
Source: Grieco and Cassidy 2001.

> Complicating the situation is that people are asked separately whether they are Hispanic or non-Hispanic. So a Hispanic person can be any race. In the 2000 Census, 94 percent indicated they were one race but 6 percent indicated two or more races; this proportion was three times higher than among non-Hispanics. Therefore, Latinos are more likely than non-Hispanics to indicate a multiracial ancestry.
>
> The Census Bureau's decision does not necessarily resolve the frustration of hundreds of thousands of people such as Stacey Davis who daily face people trying to place them in some racial or ethnic category convenient for them. However, it does underscore the complexity of social construction and trying to apply arbitrary definitions to the diversity of the human population.
>
> *Source:* El Nasser 1997; Grieco and Cassidy 2001; Jones and Smith 2001; Tafoya, Johnson, and Hill 2004; Williams 2005.

distinctive culture will become submerged. Although many Hispanics share the Spanish language and many are united by Roman Catholicism, only one in four native-born people of Mexican, Puerto Rican, or Cuban descent prefers a panethnic label to nationality or ethnic identity. Yet the growth of a variety of panethnic associations among many groups, including Hispanics, continued through the 1990s (de la Garza et al. 1992; Espiritu 1992).

Add to this cultural mix the many peoples with clear social identities that are not yet generally recognized in the United States. Arabs are a rapidly growing segment whose identity is heavily subject to stereotypes or, at best, is still ambiguous. Haitians and Jamaicans affirm that they are Black but rarely accept the identity of African American. Brazilians, who speak Portuguese, often object to being called Hispanic because of that term's association with Spain. Similarly, there are White Hispanics and non–White Hispanics, some of the latter being Black and others Asian (Bennett 1993; Omi and Winant 1994, 162).

Another challenge to identity is **marginality,** the status of being between two cultures, as in the case of a person whose mother is a Jew and whose father is a Christian. Du Bois (1903) spoke eloquently of the "double consciousness" that Black Americans feel—caught between the concept of being a citizen of the United States but viewed as something quite apart from the dominant social forces of society. Incomplete assimilation by immigrants also results in marginality. Although a Filipino woman migrating to the United States may take on the characteristics of her new host society, she may not be fully accepted and may, therefore, feel neither Filipino nor American. The marginalized person finds himself or herself being perceived differently in different environments, with varying expectations (Billson 1988; Park 1928; Stonequist 1937).

As we seek to understand diversity in the United States, we must be mindful that ethnic and racial labels are just that: labels that have been socially constructed. Yet these social constructs can have a powerful impact, whether self-applied or applied by others.

Celebrities such as Mariah Carey are unable to protect their privacy. Much has been made about her racial and ethnic identity. She told *Ebony* magazine that she is very aware of her African American heritage, "and I think sometimes it bothers people that I don't say, 'I'm black' and that's it . . . So when people ask, I say I'm black, Venezuelan, and Irish, because that's who I am" (Carberry 2006:5).

Matrix of Domination: Minority Women

Many women experience differential treatment not only because of their gender but also because of race and ethnicity. These citizens face a subordinate status twice defined. A disproportionate share of this low-status group also is poor. The African American feminist Patricia Hill Collins (2000) has termed this the **matrix of domination** (Figure 1.9, p.40). Whites dominate non-Whites; men dominate women, and the affluent dominate the poor.

Gender, race, and social class are not the only systems of oppression, but they do profoundly affect women and people of color in the United States. Other forms of categorization and stigmatization can also be included in this matrix, such as sexual orientation, religion, disability status, and age. If we

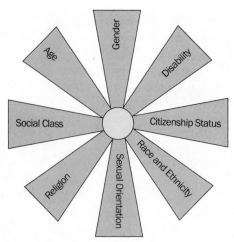

Figure 1.9 Matrix of Domination
The matrix of domination illustrates how several
social factors including gender, social class, and
race and ethnicity, can converge to create a
cumulative impact on a person's social standing.

turn to a global stage, added to oppression can be citizenship status or
being perceived as a "colonial subject" even after colonialism has ended
(Winant 2006).

Feminists have addressed themselves to the needs of minority women, but
the oppression of these women because of their sex is overshadowed by the
subordinate status that both White men and White women impose on them
because of their race or ethnicity. The question for the Latina (Hispanic
woman), African American woman, Asian American woman, Native American
woman, and so on appears to be whether she should unify with her brothers
against racism or challenge them for their sexism. The answer is that society
cannot afford to let up on the effort to eradicate both sexism and racism as
well as other forces that stigmatize and oppress (Beisel and Kay 2004; Epstein
1999; MacLean and Williams 2008).

The discussion of gender roles among African Americans has always provoked controversy. Advocates of Black nationalism contend that feminism
only distracts women from full participation in the African American struggle.
The existence of feminist groups among Blacks, in their view, simply divides the
Black community and thereby serves the dominant White society. By contrast,
Black feminists such as Bell Hooks (1994) argue that little is to be gained by
accepting the gender-role divisions of the dominant society that place women
in a separate, subservient position. African American journalist Patricia Raybon
(1989) has noted that the media commonly portray Black women in a negative

light: as illiterates, as welfare mothers, as prostitutes, and so forth. Black feminists emphasize that it is not solely Whites and White-dominated media that focus on these negative images; Black men (most recently, Black male rap artists) have also been criticized for the way they portray African American women (Threadcraft 2008).

Native Americans stand out as a historical exception to the North American patriarchal tradition. At the time of the arrival of the European settlers, gender roles varied greatly from tribe to tribe. Southern tribes, for reasons unclear to today's scholars, usually were matriarchal and traced descent through the mother. European missionaries sought to make the native peoples more like the Europeans, and this aim included transforming women's role. Some Native American women, like members of other groups, have resisted gender stereotypes (Marubbio 2006).

The plight of Latinas usually is considered part of either the Hispanic or feminist movements, and the distinctive experience of Latinas is ignored. In the past, they have been excluded from decision making in the two social institutions that most affect their daily lives: the family and the church. The Hispanic family, especially in the lower class, feels the pervasive tradition of male domination. The Catholic Church relegates women to supportive roles while reserving for men the leadership positions (Browne 2001; De Anda 2004).

By considering the matrix of domination, we recognize that issues of gender domination must be included to fully understand what women of color experience.

Resistance and Change

By virtue of wielding power and influence, the dominant group may define the terms by which all members of society operate. This is particularly evident in a slave society, but even in contemporary industrialized nations, the dominant group has a disproportionate role in shaping immigration policy, the curriculum of the schools, and the content of the media.

Subordinate groups do not merely accept the definitions and ideology proposed by the dominant group. A continuing theme in dominant–subordinate relations is the minority group's challenge to its subordination. Resistance by subordinate groups is well documented as they seek to promote change that will bring them more rights and privileges, if not true equality. Often traditional notions of racial formation are overcome not only through panethnicity but also because Black people with Latinos and sympathetic Whites join in (Moulder 1996; Winant 2004).

Resistance can be seen in efforts by racial and ethnic groups to maintain their identity through newspapers and organizations and in today's technological age through cable television stations, blogs, and Internet sites. Resistance manifests itself in social movements such as the civil rights movement, the feminist movement, and gay rights efforts. The passage of such legislation as the Age Discrimination Act or the Americans with Disabilities Act marks the success of oppressed groups in lobbying on their own behalf.

Resistance efforts may begin through small actions. For example, residents of a reservation question a toxic waste dump being located on their land. Although it may bring in money, they question the wisdom of such a move. Their concerns lead to further investigations of the extent to which American Indian lands are used disproportionately to house dangerous materials. This action in turn leads to a broader investigation of the way in which minority-group people often find themselves "hosting" dumps and incinerators. As we will discuss later, these local efforts eventually led the Environmental Protection Agency to monitor the disproportionate placement of toxic facilities in or near racial and ethnic minority communities. There is little reason to expect that such reforms would have occurred if we had relied on traditional decision-making processes alone.

Change has occurred. At the beginning of the twentieth century, lynching was practiced in many parts of the country. At the beginning of the twenty-first century, laws punishing hate crimes were increasingly common and embraced a variety of stigmatized groups. Although this social progress should not be ignored, the nation needs to focus concern ahead on the significant social inequalities that remain. It is too easy to look at the race of Barack Obama and Hillary Clinton and conclude "mission accomplished" in terms of racial and gender injustices (Best 2001).

An even more basic form of resistance is to question societal values. In this book, we avoid using the term American to describe people of the United States because geographically Brazilians, Canadians, and El Salvadorans are Americans as well. It is very easy to overlook how our understanding of today has been shaped by the way institutions and even the very telling of history have been presented by members of the dominant group. African American studies scholar Molefi Kete Asante (2007, 2008) has called for an **Afrocentric perspective** that emphasizes the customs of African cultures and how they have pervaded the history, culture, and behavior of Blacks in the United States and around the world. Afrocentrism counters Eurocentrism and works toward a multiculturalist or pluralist orientation in which no viewpoint is suppressed. The Afrocentric approach could become part of our school curriculum, which has not adequately acknowledged the importance of this heritage.

The Afrocentric perspective has attracted much attention in education. Opponents view it as a separatist view of history and culture that distorts both past and present. Its supporters counter that African peoples everywhere can come to full self-determination only when they are able to overthrow White or Eurocentric intellectual interpretations (Conyers 2004).

In considering the inequalities present today, as we will in the chapters that follow, it is easy to forget how much change has taken place. Much of the resistance to prejudice and discrimination in the past, either to slavery or to women's prohibition from voting, took the active support of members of the dominant group. The indignities still experienced by subordinate groups continue to be resisted as subordinate groups and their allies among the dominant group seek further change.

Conclusion

One hundred years ago, sociologist and activist W. E. B. Du Bois took another famed Black activist, Booker T. Washington, to task for saying that the races could best work together apart, like fingers on a hand. Du Bois felt that Black people had to be a part of all social institutions and not create their own. Today among African Americans, Whites, and other groups, the debate persists as to what form society should take. Should we seek to bring everyone together into an integrated whole? Or do we strive to maintain as much of our group identities as possible while working cooperatively as necessary?

In this chapter, we have attempted to organize our approach to subordinate–dominant relations in the United States. We observed that subordinate groups do not necessarily contain fewer members than the dominant group. Subordinate groups are classified into racial, ethnic, religious, and gender groups. Racial classification has been of interest, but scientific findings do not explain contemporary race relations. Biological differences of race are not supported by scientific data. Yet as the continuing debate over standardized tests demonstrates, attempts to establish a biological meaning of race have not been swept entirely into the dustbin of history. However, the social meaning given to physical differences is very significant. People have defined racial differences in such a way as to encourage or discourage the progress of certain groups.

The oppression of selected racial and ethnic groups may serve some people's vested interests. However, denying opportunities or privileges to an entire group only leads to conflict between dominant and subordinate groups. Societies such as the United States develop ideologies to justify privileges given to some and opportunities denied to others. These ideologies may be subtle, such as assimilation (i.e., "You should be like us"), or overt, such as racist thought and behavior.

Subordinate groups generally emerge in one of three ways: migration, annexation, or colonialism. Once a group is given subordinate status, it does not necessarily keep it indefinitely. Extermination, expulsion, secession, segregation, fusion, and assimilation remove the status of subordination, although inequality still persists.

Subordinate-group members' reactions include the seeking of an alternative avenue to acceptance and success: "Why should we forsake what we are to be accepted by them?" In response to this question, there has been a resurgence of ethnic identification. Pluralism describes a society in which several different groups coexist, with no dominant or subordinate groups. The hope for such a society remains unfulfilled, except perhaps for isolated exceptions.

Race and ethnicity remains the single most consistent social indicator of where we live, whom we date, what media we watch, where we worship, and even how we vote (Younge 2004).

Subordinate groups have not and do not always accept their second-class status passively. They may protest, organize, revolt, and resist society as defined by the dominant group. Patterns of race and ethnic relations are changing, not stagnant.

Racial, ethnic, and religious groups and women have always questioned their second-class status. Muslim Americans are among the most recent. Here student and community leaders gathered in 2005 at the Massachusetts State House to condemn then Governor Mitt Romney's remarks that surveillance of foreign students and wiretapping of mosques should be considered as a part of the homeland security effort.

Furthermore, in many nations, including the United States, the nature of race and ethnicity changes through migration. Indicative of the changing landscape, biracial and multiracial children present us with new definitions of identity emerging through a process of racial formation, reminding us that race is socially constructed.

The two significant forces that are absent in a truly pluralistic society are prejudice and discrimination. In an assimilation society, prejudice disparages outgroup differences, and discrimination financially rewards those who shed their past. In the next two chapters, we will explore the nature of prejudice and discrimination in the United States.

Key Terms

Afrocentric perspective 42	class 17	ethnic cleansing 27
amalgamation 30	colonialism 24	ethnic group 9
assimilation 31	conflict perspective 20	functionalist perspective 19
biological race 13	dysfunction 20	fusion 30
blaming the victim 21	emigration 23	genocide 27

globalization   24
immigration   23
intelligence quotient
    (IQ)   13
internal colonialism   26
labeling theory   21
marginality   38
matrix of domination   39

melting pot   31
migration   23
minority group   6
panethnicity   36
pluralism   33
racial formation   16
racial group   8
racism   16

resegregation   29
segregation   28
self-fulfilling prophecy   22
sociology   17
stereotypes   21
stratification   17
world systems theory   25

Review Questions

1. In what ways have you seen issues of race and ethnicity emerge? Identify groups that have been subordinated for reasons other than race, ethnicity, or gender.

2. How can a significant political or social issue (such as bilingual education) be viewed in assimilationist and pluralistic terms?

3. How do the concepts of "biracial" and "multiracial" relate W. E. B. Du Bois's notion of a "color line"

Critical Thinking

1. How diverse is your city? Can you see evidence that some group is being subordinated? What social construction of categories do you see that may be different in your community as compared to elsewhere?

2. In 2006, "Nuestro Himno" ("Our Anthem") hit the airwaves as a Spanish-language version of Francis Scott Key's original words. Do you think this represents a positive development or a step backward? How does it relate to the Intergroup Relations Continuum pictured in Figure 1.4?

3. Identify some protest and resistance efforts by subordinated groups in your area. Have they been successful? Why are some people who say they favor equality uncomfortable with such efforts? How can people unconnected with such efforts either help or hinder such protests?

Internet Connections—Research Navigator™

1. The *Pearson Guide to Research Navigator*™ focuses on using Research Navigator™—Pearson's own gateway to databases including the EBSCO/ContentSelect Academic Journal and Abstract Database, Link Library, the *Financial Times* Archive and Company Financials, and a link to the *New York Times*. It also includes an appendix on documenting online sources and avoiding plagiarism. This supplement—which includes an access code to the Research Navigator™ Web site—is available at no additional charge when packaged with a new text. Visit our Research Navigator™ Web site at www.Research-Navigator.com. Once at this Web site, click on Register under New Users and enter your

access code to create a personal login name and password. (When revisiting the web site, use the same login name and password.) Browse the features of the Research Navigator™ Web site and search the databases of academic journals, newspapers, magazines, and Web links.

2. For further information relevant to Chapter 1, you may wish to use such keywords as "ethnicity," "IQ," and "biracial," and the search engine will supply relevant and recent scholarly and popular press publications. Use the New York Times Search-by-Subject Archive to find recent news articles related to sociology and the Link Library feature to locate relevant Web links organized by the key terms associated with this chapter.

2 Prejudice

CHAPTER OUTLINE

──────────────⟨ H I G H L I G H T S ⟩──────────────

Prejudice is a negative attitude that rejects an entire group; discrimination is behavior that deprives a group of certain rights or opportunities. Prejudice does not necessarily coincide with discrimination, as is made apparent by a typology developed by sociologist Robert Merton. Several theories have been advanced to explain prejudice: scapegoating, authoritarian personality, exploitation, and the normative approach. Although widespread expression of prejudice has declined, color-blind racism allows the status quo of racial and ethnic inequality to persist. Prejudice is not limited to the dominant group; members of subordinate groups often dislike one another. The mass media seem to be of limited value in reducing prejudice and may even intensify ill feeling. Equal-status contact and the shared-coping approach may reduce hostility between groups, but data show few friendships cross racial lines. In response to increasing diversity in the workplace, corporations and organizations have mounted diversity training programs to increase organizational effectiveness and combat prejudice. There are also ten identifiable steps that we as individuals can take to stop prejudice and hatred.

The immigration debate has persisted for years with little action on a complex issue. Some have advocated measures to allow long-term illegal residents a way to become permanent residents, but loud cries have been made taking a "What part of illegal don't they get." Not too surprisingly, hate crimes against Latinos has increased by 35 percent over the last three years. The rhetoric over immigration has often stigmatized, or dehumanized, immigrants (even legal arrivals at times) as "invaders," "criminal aliens," and "cockroaches."

Imagine one is a "shooter" faced with making a decision whether to shoot a threatening, potentially dangerous person. Social psychologists have created such a situation for police, everyday community residents, and even volunteer college students using a video simulation they constructed. As one might expect, the police as "shooters" were faster in responding and were more accurate in determining whether the "criminal" was armed with a gun. But what if the situation sometimes shows the target to be Black and sometimes he or she is White? Reflecting general stereotypes, response time is fastest to decide whether to shoot or hold fire if the White target is unarmed and the Black target is armed. Yet when the image does not follow the notion that Black people are less trustworthy, response time falls. People hesitate to shoot armed White targets and take longer to decide whether to shoot unarmed Black targets. This measured bias seems to be across race and ethnicity in that there were no significant differences based on whether the "shooter" themselves were White or Black or Hispanic. Particularly troubling was the finding that police assigned to predominantly Black neighborhoods than White communities are even quicker to shoot armed Black targets and more hesitant to fire at armed White targets.

These results were not unusual. In a similar study at the University of Washington, psychologists asked college students to distinguish virtual citizens and police officers from armed criminals. They found that subjects were more likely to misperceive and shoot images of Black men than of White men in the video game they created. For the last three decades, in fact, research has suggested that people in the United States are more likely to see Black men as being violent than White men, which translated in this study for the Black men to be more likely to be "shot" at.

Are there limits for this hostility? Apparently not. In the commercially successful "Grand Theft Auto (GTA) IV" video game, where Nikolai Bellic, "an Eastern European" arrives in Liberty City (i.e., New York City) to pursue the American Dream, which has been presented to him as fast money and fast women. In the various editions of GTA, players are encouraged to take very violent actions against a variety of images. At one point, players are informed that they have come across a "Stinking nest of Haitians. We gonna kill them all. Kill all the Haitians." Why? "Kill all the Haitians, they are all drug dealers." This game, the latest version released by Rockstar Video in 2008, bore a parental code declaring that its use was inappropriate for children under 17, but aside from the fact that so many youth access such games, we might be left to ponder why such a "game" with this dialogue would be marketed even to young adults (Correll et al. 2007a, 2007b; Mock 2008; Rockstar Games 2008; Southern Poverty Law Center 2006).

Prejudice is so prevalent that it is tempting to consider it inevitable or, even more broadly, just part of human nature. Such a view ignores its variability from individual to individual and from society to society. People must learn prejudice as children before they exhibit it as adults. Therefore, prejudice is a social phenomenon, an acquired characteristic. A truly pluralistic society would lack unfavorable distinctions made through prejudicial attitudes among racial and ethnic groups.

Ill feeling between groups may result from ethnocentrism. **Ethnocentrism** is the tendency to assume that one's culture and way of life are superior to all others. The ethnocentric person judges other groups and other cultures by the standards of his or her own group. This attitude leads people quite easily to

Imagine seeing this billboard. What is it for? It is an expression of prejudice. One would easily find that it is making a case for an organization that argues White Americans have an unconditional right to territorial and political self-determination.

view other cultures as inferior. We see a woman with a veil and may regard it as strange and backward, yet find it baffling when other societies see U.S. women in short skirts and view the dress as inappropriate. Ethnocentrism and other expressions of prejudice are voiced very often, but unfortunately, they also become the motivation for criminal acts.

Hate Crimes

Although prejudice certainly is not new in the United States, it is receiving increased attention as it manifests itself in neighborhoods, at meetings, and on college campuses. The Hate Crime Statistics Act, which became law in 1990, directs the Department of Justice to gather data on hate or bias crimes. The government defines an ordinary crime as a **hate crime** when offenders are motivated to choose a victim because of some characteristic—for example, race, ethnicity, religion, sexual orientation, or disability—and provide evidence that hatred prompted them to commit the crime. Hate crimes are also sometimes referred to as bias crimes (Department of Justice 2008).

This law created a national mandate to identify such crimes, whereas previously only twelve states had monitored hate crimes. In 1994, the act was amended to include disabilities, both physical and mental, as factors that could be considered a basis for hate crimes.

In 2006, law enforcement agencies released hate crime data submitted by police agencies covering 85 percent of the United States. Even though many, many hate crimes are not reported (less than one in seven participating agencies reported an incident), a staggering number of offenses that came to law agencies' attention were motivated by hate. There were official reports of more than 7,700 hate crimes and bias-motivated incidents. As indicated in Figure 2.1, race was the apparent motivation for the bias in about 52 percent of the reports, and religion, sexual orientation, and ethnicity accounted for 13 to 19 percent each. Vandalism and intimidation were the most common, but 54 percent of the incidents against people involved assault, rape, or murder.

The vast majority of hate crimes are directed by members of the dominant group toward those who are, relatively speaking, powerless, but that does not account for every hate crime. One in five bias incidents based on race are anti-White. Hate crimes, except for those that are most horrific, receive little media attention and anti-White incidents probably receive even less. Hostility based on race knows no boundaries (Department of Justice 2007; Witt 2007).

The official reports of hate or bias crimes appear to be only the tip of the iceberg. Government-commissioned surveys conducted over a national cross section indicate that, annually, people say they have been victims of 192,000 hate crimes of which only half get reported to police. Of these, only one out of ten, according to the victims, are confirmed as hate crimes. Although definitions vary, there is obviously a lot of racial hostility in the country that becomes violent (Harlow 2005; Perry 2003).

National legislation and publicity have made hate crime a meaningful term, and we are beginning to recognize the victimization associated with such incidents. A current proposal would make a violent crime into a federal crime if the crime were motivated by racial or religious bias. Although passage is uncertain, the serious consideration of the proposal indicates a willingness to consider a major expansion of federal jurisdiction. Currently, federal law prohibits crimes

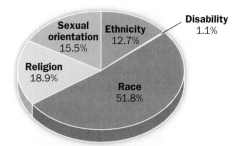

Figure 2.1 Distribution of Reported Hate Crimes in 2006

Source: Department of Justice, 2007.

motivated by race, color, religion, or national origin only if they involve violation of a federally guaranteed right, such as voting.

Victimized groups are not merely observing hate crimes and other acts of prejudice. Watchdog organizations play an important role in documenting bias-motivated violence; among such groups are the Anti-Defamation League (ADL), the National Institute Against Prejudice and Violence, the Southern Poverty Law Center (SPLC), and the National Gay and Lesbian Task Force.

Established hate groups have even set up propaganda sites on the World Wide Web. This also creates opportunities for previously unknown haters and hate groups to promote themselves. However, hate crime legislation does not affect such outlets because of legal questions involving freedom of speech. An even more recent technique has been to use instant messaging software, which enables Internet users to create a private chat room with another individual. Enterprising bigots use directories to target their attacks through instant messaging, much as harassing telephone calls were placed in the past (Working 2007).

What causes people to dislike entire groups of other people? Is it possible to change attitudes? This chapter tries to answer these questions about prejudice. Chapter 3 focuses on discrimination.

Prejudice and Discrimination

Prejudice and discrimination are related concepts but are not the same. **Prejudice** is a negative attitude toward an entire category of people. The two important components in this definition are attitude and entire category. Prejudice involves attitudes, thoughts, and beliefs, not actions. Prejudice often is expressed through the use of **ethnophaulisms,** or ethnic slurs, which include derisive nicknames such as honky, gook, or wetback. Ethnophaulisms also include speaking about or to members of a particular group in a condescending way ("José does well in school for a Mexican American") or referring to a middle-aged woman as "one of the girls."

A prejudiced belief leads to categorical rejection. Prejudice is not disliking someone you meet because you find his or her behavior objectionable. It is disliking an entire racial or ethnic group, even if you have had little or no contact with that group. A college student who requests a room change after three weeks of enduring his roommate's sleeping all day, playing loud music all night, and piling garbage on his desk is not prejudiced. However, he is displaying prejudice if he requests a change on arriving at school and learning that his new roommate is of a different nationality.

Prejudice is a belief or attitude; discrimination is action. **Discrimination** is the denial of opportunities and equal rights to individuals and groups because of prejudice or for other arbitrary reasons. Unlike prejudice, discrimination involves *behavior* that excludes members of a group from certain rights, opportunities, or privileges. Like prejudice, it is categorical, perhaps making for a few rare exceptions. If an employer refuses to hire as a computer analyst an Italian American who is illiterate, it is not discrimination. If an employer refuses to hire any Italian American because he or she thinks they are incompetent and does not make the effort to see whether an applicant is qualified, it is discrimination.

Merton's Typology

Prejudice does not necessarily coincide with discriminatory behavior. In exploring the relationship between negative attitudes and negative behavior, sociologist Robert Merton (1949, 1976) identified four major categories (Figure 2.2). The label added to each of Merton's categories may more readily identify the type of person being described. These are

1. the unprejudiced nondiscriminator: all-weather liberal,
2. the unprejudiced discriminator: reluctant liberal,
3. the prejudiced nondiscriminator: timid bigot, and
4. the prejudiced discriminator: all-weather bigot.

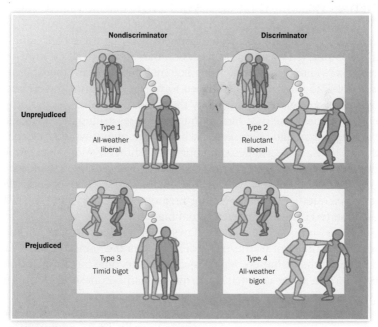

Figure 2.2 Prejudice and Discrimination
As sociologist Robert Merton's formulation shows, prejudice and discrimination are related to each other but are not the same.

As the term is used in types 1 and 2, liberals are committed to equality among people. The all-weather liberal believes in equality and practices it. Merton was quick to observe that all-weather liberals may be far removed from any real competition with subordinate groups such as African Americans or women. Furthermore, such people may be content with their own behavior and may do little to change themselves. The reluctant liberal is not that committed to equality between groups. Social pressure may cause such a person to discriminate. Fear of losing employees may lead a manager to avoid promoting women to supervisory capacities. Equal-opportunity legislation may be the best way to influence the reluctant liberals.

Types 3 and 4 do not believe in equal treatment for racial and ethnic groups, but they vary in their willingness to act. The timid bigot, type 3, will not discriminate if discrimination costs money or reduces profits or if he or she is pressured not to by peers or the government. The all-weather bigot unhesitatingly acts on the prejudiced beliefs he or she holds.

LaPiere's Study

Merton's typology points out that attitudes should not be confused with behavior. People do not always act as they believe. More than a half century ago, Richard LaPiere (1934, 1969) exposed the relationship between racial attitudes and social conduct. From 1930 to 1932 LaPiere traveled throughout the United States with a Chinese couple. Despite an alleged climate of intolerance of Asians, LaPiere observed that the couple were treated courteously at hotels, motels, and restaurants. He was puzzled by the good reception they received; all the conventional attitude surveys showed extreme prejudice by Whites toward the Chinese.

Was it possible that LaPiere had been fortunate during his travels and consistently stopped at places operated by the tolerant members of the dominant group? To test this possibility, he sent questionnaires asking the very establishments at which they had been served whether the owner would "accept members of the Chinese race as guests in your establishment." More than 90 percent responded no, even though LaPiere's Chinese couple had been treated politely at all the establishments. How can this inconsistency be explained? People who returned questionnaires reflecting prejudice were unwilling to act based on those asserted beliefs; they were timid bigots.

The LaPiere study is not without flaws. First, he had no way of knowing whether the respondent to the questionnaire was the same person who had served him and the Chinese couple. Second, he accompanied the couple, but the questionnaire suggested that the arrival would be unescorted (and, in the minds of some, uncontrolled) and perhaps would consist of many Chinese people. Third, personnel may have changed between the time of the visit and the mailing of the questionnaire (Deutscher, Pestello, and Pestello 1993).

The LaPiere technique has been replicated with similar results. This technique raises the question of whether attitudes are important if they are not completely reflected in behavior. But if attitudes are not important in small matters, they are important in other ways: Lawmakers legislate and courts may reach decisions based on what the public thinks.

This is not just a hypothetical possibility. Legislators in the United States often are persuaded to vote in a certain way by what they perceive as changed attitudes toward immigration, affirmative action, and prayer in public schools. Sociologists have enumerated some of prejudice's functions. For the majority group, it serves to maintain privileged occupations and more power for its members.

The following sections examine the theories of why prejudice exists, and discuss the content and extent of prejudice today.

Theories of Prejudice

Prejudice is learned. Friends, relatives, newspapers, books, movies, television, and the Internet all teach it. Awareness begins at an early age that there are differences between people that society judges to be important. Several theories

Many would regard this statue of colonialist Hannah Duston in Massachusetts as perpetuating stereotypes about American Indians. She is honored for killing and scalping ten Abeenaki Indians in 1697 while defending her family. Believed to be the first woman ever honored in the United States with a monument, it portrays her holding a hatchet in her right hand.

have been advanced to explain the rejection of certain groups in a society. We will examine four theoretical explanations. The first two (scapegoating and authoritarian personality) tend to be psychological, emphasizing why a particular person harbors ill feelings. The second two are more sociological (exploitation and normative), viewing prejudice in the context of our interaction in a larger society.

Scapegoating Theory

Scapegoating theory says that prejudiced people believe they are society's victims. The term *scapegoat* comes from a biblical injunction telling the Hebrews to send a goat into the wilderness to symbolically carry away the people's sins. Similarly, the theory of scapegoating suggests that, rather than accepting guilt for some failure, a person transfers the responsibility for failure to some vulnerable group. In the major tragic twentieth-century example, Adolf Hitler used the Jews as the scapegoat for all German social and economic ills in the 1930s. This premise led to the passage of laws restricting Jewish life in pre–World War II Germany and eventually escalated into the mass extermination of Europe's Jews.

Today in the United States, immigrants, whether legal or illegal, often are blamed by "real Americans" for their failure to secure jobs or desirable housing. The immigrant becomes the scapegoat for one's own lack of skills, planning, or motivation. It is so much easier to blame someone else.

? Ask Yourself

Suppose you encounter a person whose prejudice is obvious? Will you say or do anything? What if it is a friend who speaks disparagingly of all members of some ethnic or religious group? Will you speak out? When do you speak out?

Public figures who should know better express their ill feelings. Longtime civil rights leader Andrew Young, in 2006, applauded the expansion of Wal-Mart noting that the big box stores were merely replacing small stores run by Jews, Koreans, and Arabs that ripped off customers. In the same year, a drunk Mel Gibson pulled over by a policeman who was Jewish and told him that "Jews are responsible for all the wars in the world." Both Young and Gibson quickly apologized for their inflammatory remarks, but finding scapegoats among racial and ethnic groups occurs all the time (McGhee 2006; McNamara 2006).

Like the exploitation theory, the scapegoating theory adds to our understanding of why prejudice exists but does not explain all its facets. For example, the scapegoating theory offers little explanation of why a specific group is selected or why frustration is not taken out on the real culprit when possible. Also, both the exploitation and the scapegoating theories suggest that every person sharing the same general experiences in society would be equally prejudiced, but that is not the case. Prejudice varies between individuals who seem to benefit equally from the exploitation of a subordinate group or who have experienced equal frustration. In an effort to explain these personality differences, social scientists developed the concept of the authoritarian personality.

Authoritarian Personality Theory

A number of social scientists do not see prejudice as an isolated trait that anyone can have. Several efforts have been made to detail the prejudiced personality, but the most comprehensive effort culminated in a volume titled *The Authoritarian Personality* (Adorno et al. 1950). Using a variety of tests and relying on more than 2,000 respondents, ranging from middle-class Whites to inmates of San Quentin (California) State Prison, the authors claimed they had isolated the characteristics of the authoritarian personality.

In these authors' view, the basic characteristics of the **authoritarian personality** are adherence to conventional values, uncritical acceptance of authority, and concern with power and toughness. With obvious relevance to the development of intolerance, the authoritarian personality was also characterized by aggressiveness toward people who did not conform to conventional norms or obey authority. According to the researchers, this personality type developed from an early childhood of harsh discipline. A child with an authoritarian upbringing obeyed and then later treated others as he or she had been raised.

This study has been widely criticized, but the very existence of such wide criticism indicates the influence of the study. Critics have attacked the study's equation of authoritarianism with right-wing politics (although liberals can also be rigid); its failure to see that prejudice is more closely related to other individual traits, such as social class, than to authoritarianism as it was defined; the research methods used; and the emphasis on extreme racial prejudice rather than on more common expressions of hostility.

Despite these concerns about specifics in the study completed sixty years ago, annual conferences continue to draw attention to how authoritarian attitudes contribute to racism, sexism, and even torture (Kinloch 1974; O'Neill 2008).

Exploitation Theory

Racial prejudice is often used to justify keeping a group in a subordinate position, such as a lower social class. Conflict theorists, in particular, stress the role of racial and ethnic hostility as a way for the dominant group to keep its position of status and power intact. Indeed, this approach maintains that even the less-affluent White working class uses prejudice to minimize competition from upwardly mobile minorities.

This **exploitation theory** is clearly part of the Marxist tradition in sociological thought. Karl Marx emphasized exploitation of the lower class as an integral part of capitalism. Similarly, the exploitation or conflict approach explains how racism can stigmatize a group as inferior so that the exploitation of that group can be justified. As developed by Oliver Cox (1942), exploitation theory saw prejudice against Blacks as an extension of the inequality faced by the entire lower class.

The exploitation theory of prejudice is persuasive. Japanese Americans were the object of little prejudice until they began to enter occupations that brought them into competition with Whites. The movement to keep Chinese out of the country became strongest during the late nineteenth century, when Chinese immigrants and Whites fought over dwindling numbers of jobs. Both the enslavement of African Americans and the removal westward of Native Americans were to a significant degree economically motivated.

Although many cases support the exploitation theory, it is too limited to explain prejudice in all its forms. First, not all minority groups are exploited economically to the same extent. Second, many groups that have been the victims of prejudice have not been persecuted for economic reasons, such as the Quakers or gays and lesbians. Nevertheless, as Gordon Allport (1979) concludes, the exploitation theory correctly points a finger at one of the factors in prejudice, that is, the rationalized self-interest of the privileged.

Normative Approach

Although personality factors are important contributors to prejudice, normative or situational factors must also be given serious consideration. The **normative approach** takes the view that prejudice is influenced by societal norms and situations that encourage or discourage the tolerance of minorities.

Analysis reveals how societal influences shape a climate for tolerance or intolerance. Societies develop social norms that dictate not only what foods are desirable (or forbidden) but also what racial and ethnic groups are to be favored (or despised). Social forces operate in a society to encourage or discourage tolerance. The force may be widespread, such as the pressure on White Southerners to oppose racial equality while there was slavery or segregation. The influence of social norms may be limited, as when one man finds himself becoming more sexist as he competes with three women for a position in a prestigious law firm.

We should not view the four approaches to prejudice summarized in Table 2.1 as mutually exclusive. Social circumstances provide cues for a person's attitudes; personality determines the extent to which people follow social cues and the likelihood that they will encourage others to do the same. Societal norms may promote or deter tolerance; personality traits suggest the degree to which a person will conform to norms of intolerance. To understand prejudice, we need to use all four approaches together.

Table 2.1 Theories of Prejudice

There is no one explanation of why prejudice exists, but several approaches taken together offer insight.

Theory	Proponent	Explanation	Example
Scapegoating	Bruno Bettelheim Morris Janowitz	People blame others for their own failures.	An unsuccessful applicant assumes that a minority member or a woman got "his" job.
Authoritarian	Adorno and associates	Child rearing leads one to develop intolerance as an adult.	The rigid personality type dislikes people who are different.
Exploitation	Oliver C. Cox Marxist theory	People use others unfairly for economic advantage.	A minority member is hired at a lower-wage level.
Normative	Thomas Pettigrew	Peer and social influences encourage tolerance or intolerance.	A person from an intolerant household is more likely to be openly prejudiced.

Stereotypes

On Christmas Day 2001, Arab American Walied Shater boarded an American Airlines flight from Baltimore to Dallas carrying a gun. Immediately, the cockpit crew refused to let him fly, fearing that Shater would take over the plane and use it as a weapon of mass destruction. Yet Walied Shater carried documentation that he was a Secret Service agent, and calls to Washington DC confirmed that he was flying to join a presidential protection force at President George W. Bush's ranch in Texas. Nevertheless, the crew could not get past the stereotype of Arab American men posing a lethal threat (Leavitt 2002).

What Are Stereotypes?

In Chapter 1, we saw that stereotypes play a powerful role in how people come to view dominant and subordinate groups. **Stereotypes** are unreliable generalizations about all members of a group that do not take individual differences into account. Numerous scientific studies have been made of these exaggerated images. This research has shown the willingness of people to assign positive and negative traits to entire groups of people, which are then applied to particular individuals. Stereotyping causes people to view Blacks as superstitious, Whites as uncaring, and Jews as shrewd. Over the last eighty years of such research, social scientists have found that people have become less willing to express such views openly, but as we will see later, prejudice persists (Quillian 2006).

❓ Ask Yourself

How do the images we see affect how we view people? On the left is a scene from the familiar motion picture *King and I*. On the right is the real monarch, King Chulalongkorn, and his son. The king in real life bore limited similarity to the portrayal made famous by the Russian-born actor Yul Brynner. Is what we know about many ethnic and religious groups more likely the result of portrayals in the popular media than any actual study of their history and customs?

If stereotypes are exaggerated generalizations, why are they so widely held, and why are some traits more often assigned than others? Evidence for traits may arise out of real conditions. For example, more Puerto Ricans live in poverty than Whites, and so the prejudiced mind associates Puerto Ricans with laziness. According to the New Testament, some Jews were responsible for the Crucifixion of Jesus, and so, to the prejudiced mind, all Jews are Christ killers. Some activists in the women's movement are lesbians, and so all feminists are seen as lesbians. From a kernel of fact, faulty generalization creates a stereotype.

Labels take on such strong significance that people often ignore facts that contradict their previously held beliefs. People who believe many Italian Americans to be members of the Mafia disregard law-abiding Italian Americans. Muslims are regularly portrayed in a violent, offensive manner that contributes to their being misunderstood and distrusted. We will consider later in this chapter how this stereotype about Muslims has become widespread since the mid-1970s but intensified after the attack on the World Trade Center on September 11, 2001.

In "Listen to Our Voices," journalist Helen Zia, born in New Jersey to immigrants from Shanghai, China, comments about how immigrant parents grapple with the prejudice their children feel. Should they teach their children their language and perhaps heighten stereotypes and ill feelings from others or push them to become American as fast as possible?

LISTEN TO OUR VOICES

Gangsters, Gooks, Geishas, and Geeks

Helen Zia

Ah so. No tickee, no washee. So sorry, so sollee.

Chinkee, Chink. Jap, Nip, zero, kamikaze. Dothead, flat face, flat nose, slant eye, slope. Slit, mamasan, dragon lady. Gook, VC, Flip, Hindoo.

By the time I was ten, I'd heard such words so many times I could feel them coming before they parted lips. I knew they were meant in the unkindest way. Still, we didn't talk about these incidents at home, we just accepted them as part of being in America, something to learn to rise above.

The most common taunting didn't even utilize words but a string of unintelligible gobbledygook that kids—and adults—would spew as they pretended to speak Chinese or some other Asian language. It was a mockery of how they imagined my parents talked to me.

Truth was that Mom and Dad rarely spoke to us in Chinese, except to scold or call us to dinner. Worried that we might develop an accent, my father insisted that we speak English at home. This, he explained, would lessen the hardships we might encounter and make us more acceptable as Americans.

I'll never know if my father's language decision was right. On the one hand, I, like most Asian Americans, have been complimented countless times on my spoken English by people who assumed I was a foreigner. "My, you speak such good English," they'd cluck. "No kidding, I ought to," I would think to myself, then wonder: should I thank them for assuming that English isn't my native language? Or should I correct them on the proper usage of "well" and "good"?

More often than feeling grateful for my American accent, I've wished that I could jump into a heated exchange of rapid-fire Chinese, volume high and spit flying. But with a vocabulary limited to "Ni hao?" (How are you?) and "Ting bu dong" (I hear but don't understand), meaningful exchanges are woefully impossible. I find myself smiling and nodding like a dashboard ornament. I'm envious of the many people I know who grew up speaking an Asian language yet converse in English beautifully.

Armed with standard English and my flat New Jersey "a," I still couldn't escape the name-calling. I became all too familiar with other names and faces that supposedly matched mine—Fu Manchu, Suzie Wong, Hop Sing, Madame Butterfly, Charlie Chan, Ming the Merciless—the "Asians" produced for mass consumption. Their faces filled me with shame whenever I saw them on TV or in the movies. They defined my face to the rest of the world: a sinister Fu, Suzie the whore, subservient Hop Sing, pathetic Butterfly, cunning Chan, and warlike Ming. Inscrutable Orientals all, real Americans none.

Source: Excerpt from pp. 109–110 in *Asian American Dreams* by Helen Zia. Copyright © 2000 by Helen Zia. Reprinted by permission of Farrar, Straus, and Giroux, LLC.

Power of Stereotypes

The labeling of individuals through negative stereotypes has strong implications for the self-fulfilling prophecy. Studies show that people are all too aware of the negative images other people have of them. When asked to estimate the prevalence of hard-core racism among Whites, one in four Blacks agrees that more than half "personally share the attitudes of groups like the Ku Klux Klan toward Blacks"; only one Black in ten says "only a few" share such views. Stereotypes not only influence how people feel about themselves but, perhaps equally important, also affect how people interact with others. If people feel that others hold incorrect, disparaging attitudes toward them, it undoubtedly will make it difficult to have harmonious relations (Sigelman and Tuch 1997).

Stereotyping persists in many forms, even in iconic images for sports teams. For several generations, a student would dress as Chief Illiniwek and appear on behalf of the University of Illinois at Champaign, Urbana until banned by the National Collegiate Athletic Association (NCAA) in tournaments. Yet for professional teams like the Washington Redskins and the Cleveland Indians with its Chief Wahoo continue the practice with an approving base of fans.

Do only dominant groups hold stereotypes about subordinate groups? The answer is clearly no. White Americans even believe generalizations about themselves, although admittedly these are usually positive. Subordinate groups also hold exaggerated images of themselves. Studies before World War II showed a tendency for Blacks to assign to themselves many of the same negative traits assigned by Whites. Today, African Americans, Jews, Asians, and other minority groups largely reject stereotypes of themselves.

Although explicit expression of stereotypes are less common, it is much too soon to write the obituary of racial and ethnic stereotypes. In Chapter 6, we will consider the persistence of two stereotypes—the model minority and acting White; and next we will consider the use of stereotypes in the contemporary practice of racial profiling.

Stereotyping in Action: Racial Profiling

Five Middle Eastern–looking men were led off the Newark-bound plane by security in 2006. Suspiciously in-flight, they had been talking among themselves in a foreign language looking at flight manuals they had aboard. Actually, as the investigation would reveal, they were Portuguese-speaking Angolan and Israeli soldiers returning from government-approved helicopter training in Texas. Reasonable precaution in these days of terrorism? Perhaps. But would air marshals have been as suspicious of White travelers or if the men had been speaking English? Suspicions raised by appearances often related to race or ethnicity are not new.

A Black dentist, Elmo Randolph, testified before a state commission that he was stopped dozens of times in the 1980s and 1990s while traveling the New Jersey Turnpike to work. Invariably state troopers asked, "Do you have guns or drugs?" "My parents always told me, be careful when you're driving on the turnpike" said Dr. Randolph, 44. "White people don't have that conversation" (Purdy 2001, 37; also see Fernandez and Fahim 2006).

Little wonder that Dr. Randolph was pulled over. Although African Americans accounted for only 17 percent of the motorists on that turnpike, they were 80 percent of the motorists pulled over. Such occurrences gave rise to the charge that a new traffic offense was added to the books: DWB or Driving While Black (Bowles 2000).

In recent years, government attention has been given to a social phenomenon with a long history: racial profiling. According to the Department of Justice, **racial profiling** is any police-initiated action based on race, ethnicity, or national origin rather than the person's behavior. Generally, profiling occurs when law enforcement officers, including customs officials, airport security, and police, assume that people fitting certain descriptions are likely to be engaged in something illegal. Beginning in the 1980s with the emergence of the crack cocaine market, skin color became a key characteristic. This profiling can be a very explicit use of stereotypes. For example, the federal antidrug initiative,

Operation Pipeline, specifically encouraged officers to look for people with dreadlocks or for Latino men traveling together.

The reliance on racial profiling persists despite overwhelming evidence that it is misleading. Whites are more likely to be found with drugs in the areas in which minority group members are disproportionately targeted. A federal study made public in 2005 found little difference nationwide in the likelihood of being stopped by officers, but African Americans were twice as likely to have their vehicles searched and Latinos were five times more likely. A similar pattern emerged in the likelihood of force being used against drivers to be three times more likely among Latinos and Blacks than White drivers. A 2007 study of New York City police found that Whites and racial minorities are equally likely to be stopped, but the officers were more likely to frisk, search, arrest, or give summonses to Black or Latino people (Lichtblau 2005; Ridgeway 2007).

Back in the 1990s, increased attention to racial profiling led not only to special reports and commissions but also to talk of legislating against it. This proved difficult. The U.S. Supreme Court in *Whren v. United States* (1996) upheld the constitutionality of using a minor traffic infraction as an excuse to stop and search a vehicle and its passengers. Nonetheless, states and other government units are discussing policies and training that would discourage racial profiling. At the same time, most law enforcement agencies reject the idea of compiling racial data on traffic stops, arguing that it would be a waste of money and staff time.

The effort to stop racial profiling came to an abrupt end after the September 11, 2001 terrorist attacks on the United States. Suspicions about Muslims and Arabs in the United States became widespread. Foreign students from Arab countries were summoned for special questioning. Legal immigrants identified as Arab or Muslim were scrutinized for any illegal activity and were prosecuted for routine immigration violations that were ignored for people of other ethnic backgrounds and religious faiths (Withrow 2006).

National surveys have found little change since 2001 in support for profiling Arab Americans at airports. In 2006, 53 percent favored requiring Arabs, including those who are U.S. citizens, to undergo special more-intensive security checks before boarding planes in the United States (Saad 2006b).

Color-Blind Racism

Over the last three generations, nationwide surveys have consistently shown growing support by Whites for integration, interracial dating, and having members of minority groups attain political office including even to be president of the United States. Yet how can this be true and the type of hatred described at the beginning of chapter persist and thousands of hate crimes occur annually?

Color-blind racism refers to the use of race-neutral principles to defend the racially unequal status quo. Yes, there should be "no discrimination for

Color-blind racism can take many forms. Why should not the United States have an official language as most nations do? Typically calls today for English as the official language reassert values superior to someone else's. Here we see a meeting at a Wisconsin county making English the official language—a move with little practical significance but that speaks loudly in terms of symbolism in an area with a large presence of the Asian ethnic group the Hmong.

college admission," yet the disparity in educational experiences means that the use of formal admissions criteria will privilege White high school graduates. "Health care is for all," but if you fail to have workplace insurance you are unlikely to afford it.

Color-blind racism has also been referred to as "laissez-faire" or "postracialism" or "aversive racism," but the common theme is not that although notions of racial inferiority are rarely expressed, the ideology that we should proceed color-blind into the future will serve to perpetuate inequality. In the post–civil rights era, people are more likely to assume discrimination is long past and express their views in ways that are more proper, that is, lacking the overt expressions of racism of the past.

An important aspect of color-blind racism is the recognition that race is rarely invoked so that one can emphasize social class or citizenship as, in effect, proxies for race. This leads many White people to declare they are not racist and that they really do not know anyone either who is racist. It leads to the mistaken conclusion that more progress has been made to racial and ethnic equality and even tolerance than has really taken place.

When we survey White attitudes toward African Americans, two conclusions are inescapable. First, attitudes are subject to change, and in periods of dramatic social upheaval, dramatic shifts can occur within one generation. Second, less progress was made in the late twentieth and the beginning of the twenty-first centuries than was made in the relatively brief period of the 1950s and 1960s.

Economically less-successful groups such as African Americans and Latinos have been associated with negative traits to the point at which issues such as urban decay, homelessness, welfare, and crime are now viewed as race issues even though race is rarely spoken of explicitly. Besides making the resolution of very difficult social issues even harder, this is another instance of blaming the victim. These perceptions come at a time when the willingness of the government to address domestic ills is limited by increasing opposition to new taxes and continuing commitments to fight terrorism here and abroad. The color line remains even if more and more people are unwilling to accept its divisive impact on everyone's lives (Ansell 2008; Bonilla-Silva 2006; Bonilla-Silva and Baiocchi 2001; Dovidio 2001; Ferber 2007; Quillian 2006; Winant 2004, 106–108).

The Mood of the Oppressed

Sociologist W. E. B. Du Bois relates an experience from his youth in a largely White community in Massachusetts. He tells how, on one occasion, the boys and girls were exchanging cards, and everyone was having a lot of fun. One girl, a newcomer, refused his card as soon as she saw that Du Bois was Black. He wrote,

> *Then it dawned upon me with a certain suddenness that I was different from others . . . shut out from their world by a vast veil. I had therefore no desire to tear down that veil, to creep through; I held all beyond it in common contempt and lived above it in a region of blue sky and great wandering shadows (Du Bois 1903, 2).*

In using the image of a veil, Du Bois describes how members of subordinate groups learn that they are being treated differently. In his case and that of many others, this leads to feelings of contempt toward all Whites, which continue for a lifetime.

Opinion pollsters have been interested in White attitudes on racial issues longer than they have measured the views of subordinate groups. This neglect of minority attitudes reflects, in part, the bias of the White researchers. It also stems from the contention that the dominant group is more important to study because it is in a better position to act on its beliefs. The results of a nation-wide survey conducted in the United States in 2007 offer insight into sharply different views on the state of race relations today (Figure 2.3). Latinos, African Americans, and Asian Americans all have strong reservations of the state of "race relations" in the United States. They are skeptical about the level of equal opportunity and perceive a lot of discrimination. Interestingly, Hispanics and Asian Americans, overwhelmingly immigrants, are more likely to feel they will succeed if they work hard. Yet the majority of all three groups have a positive outlook for the next ten years (New America Media 2007; Preston 2007b).

We have focused so far on what usually comes to mind when we think about prejudice: one group hating another group. But there is another form of prejudice: A group may come to hate itself. Members of groups held in low esteem

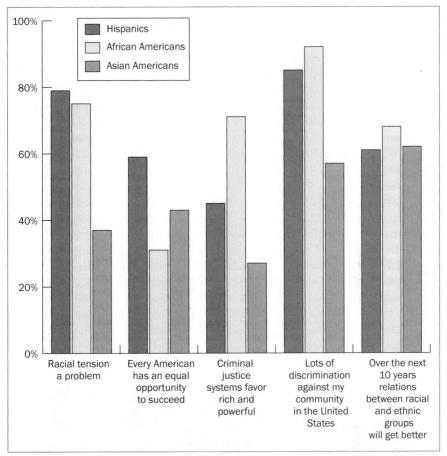

Figure 2.3 What Is the State of Race Relations? Three Views

Note: Answers of "very important problem" or "strongly agree" with statements listed. Based on 1,105 interviews in August–September 2007 with bilingual questionners used as necessary.

Source: New America Media 2007, pp. 6, 12, 14, 24, 26.

by society may, as a result, have low self-esteem themselves. Many social scientists once believed that members of subordinate groups hated themselves or at least had low self-esteem. Similarly, they argued that Whites had high self-esteem. High self-esteem means that an individual has fundamental respect for himself or herself, appreciates his or her own merits, and is aware of personal faults and will strive to overcome them.

The research literature of the 1940s through the 1960s emphasized the low self-esteem of minorities. Usually, the subject was African Americans, but the argument has also been generalized to include any subordinate racial, ethnic, or nationality group. This view is no longer accepted. We should not assume that minority status influences personality traits in either a good or a bad way.

First, such assumptions may create a stereotype. We cannot describe a Black personality any more accurately than we can a White personality. Second, characteristics of minority-group members are not entirely the result of subordinate racial status; they are also influenced by low incomes, poor neighborhoods, and so forth. Third, many studies of personality imply that certain values are normal or preferable, but the values chosen are those of dominant groups.

If assessments of a subordinate group's personality are so prone to misjudgments, why has the belief in low self-esteem been so widely held? Much of the research rests on studies with preschool-age Black children asked to express preferences among dolls with different facial colors. Indeed, one such study, by psychologists Kenneth and Mamie Clark (1947), was cited in the arguments before the U.S. Supreme Court in the landmark 1954 case *Brown v. Board of Education.* The Clarks' study showed that Black children preferred White dolls, a finding suggesting that the children had developed a negative self-image. Although subsequent doll studies have sometimes shown Black children's preference for white-faced dolls, other social scientists contend that this shows a realization of what most commercially sold dolls look like rather than documenting low self-esteem (Bloom 1971; Powell-Hopson and Hopson 1988).

Because African American children, as well as other subordinate groups' children, can realistically see that Whites have more power and resources and, therefore, rate them higher does not mean that they personally feel inferior. Indeed, studies, even with children, show that when the self-images of

How do children come to develop an image about themselves? Toys and playthings play an important role, and for many children of racial and ethnic minorities it is unusual to find a toy that looks like themselves. In 2005, a new doll was released called Fulla—an Arab girl who reflects modesty, piety, and respect, yet underneath she wears more chic clothes as might be typically worn by Muslim women in private.

middle-class or affluent African Americans are measured, their feelings of self-esteem are more positive than those of comparable Whites (Gray-Little and Hafdahl 2000).

Intergroup Hostility

Prejudice is as diverse as the nation's population. It exists not only between dominant and subordinate peoples but also between specific subordinate groups. Unfortunately, until recently little research existed on this subject except for a few social distance scales administered to racial and ethnic minorities.

A national survey revealed that, like Whites, many African Americans, Hispanic Americans, and Asian Americans held prejudiced and stereotypical views of other racial and ethnic minority groups:

- Majorities of Black, Hispanic, and Asian American respondents agreed that Whites are "bigoted, bossy, and unwilling to share power." Majorities of these non-White groups also believed that they had less opportunity than Whites to obtain a good education, a skilled job, or decent housing.
- Forty-six percent of Hispanic Americans and 42 percent of African Americans agreed that Asian Americans are "unscrupulous, crafty, and devious in business."
- Sixty-eight percent of Asian Americans and 49 percent of African Americans believed that Hispanic Americans "tend to have bigger families than they are able to support."
- Thirty-one percent of Asian Americans and 26 percent of Hispanic Americans agreed that African Americans "want to live on welfare."

Members of oppressed groups obviously have adopted the widely held beliefs of the dominant culture concerning oppressed groups. At the same time, the survey also revealed positive views of major racial and ethnic minorities:

- More than 80 percent of respondents admired Asian Americans for "placing a high value on intellectual and professional achievement" and "having strong family ties."
- A majority of all groups surveyed agreed that Hispanic Americans "take deep pride in their culture and work hard to achieve a better life."
- Large majorities from all groups stated that African Americans "have made a valuable contribution to American society and will work hard when given a chance" (National Conference of Christians and Jews 1994).

Do we get along? Although this question often is framed in terms of the relationships between White Americans and other racial and ethnic groups, we should recognize the prejudice between groups. In a national survey conducted in 2000, people were asked whether they felt they could generally get along with members of other groups. In Figure 2.4, we can see that Whites felt they had the most difficulty getting along with Blacks. We also see the different views that Blacks, Latinos, Asian Americans, and American Indians hold toward other groups.

Curiously, we find that some groups feel they get along better with Whites than with other minority groups. Why would that be? Often, low-income people are competing daily with other low-income people and do not readily see the larger societal forces that contribute to their low status. As we can see from the survey results, many Hispanics are more likely to see Asian Americans as getting in their way than the White Americans who are actually the real decision makers in their community.

Reducing Prejudice

Focusing on how to eliminate prejudice involves an explicit value judgment: Prejudice is wrong and causes problems for those who are prejudiced and for their victims. The obvious way to eliminate prejudice is to eliminate its causes: the desire to exploit, the fear of being threatened, and the need to blame others for one's own failure. These might be eliminated by personal therapy, but therapy, even if it works for every individual, is no solution for an entire society in which prejudice is a part of everyday life.

The answer appears to rest with programs directed at society as a whole. Prejudice is attacked indirectly when discrimination is attacked. Despite prevailing beliefs to the contrary, we can legislate against prejudice: Statutes and decisions do affect attitudes. In the past, people firmly believed that laws could not overcome norms, especially racist ones. Recent history, especially after the civil rights movement began in 1954, has challenged that common wisdom. Laws and court rulings that have equalized the treatment of Blacks and Whites have led people to reevaluate their beliefs about what is right and wrong. The increasing tolerance by Whites during the civil rights era, from 1954 to 1965, seems to support this conclusion.

Much research has been done to determine how to change negative attitudes toward groups of people. The most encouraging findings point to education, mass media, intergroup contact, and workplace training programs.

Education

Research on education and prejudice considers both special programs aimed at promoting mutual respect and on what effect more formal schooling generally has on expressions of bigotry.

Most research studies show that well-constructed programs do have some positive effect in reducing prejudice, at least temporarily. The reduction is rarely as much as one might wish, however. The difficulty is that a single

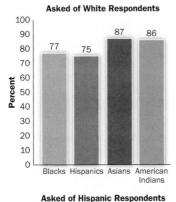

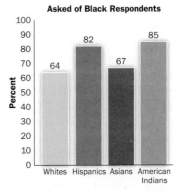

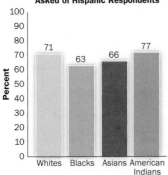

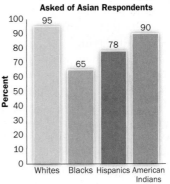

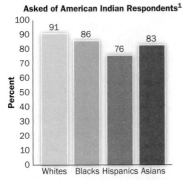

Figure 2.4 Do We Get Along?

Percentage saying groups get along with each other (Don't Knows excluded).

[1]Sample size for American Indians is very small and subject to large sample variance.

Note: The wording of the question was "We hear a lot these days about how various groups in society get along with each other. I'm going to mention several groups and ask whether you think they generally get along with each other or generally do not get along with each other." So, in the Asked of White Respondents graph, Whites are asked how Whites get along with each ethnic group; in the Asked of Black Respondents graph, Blacks are asked how Blacks get along with each ethnic group, and so on.

Source: From *Taking America's Pulse III: NCCJ's 2005 Survey of Intergroup Relations in the United States* by Tom W. Smith, 2006, p. 65. Reprinted by permission of the author.

program is insufficient to change lifelong habits, especially if little is done to reinforce the program's message once it ends. Persuasion to respect other groups does not operate in a clear field because, in their ordinary environments, people are still subjected to situations that promote prejudicial feelings. Children and adults are encouraged to laugh at Polish jokes and cheer for a team named "Redskins." Black adolescents may be discouraged by peers from befriending a White youth. All this undermines the effectiveness of prejudice reduction programs (Allport 1979).

Studies document that increased formal education, regardless of content, is associated with racial tolerance. Research data show that highly educated people are more likely to indicate respect and liking for groups different from themselves. Why should more years of schooling have this effect? It could be that more education gives a broader outlook and makes a person less likely to endorse myths that sustain racial prejudice. Formal education teaches the importance of qualifying statements and the need to question rigid categorizations, if not reject them altogether. Colleges are increasingly including as a graduation requirement a course that explores diversity or multiculturalism. Another explanation is that education does not actually reduce intolerance but simply makes people more careful about revealing it. Formal education may simply instruct people in the appropriate responses, which in some settings could even be prejudiced views. Despite the lack of a clear-cut explanation, either theory suggests that the continued trend toward a better-educated population will contribute to a reduction in overt prejudice.

However, college education may not reduce prejudice uniformly. For example, some White students will come to believe that minority students did not earn their admission into college. Students may feel threatened to see large groups of people of different racial and cultural backgrounds congregating together and forming their own groups. Racist confrontations do occur outside the classroom and, even if they do involve only a few, the events themselves will be followed by hundreds. Therefore, some aspects of the college experience may only foster "we" and "they" attitudes (Schaefer 1986, 1996).

Mass Media

The mass media, like schools, may reduce prejudice without the need for specially designed programs. Television, radio, motion pictures, newspapers, magazines, and the Internet present only a portion of real life, but what effect do they have on prejudice if the content is racist or antiracist, sexist or antisexist? As with measuring the influence of programs designed to reduce prejudice, coming to strong conclusions on the mass media's effect is hazardous, but the evidence points to a measurable effect.

Today, 40 percent of all youths in the nation are children of color, yet few of the faces they see on television reflect their race or cultural heritage. As of Spring 2007, only five of the early sixty primetime series carried on the four major networks featured performers of color in leading roles, and only two—*Ugly Betty*

Members of racial and ethnic minorities do not often appear on a regular basis in staring roles on television drama and comedy shows, and when they do, it is often in roles reflecting negative stereotypes. (Lalo Alcaraz © 2001 Dist. by Universal Press Syndicate. Reprinted with permission. All Rights Reserved).

and *George Lopez*—centered on minority performers. What is more, the programs that show earlier in the evening, when young people are most likely to watch television, are the least diverse of all.

Why the underrepresentation? Incredibly, network executives seemed surprised by the research demonstrating an all-White season. Producers, writers, executives, and advertisers blamed each other for the alleged oversight. In recent years, the rise of both cable television and the Internet has fragmented the broadcast entertainment market, siphoning viewers away from the general-audience sitcoms and dramas of the past. With the proliferation of cable channels such as Black Entertainment Television (BET) and the Spanish-language Univision and Web sites that cater to every imaginable taste, there no longer seems to be a need for broadly popular series such as *The Cosby Show,* whose tone and content appealed to Whites as well as Blacks in a way that the newer series do not. The result of these sweeping technological changes has been a sharp divergence in viewer preferences.

It is not surprising that these mainstream writers and producers, most of whom live far from ethnically and racially diverse inner-city neighborhoods, tend to write and prefer stories about people like themselves. Even urban-based programs such as the successful *Seinfeld* and *Frazier* lasted years on television with almost no people of color crossing the screen.

Television series are only part of the picture. Newscasting and print journalists are overwhelmingly done by Whites and local news emphasizes crime often featuring Black or Hispanic perpetrators. This is especially troubling given another finding in the study discussed at the beginning of the chapter. Research showed that people were quicker to "shoot" an armed Black person than a White man in a video stimulation. In another variation of that same study, the researchers showed subjects fake newspaper articles describing a string of armed robberies that showed either Black or White suspects. The subjects were quicker to "shoot" the armed suspect if he was Black but had no impact on their willingness to "shoot" the armed White criminal. This is a troubling aspect of the potential impact that media content may have (Correll et al. 2007b).

Avoidance versus Friendship

Do we get along? In Research Focus, we consider the degree to which people have close friends of different racial and ethnic backgrounds. Two parallel paths have been taken to consider intergroup contact—social distance and equal-status contact.

The Social Distance Scale   Robert Park and Ernest Burgess first defined **social distance** as the tendency to approach or withdraw from a racial group (1921, 440). Emory Bogardus (1968) conceptualized a scale that could measure social distance empirically. His social distance scale is so widely used that it is often called the **Bogardus scale.**

The scale asks people how willing they would be to interact with various racial and ethnic groups in specified social situations. The situations describe different degrees of social contact or social distance. The items used, with their corresponding distance scores, follow. People are asked whether they would be willing to work alongside, be a neighbor, and, showing the least amount of

RESEARCH FOCUS

Few of My Best Friends Are ...

Do people really have close friends of different racial and ethnic backgrounds? Some sociologists have attempted to gauge the degree of White–Black interaction in the United States. They indicate that many people overestimate the degree of "racial togetherness" in our society.

Sociologist Tom Smith, who directs the respected General Social Survey, has noticed that a high proportion of both White and African American respondents claim to have close friends of another race. But is that really true? When Smith and fellow researchers analyzed the survey data, they found that response rates varied with the way the question was phrased. When asked whether any of the friends they felt close to was Black, 42.1 percent of Whites said yes. Yet when asked to give the names of friends they felt close to, only 6 percent of Whites listed a close friend of a different race or ethnicity. (Figure 2.5)

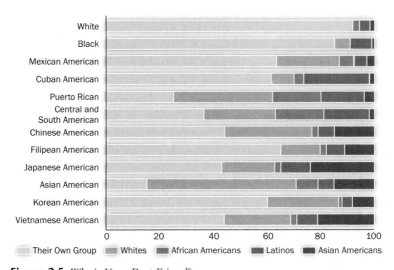

Figure 2.5 Who's Your Best Friend?

Source: Adapted from Kao and Joyner 2004, Table 1.

When asked the race of their best same-sex friend, most Americans choose someone of the same race as themselves. In a national study of adolescents, over 91 percent of non–Hispanic Whites claimed a non–Hispanic White as their best same-sex friend. The General Social Survey yielded almost the same result for all adults. Given the fact that over a third of the teens in the United States are either non-White or Hispanic, we might have expected to find more cross-race friendships. Members of minority groups seem more willing than Whites to cross racial and ethnic boundaries, however. A slightly lower 85 percent of Black adolescents selected a Black for a best friend, and a markedly lower 62 percent of Mexican Americans named another Mexican American.

In yet another study, sociologists Grace Kao and Kara Joyner released a study in 2004 that considered the responses of more than 90,000 adolescents nationwide in an in-school survey. Among many questions, students were asked to identify their best friend and later to identify that person's race and ethnicity. As we can see in Figure 2.4, most people for their primary friendships chose someone of the same race or ethnicity.

We can see that over 81 percent of White youths had as their best friend someone who was also White. Other racial and ethnic groups are more likely to venture outside their group's boundaries but friendships within racial and ethnic groups still dominate, especially when one considers the potential to befriend a member of the numerous White majority.

Research of the last ten years shows that regardless of one's racial or ethnic group, friendships that cross racial and ethnic boundaries are less likely than others to involve visits to each other's homes. They are also less likely than others to feature a sharing of personal problems.

In sum, careful research shows that to a great degree, our society's growing diversity is not necessarily reflected in our choice of friends.

Source: Briggs 2007; Hamm, Brown, and Heck 2005; Kao and Joyner 2004; Kao and Vaquera 2006; Mouw and Entwisle 2006; Smith 1999.

social distance, be related through marriage. Over the seventy-year period the tests were administered, certain patterns emerged. In the top third of the hierarchy are White Americans and northern Europeans. Held at greater social distance are eastern and southern Europeans, and generally near the bottom are racial minorities (Bogardus 1968; Song 1991).

Generally, the researchers also found that among the respondents who had friends of different racial and ethnic origin, they were more likely to show greater social distance—that is, they were less likely to have been in each other's homes, share in fewer activities, and were less likely to talk about their problems with each other. This is unlikely to promote mutual understanding.

Equal-Status Contact An impressive number of research studies have confirmed the **contact hypothesis,** which states that intergroup contact between people of equal status in harmonious circumstances will cause them to become less prejudiced and to abandon previously held stereotypes. Most studies indicate that such contact also improves the attitude of subordinate-group members. The importance of equal status in the interaction cannot be stressed enough. If a Puerto Rican is abused by his employer, little interracial harmony is promoted. Similarly, the situation in which contact occurs must be pleasant, making a positive evaluation likely for both individuals. Contact between two nurses, one Black and the other White, who are competing for one vacancy as a supervisor may lead to greater racial hostility (Schaefer 1976).

The key factor in reducing hostility, in addition to equal-status contact, is the presence of a common goal. If people are in competition, as already noted, contact may heighten tension. However, bringing people together to share a common task has been shown to reduce ill feelings when these people belong to different racial, ethnic, or religious groups. A study released in 2004 traced the transformations that occurred over the generations in the composition of the Social Service Employees Union in New York City. Always a mixed membership, the union was founded by Jews and Italian Americans, only to experience an influx of Black Americans. More recently, it is comprised of Latin Americans, Africans, West Indians, and South Asians. At each point, the common goals of representing the workers effectively overcame the very real cultural differences among the rank-and-file of Mexican and El Salvadoran immigrants in Houston. The researchers found when the new arrivals had contact with African Americans, intergroup relations generally improved, and the absence of contact tended to foster ambivalent, even negative, attitudes (Fine 2008; Foerstrer 2004; Sherif and Sherif 1969).

Such studies are encouraging but what is troubling is still how little significant intergroup contact exists. In "Research Focus," we consider recent efforts to measure how much contact occurs.

The limited amount of intergroup contact is of concern given the power of the contact hypothesis. If there is not positive contact, how can we expect there to be less prejudice. National surveys show prejudice directed toward Muslim Americans, but social contact bridges that hatred. In a 2006 survey, 50 percent of people who are not acquainted with a Muslim favor special identification for Muslim Americans, but only 24 percent of those who know a Muslim embrace that same view. Similarly, people personally familiar with Muslims are a more than a third less likely to endorse special security checks just for Muslims and are nervous to see a Muslim man on the same flight with themselves. Although negative views are common toward Muslim Americans today, they are much less likely to be endorsed by people who have had intergroup contact (Saad 2006a).

As African Americans and other subordinate groups slowly gain access to better-paying and more responsible jobs, the contact hypothesis takes on greater significance. Usually, the availability of equal-status interaction is taken for granted, yet in everyday life, intergroup contact does not conform to the equal-status idea of the contact hypothesis. Furthermore, as we have seen, in a highly segregated society such as the United States, contact, especially between Whites and minorities, tends to be brief and superficial. The apartheid-like friendship patterns prevent us from learning firsthand not just to get along but to revel in interracial experiences (Bonilla-Silva and Embrick 2007; Miller 2002).

Corporate Response: Diversity Training

Prejudice carries a cost. This cost is not only to the victim but also to any organization that allows prejudice to interfere with its functioning. Workplace hostility can lead to lost productivity and even attrition. Furthermore, if left unchecked, an organization, whether a corporation, government agency, or nonprofit enterprise, can develop a reputation for having a "chilly climate." This reputation of a business unfriendly to people of color or to women discourages both qualified people from applying for jobs and potential clients from seeking products or services.

In an effort to improve workplace relations, most organizations have initiated some form of diversity training. These programs are aimed at eliminating circumstances and relationships that cause groups to receive fewer rewards, resources, or opportunities. Typically, programs aim to reduce ill treatment based on race, gender, and ethnicity. In addition, diversity training may deal with (in descending order of frequency) age, disability, religion, and language, as well as other aspects, including citizenship status, marital status, and parental status (Society for Human Resource Management 2002).

It is difficult to make any broad generalization about the effectiveness of diversity training programs because they vary so much in structure between organizations. At one extreme are short presentations that seem to have little support from management. People file into the room feeling that this is something they need to get through quickly. Such training is unlikely to be effective

Efforts are beginning in the workplace to reduce hostility among workers based on prejudice.

and may actually be counterproductive by heightening social tensions. At the other end of the continuum is a diversity training program that is integrated into initial job training, reinforced periodically, and presented as part of the overall mission of the organization, with full support from all levels of management. In these businesses, diversity is a core value, and management demands a high degree of commitment from all employees (Ely, Meyerson, and Davidson 2006; Lindsley 1998).

As shown in Figure 2.6, the workforce is becoming more diverse, and management is taking notice. An increasing proportion of the workforce is foreign-born and the numbers of U.S.-born African Americans, Latinos, and Asian Americans is also growing. Growing research in business and the social sciences is documenting that diversity is an asset in bringing about creative changes. The benefits of workplace diversity is especially true at management levels where leadership teams can develop innovative solutions (DiTomaso, Post, and Parks-Yancy 2007; Page 2007).

It is not in an organization's best interests if employees start to create barriers based on, for example, racial lines. We saw in the previous section that equal-status contact can reduce hostility. However, in the workplace, people compete for promotions, desirable work assignments, and better office space, to name a few sources of friction. When done well, an organization undertakes diversity training to remove ill feelings among workers, often reflected in the prejudices present in larger society.

The content of diversity training also varies. Generally, it includes sharing information about the diverse composition of the service region, the company, and potential clientele today and in the future. Videotapes are sometimes used

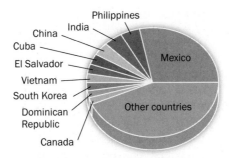

Figure 2.6 Foreign-Born Workers in the
United States by Country
About 15 percent of the civilian labor force is
foreign-born with Mexico the largest source.
Source: Data for 2004 from the Bureau of Labor
Statistics in Mosisa 2006, 48.

that usually compare proper and awkward ways to handle a situation. Training sessions may break up into smaller group interactions where problem solving and team building are also encouraged.

If it is to have a lasting impact on an organization, diversity training should not be separated from other aspects of the organization. For example, even the most inspired program will have little effect on prejudice if the organization promotes a sexist or ethnically offensive image in its advertising. The University of North Dakota launched an initiative in 2001 to become one of the top institutions for Native Americans in the nation. Yet at almost the same time, the administration reaffirmed its commitment, despite tribal objections, to having as its mascot for athletic teams the "Fighting Sioux." It does little to do diversity training if overt actions by an organization propel it in the opposite direction. In 2005, the National Collegiate Athletic Association began a review of logos and mascots that could be considered insulting to Native Americans. Some colleges have resisted suggestions to change or alter their publicity images although others have abandoned the practice (Brownstein 2001; NCAA 2005).

Although diversity training is increasingly common in the workplace, it may be undertaken primarily in response to major evidence of wrongdoing. In recent years, companies as diverse as Avis Rent-a-Car, Circuit City, Coca-Cola, Mitsubishi, Denny's Restaurants, Morgan Stanley, and Texaco have become synonymous with racism or sexual harassment. Generally, as a part of multimillion-dollar settlements, organizations agree to conduct comprehensive diversity training programs. So common is this pattern that a human resources textbook even cautions that a company should "avoid beginning such training too soon" after a complaint of workplace prejudice or discrimination (Carrell, Elbert, and Hatfield 2000, 266).

Despite the problems inherent in confronting prejudice, an organization with a comprehensive, management-supported program of diversity training can go a long way toward reducing prejudice in the workplace. The one major qualifier is that the rest of the organization must also support mutual respect.

Ways to Fight Hate

What can schools do? Television and movie producers? Corporate big shots? It is easy to shift the responsibility for confronting prejudice to the movers and shakers, and certainly they do play a critical role. Yet there definitely are actions one can take in the course of everyday day life to challenge intergroup hostility.

The SPLC, founded in 1971 and based in Montgomery, Alabama, organized committed activists all over the country to mount legal cases and challenges against hate groups such as the Ku Klux Klan. The center's courtroom-challenges led to the end of many discriminatory practices. Its cases have now gone beyond conventional race-based cases because the center has won equal benefits for women in the armed forces, ended involuntary sterilization of women on welfare, and reformed prison and mental health conditions.

Recognizing that social change can also begin at the individual level, the SPLC has identified ten ways to fight hate on the basis of its experience working at the community level (Carrier 2000):

1. *Act.* Do something. In the face of hatred, apathy will be taken as acceptance even by the victims of prejudice themselves. The SPLC tells of a time when a cross was burned in the yard of a single mother of Portuguese descent in Missouri; one person acted and set in motion a community uprising against hatred.

2. *Unite.* Call a friend or coworker. Organize a group of like-thinking friends from school or your place of worship or club. Create a coalition that is diverse and includes the young, the old, law enforcement representatives, and the media. Frustrated when a neo-Nazi group got permission to march in Springfield, Illinois, in 1994, a Jewish couple formed Project Lemonade. Money raised helps to create education projects or monuments in communities that witness such decisive events.

3. *Support the Victims.* Victims of hate crimes are especially vulnerable. Let them know you care by words, by e-mail. If you or your friend is a victim, report it. In the wake of an outbreak of anti–Native American and anti-Jewish activity in Billings, Montana, a manager of a local sports shop replaced all his usual outdoor advertising and print advertisements with "Not in Our Town," which soon became a community rallying point for a support network of hate victims.

4. *Do Your Homework.* If you suspect a hate crime has been committed, do your research to document it. An Indiana father spotted his son receiving a "pastor's license," did some research, and found that the source was a White supremacist group disguised as a church. It helped explain the

boy's recent fascination with Nazi symbols. The father wrote to the "church," demanded that the contacts be stopped, and threatened suit.

5. *Create an Alternative.* Never attend a rally where hate is a part of the agenda. Find another outlet for your frustration, whatever the cause. When the Ku Klux Klan held a rally in Madison, Wisconsin, a coalition of ministers organized citizens to spend the day in minority neighborhoods.

6. *Speak Up.* You too have First Amendment rights. Denounce the hatred, the cruel jokes. If you see a news organization misrepresenting a group, speak up. When a newspaper exposed the 20-year-old national leader of the Aryan Nation in Canada, he resigned and closed his Web site.

7. *Lobby Leaders.* Persuade policy makers, business heads, community leaders, and executives of media outlets to take a stand against hate. Levi Strauss contributed $5 million to an antiprejudice project and a program that helps people of color to get loans in communities where it has plants: Knoxville, Albuquerque, El Paso, Valdosta, and Georgia.

8. *Look Long Range.* Participate or organize events such as annual parades or cultural fairs to celebrate diversity and harmony. Supplement it with a Web site that can be a 24/7 resource. In Selma, Alabama, a major week-end street fair is held on the anniversary of Bloody Sunday, when voting-rights activists attempting to walk across a bridge to Montgomery were beaten back by police.

9. *Teach Tolerance.* Prejudice is learned and parents and teachers can influence the content of curriculum. In Brooklyn, New York, an interra-cial basketball program called Flames was founded in the mid-1970s. Since then, it has brought together more than 10,000 youths of diverse backgrounds.

10. *Dig Deeper.* Look into the issues that divide us—social inequality, immigra-tion, and sexual orientation. Work against prejudice. Dig deep inside your-self for prejudices and stereotypes you may embrace. Find out what is happening and act! As former White supremacist Floyd Cochran declared, "It is not enough to hold hands and sing Kumbaya" (Carrier 2000, 22).

Expressing prejudice and expressing tolerance are fundamentally personal decisions. These steps recognize that we have the ability to change our atti-tudes, resist ethnocentrism and prejudice, and avoid the use of ethnophaulisms and stereotypes.

Conclusion

This chapter has examined theories of prejudice and measurements of its extent. Prejudice should not be confused with discrimination. The two concepts are not the same: Prejudice consists of negative attitudes, and discrimination consists of negative behavior toward a group.

Several theories try to explain why preju-dice exists. Some emphasize economic con-cerns (the exploitation and scapegoating theories), whereas other approaches stress personality or normative factors. No one explanation is sufficient. Surveys conducted in the United States over the past sixty years point to a reduction of prejudice as measured by the willingness to express stereotypes or maintain social distance. Survey data also show that African Americans, Latinos, Asian Americans, and American Indians do not necessarily feel comfortable with each other. They have adopted attitudes toward other oppressed groups similar to those held by many White Americans.

The absence of widespread public expression of prejudice does not mean it is absent by any means. Recent prejudice aimed at Hispanics, Asian Americans, and large recent immigrant groups such as Arab Americans and Muslim Americans is well documented. Issues such as immigration and affirmative action reemerge and cause bitter resentment. Furthermore, ill feelings exist between subordinate groups in schools, in the streets, and in the workplace. Color-blind racism allows one to appear to be tolerant while allowing racial and ethnic inequality to persist.

Equal-status contact may reduce hostility between groups. However, in a highly segregated society defined by inequality, such opportunities are not typical. The mass media can be of value in reducing discrimination but have not done enough and may even intensify ill feeling by promoting stereotypical images. Although strides are being made in increasing the appearance of minorities in positive roles in television and films, one would not realize how diverse our society is by sampling advertisements, television programs, or movies.

Even though we can be encouraged by the techniques available to reduce intergroup hostility, there are still sizable segments of the population that do not want to live in integrated neighborhoods, do not want to work for or be led by someone of a different race, and certainly object to the idea of their relatives marrying outside their own group. People still harbor stereotypes toward one another, and this tendency includes racial and ethnic minorities having stereotypes about one another.

Reducing prejudice is important because it can lead to support for policy change. There are steps we can take as individuals to confront prejudice and overcome hatred. Another real challenge and the ultimate objective is to improve the social condition of oppressed groups in the United States. To consider this challenge, we turn to discrimination in Chapter 3. Discrimination's costs are high to both dominant and subordinate groups. With this fact in mind, we will examine some techniques for reducing discrimination.

Key Terms

authoritarian personality 57	ethnocentrism 49	prejudice 52
Bogardus scale 74	ethnophaulism 52	racial profiling 63
color-blind racism 64	exploitation theory 58	scapegoating theory 56
contact hypothesis 76	hate crime 50	social distance 74
discrimination 52	normative approach 58	stereotypes 59

Review Questions

1. How are prejudice and discrimination both related and unrelated to each other?
2. How do theories of prejudice relate to different expressions of prejudice?

3. How is color-blind racism expressed?

4. Are there steps that you can identify that have been taken against prejudice in your community?

Critical Thinking

1. Identify stereotypes associated with a group of people, such as older adults or people with physical disabilities.

2. What social issues do you think are most likely to engender hostility along racial and ethnic lines?

3. Consider the television programs you have watched the most. In terms of race and ethnicity, how well do the programs you watch tend to reflect the diversity of the population in the United States?

Internet Connections—Research Navigator™

Follow the instructions given in "Internet Connections—Research Navigator™" in Chapter 1 of this text to access the features of Research Navigator™. Once at the Web site, enter your login name and password. Then, to use the ContentSelect database, enter keywords such as "racism," "racial profiling," and "diversity training," and the research engine will supply relevant and recent scholarly and popular press publications. Use the New York Times Search-by-Subject Archive to find recent news articles related to sociology and the Link Library feature to locate relevant Web links organized by the key terms associated with this chapter.

3 Discrimination

CHAPTER OUTLINE

───────────── ⟨ HIGHLIGHTS ⟩ ─────────────

Just as social scientists have advanced theories to explain why prejudice exists, they have also presented explanations of why discrimination occurs. Social scientists look more and more at the manner in which institutions, not individuals, discriminate. Institutional discrimination is a pattern in social institutions that produces or perpetuates inequalities, even if individuals in the society do not intend to be racist or sexist. Income data document that gaps exist between racial and ethnic groups. Historically, attempts have been made to reduce discrimination, usually through strong lobbying efforts by minorities themselves. Patterns of total discrimination make solutions particularly difficult for people in the informal economy or the underclass. Affirmative action was designed to equalize opportunity but has encountered significant resentment by those who charge that it constitutes reverse discrimination. Despite many efforts to end discrimination, glass ceilings and glass walls remain in the workplace.

The human casualties from natural disasters are well documented. This has been especially true with the impact of Hurricane Katrina on the Gulf Coast in 2005. Also well-known now are the ill-planned evacuation plan in New Orleans, the subsequent high death toll, the ineffectiveness of levee construction and maintenance, and the slow response initially and the subsequent prolonged recovery especially for low-income residents.

The persistent role of discrimination in the aftermath has been less a part of the national consciousness. Although Hurricane Katrina made victims of everyone, poor minority people have been especially victimized. Rural tribal Native American groups and Vietnamese American Gulf residents fell through the cracks of recovery plans. Latino workers who came to the area in the aftermath have been disadvantaged.

The storms destroyed more than 200,000 homes and apartments in Louisiana. Therefore, housing for those who wish to remain or move back is at a premium. But if you are Black and especially of modest means, the ability to reestablish a homestead is much more difficult in metropolitan New Orleans.

Courts have had to intervene to restrain St. Bernard Parish, a county just outside New Orleans which is 93 percent White, from limiting rentals to only blood relatives and limiting new residential construction to single-family homes.

On March 8, 2007, an African American responds to a housing advertisement in another area but is told the owner is out of state and will send information when he or she is back in town and can show the property. Nothing ever happens. A White person responds to the same advertisement the next day and learns from the same person that he or she will be in town that weekend and can arrange to show the property. The absentee landlord tells the person that he or she can apply immediately and states "We don't want any loud rap music," and we are looking for people "that are more settled."

This is just one example from a 2007 study that sent Black and White well-trained testers presenting similar financial circumstances and family types out to attempt to rent housing throughout metropolitan New Orleans. When discrimination appeared to be present, follow-up testing occurred. In the final analysis, six out of every ten cases, African American testers faced differential treatment. Whites were granted appointments when Blacks were not. Whites were told about available apartments, Blacks were told nothing was available. Blacks were frequently quoted a higher monthly rental charge. White testers' voicemail requests for information were returned, whereas many Black testers did not receive callbacks. Recovery is a much harder road if you are a person of color (Greater New Orleans Fair Housing Center 2007; Kao 2006; Simmons 2007; Trujillo-Pagan 2006).

Studies document that African Americans seeking to find housing in New Orleans encounter differential treatment compared to Whites in the same income, financial history, and household size.

Discrimination has a long history, right up to the present, of taking its toll on people. We will examine the many faces of discrimination, its many victims, and the many ways scholars have documented its presence today in the United States. We will return to more examples of discrimination in housing, but also look at differential treatment in employment opportunities, wages, voting, vulnerability to environmental hazards, and even access to membership in private clubs.

Understanding Discrimination

Discrimination is the denial of opportunities and equal rights to individuals and groups because of prejudice or for other arbitrary reasons. Some people in the United States find it difficult to see discrimination as a widespread phenomenon. "After all," it is often said, "these minorities drive cars, hold jobs, own their homes, and even go to college." Yet this view also fails to recognize the lingering legacy of past discrimination. Recently, scholarly research documented the history of "sundown towns," communities that for decades had explicit rules ordering Black people out at sundown. They could work and spend their money in these towns, but they could not socialize or live there. Asians and American Indians were also victims of such policies. Although this explicit practice ended in the post–World War II era, most of these communities still remained all White well into the twenty-first century (Loewen 2005; Loewen and Schaefer 2008).

Even today discrimination is not rare. An understanding of discrimination in modern industrialized societies such as the United States must begin by distinguishing between relative and absolute deprivation.

Relative versus Absolute Deprivation

Conflict theorists have said correctly that it is not absolute, unchanging standards that determine deprivation and oppression. Although minority groups may be viewed as having adequate or even good incomes, housing, health care, and educational opportunities, it is their position relative to some other group that offers evidence of discrimination.

Relative deprivation is defined as the conscious experience of a negative discrepancy between legitimate expectations and present actualities. After settling in the United States, immigrants often enjoy better material comforts and more political freedom than were possible in their old country. If they compare themselves with most other people in the United States, however, they will feel deprived because, although their standard has improved, the immigrants still perceive relative deprivation.

Absolute deprivation, on the other hand, implies a fixed standard based on a minimum level of subsistence below which families should not be expected to exist. Discrimination does not necessarily mean absolute deprivation.

In this often-reproduced photograph, civil rights hero Rosa Parks is shown defying de jure segregation by sitting in the White section of the bus, which launched the Montgomery, Alabama, bus boycott in 1955. Actually, although the event was very real, there were no journalists present at the time, and this iconic photography was a recreation with an Associated Press reporter seated behind Rosa Parks.

A Japanese American who is promoted to a management position may still be a victim of discrimination if he or she had been passed over for years because of corporate reluctance to place an Asian American in a highly visible position.

Dissatisfaction is also likely to arise from feelings of relative deprivation. The members of a society who feel most frustrated and disgruntled by the social and economic conditions of their lives are not necessarily worse off in an objective sense. Social scientists have long recognized that what is most significant is how people perceive their situations. Karl Marx pointed out that, although the misery of the workers was important in reflecting their oppressed state, so was their position relative to the ruling class. In 1847, Marx wrote, "Although the enjoyment of the workers has risen, the social satisfaction that they have has fallen in comparison with the increased enjoyment of the capitalist" (Marx and Engels 1955, 94).

This statement explains why the groups or individuals who are most vocal and best organized against discrimination are not necessarily in the worst economic and social situation. However, they are likely to be those who most strongly perceive that, relative to others, they are not receiving their fair share. Resistance to perceived discrimination, rather than the actual amount of absolute discrimination, is the key.

LISTEN TO OUR VOICES

Of Race and Risk

Patricia J. Williams

Several years ago, at a moment when I was particularly tired of the unstable lifestyle that academic careers sometimes require, I surprised myself and bought a real house. Because the house was in a state other than the one where I was living at the time, I obtained my mortgage by telephone. I am a prudent little squirrel when it comes to things financial, always tucking away stores of nuts for the winter, and so I meet the criteria of a quite good credit risk. My loan was approved almost immediately.

A little while later, the contract came in the mail. Among the papers the bank forwarded were forms documenting compliance with the Fair Housing Act, which outlaws racial discrimination in the housing market. The act monitors lending practices to prevent banks from redlining—redlining being the phenomenon whereby banks circle certain neighborhoods on the map and refuse to lend in those areas. It is a practice for which the bank with which I was dealing, unbeknownst to me, had been cited previously—as well as since. In any event, the act tracks the race of all banking customers to prevent such discrimination. Unfortunately, and with the creative variability of all illegality, some banks also use the racial information disclosed on the fair housing forms to engage in precisely the discrimination the law seeks to prevent.

I should repeat that to this point my entire mortgage transaction had been conducted by telephone. I should also note that I speak a Received Standard English, regionally marked as Northeastern perhaps, but not easily identifiable as black. With my credit history, my job as a law professor, and, no doubt, with my accent, I am not only middle class but apparently match the cultural stereotype of a good white person. It is thus, perhaps, that the loan officer of the bank, whom I had never met, had checked off the box on the fair housing form indicating that I was white.

Race shouldn't matter, I suppose, but it seemed to in this case, so I took a deep breath, crossed out "white" and sent the contract back. That will teach them to presume too much, I thought. A done deal, I assumed. But suddenly the transaction came to a screeching halt. The bank wanted more money, more points, and a higher rate of interest. Suddenly I found myself facing great resistance and much more debt. To make a long story short, I threatened to sue under the act in question, the bank quickly backed down, and I procured the loan on the original terms. What was interesting about all this was that the reason the bank gave for its newfound recalcitrance was not race, heaven forbid. No, it was all about economics and increased risk: The reason they gave was that property values in that neighborhood were suddenly falling. They wanted more money to buffer themselves against the snappy winds of projected misfortune.

Initially, I was surprised, confused. The house was in a neighborhood that was extremely stable. I am an extremely careful shopper; I had uncovered absolutely nothing to indicate that prices were falling. It took my realtor to make me see the light. "Don't you get it," he sighed. "This is what always happens." And even though I suppose it was a little thick of me, I really hadn't gotten it: For, of course, I was the reason the prices were in peril. . . .

In retrospect, what has remained so fascinating to me about this experience was the way it so exemplified the problems of the new rhetoric of racism. For starters, the new rhetoric of race never mentions race. It wasn't race but risk with which the bank was so concerned. . . .

By this measure of mortgage-worthiness, the ingredient of blackness is cast not just as a social toll but also as an actual tax. A fee, an extra contribution at the door, an admission charge for the high costs of handling my dangerous propensities, my inherently unsavory properties. I was not judged based on my independent attributes or financial worth; not even was I judged by statistical profiles of what my group actually does. (For, in fact, anxiety-stricken, middle-class black people make good cake-baking neighbors when not made to feel defensive by the unfortunate historical strategies of bombs, burnings, or abandonment.) Rather, I was being evaluated based on what an abstraction of White Society writ large thinks we—or I—do, and that imagined "doing" was treated and thus established as a self-fulfilling prophecy. It is a dispiriting message: that some in society apparently not only devalue black people but devalue themselves and their homes just for having us as part of their landscape.

"I bet you'll keep your mouth shut the next time they plug you into the computer as white," laughed a friend when he heard my story. It took me aback, this postmodern pressure to "pass," even as it highlighted the intolerable logic of it all. For by these "rational" economic measures, an investment in my property suggests the selling of myself.

Source: Excerpt from "Of Race and Risk" by Patricia J. Williams. Reprinted with permission from the December 29, 1997 issue of *The Nation.* For subscription information, call 1-800-333-8536. Portions of each week's Nation magazine can be accessed at http://www.thenation.com.

Total Discrimination

Social scientists—and increasingly policy makers—have begun to use the concept of total discrimination. **Total discrimination,** as shown in Figure 3.1, refers to current discrimination operating in the labor market and past discrimination. Past discrimination experienced by an individual includes the poorer education and job experiences of racial and ethnic minorities compared with those of many White Americans. When considering discrimination, therefore, it is not enough to focus only on what is being done to people now. Sometimes a person may be dealt with fairly but may still be at a disadvantage because he or she suffered from poorer health care, inferior counseling in the school system, less access to books and other educational materials, or a poor job record resulting from absences to take care of brothers and sisters.

Discrimination casts a wide net. Although the poor and less educated are most vulnerable and unable to access resources that might help them, discrimination also is faced by the affluent with professional degrees. In "Listen to Our Voices," respected law professor Patricia J. Williams, an African American,

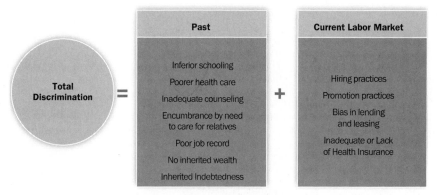

Figure 3.1 Total Discrimination

describes her inability to secure a mortgage despite initial approval after an analysis of her financial status but before the bank realized she was Black. Her recent experience is not unusual and helps to explain the persistence of discrimination.

William's experience is not unusual. A study released by the National Fair Housing Alliance and the federal Department of Housing and Urban Development found that discriminatory housing practices were routine. Consider the sobering results of a two-year study conducted in twelve metropolitan areas with seventy-three real estate firms: White real estate shoppers are steered away from houses in mixed neighborhoods even when they express interest in integrated areas. Latinos and African Americans looking for housing are steered toward minority neighborhoods even when their incomes justify seeing more affluent neighborhoods. The challenge to being a minority homebuyer does not stop there. Studies document that Black and Hispanic homebuyers tend to pay higher interest rates than Whites with similar credit ratings. All things are hardly equal in home buying (Bocian, Ernst, and Li 2006).

We find another variation of this past-in-present discrimination when apparently nondiscriminatory present practices have negative effects because of prior intentionally biased practices. Although unions that purposely discriminated against minority members in the past may no longer do so, some people are still prevented from achieving higher levels of seniority because of those past practices. Personnel records include a cumulative record that is vital in promotion and selection for desirable assignments. Blatantly discriminatory judgments and recommendations in the past remain part of a person's record.

Institutional Discrimination

Individuals practice discrimination in one-to-one encounters, and institutions practice discrimination through their daily operations. Indeed, a consensus is growing today that this institutional discrimination is more significant than acts committed by prejudiced individuals.

Despite numerous laws and steep penalties, discrimination continues in the housing market.

Social scientists are particularly concerned with the ways in which patterns of employment, education, criminal justice, housing, health care, and government operations maintain the social significance of race and ethnicity. **Institutional discrimination** is the denial of opportunities and equal rights to individuals and groups that results from the normal operations of a society.

Civil rights activist Stokely Carmichael and political scientist Charles Hamilton are credited with introducing the concept of institutional racism. Individual discrimination refers to overt acts of individual Whites against individual Blacks; Carmichael and Hamilton reserved the term *institutional racism* for covert acts committed collectively against an entire group. From this perspective, discrimination can take place without an individual intending to deprive others of privileges and even without the individual being aware that others are being deprived (Ture and Hamilton 1992).

How can discrimination be widespread and unconscious at the same time? The following are a few documented examples of institutional discrimination:

1. Standards for assessing credit risks work against African Americans and Hispanics seeking to establish businesses because many lack conventional

credit references. Businesses in low-income areas where these groups often reside also have much higher insurance costs.

2. IQ testing favors middle-class children, especially the White middle class, because of the types of questions included.

3. The entire criminal justice system, from the patrol officer to the judge and jury, is dominated by Whites who find it difficult to understand life in poverty areas.

4. Hiring practices often require several years' experience at jobs only recently opened to members of subordinate groups.

5. Many jobs automatically eliminate a person with felony records or past drug offenses, which disproportionately reduces employment opportunities for people of color.

Institutional discrimination is so systemic that it takes on the pattern of what has been termed "woodwork racism" in that racist outcomes become so widespread that African Americans, Latinos, Asian Americans, and others endure them as a part of everyday life (Feagin and McKinney 2003).

In some cases, even apparently neutral institutional standards can turn out to have discriminatory effects. African American students at a midwestern state university protested a policy under which fraternities and sororities that wanted to use campus facilities for a dance were required to post a $150 security deposit to cover possible damage. The Black students complained that this policy had a discriminatory impact on minority student organizations. Campus police countered that the university's policy applied to all student groups interested in using these facilities. However, because, overwhelmingly, White fraternities and sororities at the school had their own houses, which they used for dances, the policy affected only African American and other subordinate groups' organizations.

Ten years later, the entire nation scrambled to make aviation safer in the wake of the September 11, 2001, terrorist attacks. The government saw airport security as a weak link and federalized airport screeners under the newly formed Transport Security Administration. Wages improved and training strengthened. The new screeners also had to be U.S. citizens. This latter provision eliminated the many legal immigrants from Asia, Africa, and Latin America who had previously worked as screeners. Airport screening went from overwhelmingly minority to 61 percent White. Clearly, this measure had the unintended consequences of discriminating against people of color (Alonso-Zaldivar and Oldhan 2002).

Even efforts to right injustices can be discriminatory in their outcome. Numerous instances are documented of low-income potential homeowners entering into very undesirable financial agreements eventually leading to foreclosure when they go to buy that first home. In an effort to protect people from being taken advantage of, beginning in 2006, the State of Illinois required buyers with poor credit records in certain areas of Chicago to go through mandatory financial counseling. As a result, over twenty lenders have curtailed granting home loans in these areas, not wanting to deal with the further restrictions. Over 80 percent of the people in the affected area are Black or Latino. A well-intentioned attempt to help people is making it very difficult for people wanting to live in an area over-whelmingly populated by racial and ethnic minorities (Umberger 2006).

The 2000 presidential election created headlines because it took weeks to resolve who won—Bush or Gore. Yet for 1.4 million African Americans who were denied the right to vote, this seemed like a national issue that had left them on the sidelines. The prohibition was not because they were Black, which would have been clearly racist and legally discriminatory, but because they were convicted felons. In eleven states, a felony conviction can result in a ban from voting for life even after their prison sentence is served. Because many of these states are in the South and have large Black populations, dis-proportionately, the voting prohibition covers African American men. Cur-rently 13 percent of the nation's Black male population is precluded from voting by such laws. Florida was the deciding state in the close 2000 elections, and more than 200,000 potential Black voters were excluded. This case of institutional discrimination may have changed the outcome of a presidential election (Cooper 2004; Sentencing Project 2008).

Institutional discrimination continuously imposes more hindrances on and awards fewer benefits to certain racial and ethnic groups than it does to others. This is the underlying and painful context of American intergroup relations.

Low-Wage Labor

Disproportionate shares of racial and ethnic minority members are either unemployed or employed in low-wage labor. Much of this low-wage labor is in a part of the labor market that provides little opportunities for improvement during one's working years and virtually no protection in terms of health insur-ance or retirement benefits.

The secondary labor market affecting many members of racial and ethnic minorities has come to be called the informal economy. The **informal economy** (also called the **irregular** or **underground economy**) consists of transfers of money, goods, or services that are not reported to the government. This label describes much of the work in inner-city neighborhoods and poverty-stricken rural areas, which is in sharp contrast to the rest of the marketplace. Workers are employed in the informal economy seasonally or infrequently. The work they do may resemble the work of traditional occupations, such as mechanic, cook, or electrician, but these workers lack the formal credentials to enter such employment. Indeed, workers in the informal economy may work sporadically or may moonlight in the regular economy. The informal economy also includes unregulated child-care services, garage sales, and the unreported income of craftspeople and street vendors.

According to the dual labor market model, minorities have been relegated to the informal economy. Although the informal economy may offer employment

Many people work in the informal economy with little prospect of moving into the primary, better-paying economy. Pictured is a street vendor in New York City.

to the jobless, it provides few safeguards against fraud or malpractice that victimizes the workers. There are also few of the fringe benefits of health insurance and pensions that are much more likely to be present in the conventional marketplace. Therefore, informal economies are criticized for promoting highly unfair and dangerous working conditions. To be consigned to the informal economy is yet another example of social inequality.

Sociologist Edna Bonacich (1972, 1976) outlined the **dual** or **split labor market** that divides the economy into two realms of employment, the secondary one being populated primarily by minorities working at menial jobs. Even when not manual, labor is still rewarded less when performed by minorities. In keeping with the conflict model, this dual market model emphasizes that minorities fare unfavorably in the competition between dominant and subordinate groups.

The workers in the informal economy are ill prepared to enter the regular economy permanently or to take its better-paying jobs. Frequent changes in employment or lack of a specific supervisor leaves them without the kind of résumé that employers in the regular economy expect before they hire. Some of the sources of employment in the informal economy are illegal, such as fencing stolen goods, narcotics peddling, pimping, and prostitution. More likely, the work is legal but not transferable to a more traditional job. An example is an "information broker," who receives cash in exchange for such information as where to find good buys or how to receive maximum benefits from public assistance programs (Pedder 1991).

Workers in the informal economy have not necessarily experienced direct discrimination. Because of past discrimination, they are unable to secure traditional employment. Working in the informal economy provides income but

RESEARCH FOCUS

Discrimination in Job Seeking

A dramatic confirmation of discrimination came with research begun by sociologist Devah Pager in 2003. She sent four men out as trained "testers" to look for entry-level jobs in Milwaukee, Wisconsin, requiring no experience or special training. Each was a 23-year-old college student, but each one presented himself as having a high school diploma with similar job histories.

The job-seeking experiences with 350 different employers were vastly different among the four men. Why was that? Two of the testers where Black and two were White. Furthermore, one tester of each pair indicated in the job application that he had served 18 months of jail time for a felony conviction (possession of cocaine with intent to distribute). As you can see in Figure 3.2, applicants with a prison record received significantly fewer callbacks. But as dramatic a difference as a criminal record made, race was clearly more important.

The differences were to the point that a White job applicant with a jail record actually received more callbacks for further consideration than a Black man with no criminal record. Whiteness has a privilege even when it comes to jail time; race, it seems, was more of a concern to potential employers than a criminal background.

"I expected there to be an effect of race, but I did not expect it to swamp the results as it did," Pager told an interviewer. Her finding was especially significant because the majority of convicts who are released from prison each year (52 percent) are, in fact, Black men. Pager's research, which was widely publicized, eventually contributed to a change in public policy. In his 2004 State of the Union address, and specifically referring to Pager's work, President George W. Bush announced a $300 million monitoring program for ex-convicts who are attempting to reintegrate into society. These findings, however, are not isolated to this one study or to one city. A similar study sending job applicants out in New York City also confirmed that a White felon has a better chance to get a call-back or an actual job offer than an African American with no criminal record.

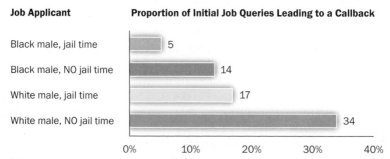

Figure 3.2 Discrimination in Job Seeking
Source: Pager 2003, 958.

Sources: Bordt 2005; Bureau of Justice Statistics 2004; Kroeger 2004; Pager 2003, 2007a, 2007b; Pager and Quillian 2005; Pager and Western 2007.

does not lead them into the primary labor market. A self-fulfilling cycle continues that allows past discrimination to create a separate work environment.

Efforts to end discrimination continue to run up against discrimination of all sorts. As described in "Research Focus," although we can document discrimination in research studies, it is often very difficult to prove even if we had the time and money to bring the incident to the attention of the legal system.

Not all low-wage laborers are a part of the informal economy, but many workers are driven into such jobs as better-paying jobs either move far away from where African Americans and Latinos live or even move abroad as globalization creates more and more of an international labor market.

The absence of jobs casts a wider shadow in poor neighborhoods beyond the lousy employment opportunities. People in poor urban neighborhoods often live in what have been called "commercial deserts" where they have little access to major grocers, pharmacies, or other retailers, but have plenty of liquor stores and fast-food restaurants nearby. Not only does this affect the quality of life but also exacerbates the exodus of good job opportunities (Gallagher 2005; Shaffer and Gottlieb 2007).

It is commonly believed that there are jobs available for the inner-city poor but that they just do not seek them. A study looked at jobs that were advertised in a help-wanted section of the *Washington Post*. The analysis showed that most of the jobs were beyond the reach of the underclass; perhaps 5 percent of all openings could even remotely be considered reasonable job prospects for people without skills or experience. During interviews with the employers, researchers found that an average of twenty-one people applied for each position, which typically was filled within three days of the time the advertisement appeared. The mean hourly wage was $6.12, 42 percent offered no fringe benefits, and the remaining positions offered meager fringe benefits after six months or one year of employment. This study, like others before it, counters the folk wisdom that there are plenty of jobs around for the underclass (Pease and Martin 1997).

Discrimination Today

In 2003, the Legal Assistance Foundation of Metropolitan Chicago sent matched pairs of a White woman and a Black woman to seek jobs in suburban Chicago. They applied for a variety of jobs that were advertised or that posted "Help Wanted" signs in the window. Many of the jobs were retail positions in shopping centers or malls. Employers were 16 percent more likely to offer jobs to Whites than to Blacks, even though the Black applicant always applied first and presented stronger job-related qualifications. Black applicants were four times as likely to be asked about their absenteeism record and nearly twice as likely to be specifically asked why they left their previous job. This was in 2003, not 1953. It was also where jobs in urban America tend to be available—the suburbs (Lodder, McFarland, and White 2003).

Discrimination is widespread in the United States. It sometimes results from prejudices held by individuals. More significantly, it is found in institutional discrimination and the presence of the informal economy. The presence of an underclass is symptomatic of many social forces, and total discrimination—past and present discrimination taken together—is one of them.

Measuring Discrimination

How much discrimination is there? As in measuring prejudice, problems arise in quantifying discrimination. Measuring prejudice is hampered by the difficulties in assessing attitudes and by the need to take many factors into account. It is further limited by the initial challenge of identifying different treatment. A second difficulty of measuring discrimination is assigning a cost to the discrimination.

Some tentative conclusions about discrimination can be made, however. Figure 3.3 uses income data to show vividly the disparity in income between African Americans and Whites and also between men and women. This encompasses all full-time workers. White men, with a median income of $51,997, earn one-third more than Black men and nearly what Hispanic women earn in wages.

Why do Asian American men earn so much if race serves as a barrier? The economic picture is not entirely positive. Some Asian American groups such as Laotians and Vietnamese have high levels of poverty. However, a significant number of Asian Americans with advanced educations have high-earning jobs

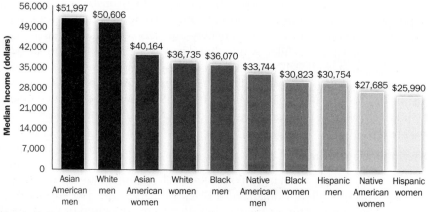

Figure 3.3 Median Income by Race, Ethnicity, and Gender
Even at the very highest levels of schooling, the income gap remains between Whites and Blacks. Education also has little apparent effect on the income gap between male and female workers. Even a brief analysis reveals striking differences in earning power between White men and other groups in the United States. Furthermore, the greater inequality is apparent for African American and Hispanic women.

Note: Data released in 2007 for income earned in 2006. Median income is from all sources and is limited to year-round, full-time workers over 25 years old. Data for White men and women are for non-Hispanics.

Source: DeNavas-Walt, Carmen, Bernadette D. Proctor, and Jessica Smith, 2007. For Native Americans, author's estimate based on Bureau of the Census data in Ogunwole 2006.

bringing up the median income. However, as we will see, given their high levels of schooling, their incomes should be even higher.

Clearly, regardless of race or ethnicity, men outpace women in annual income. This disparity between the incomes of Black women and White men has remained unchanged over the more than fifty years during which such data have been tabulated. It illustrates yet another instance of the greater inequality experienced by minority women. Also, Figure 3.3 includes only data for full-time, year-round workers; it excludes homemakers and the unemployed. Even in this comparison, the deprivation of Blacks, Hispanics, and women is confirmed again.

Are these differences entirely the result of discrimination in employment? No, individuals within the four groups are not equally prepared to compete for high-paying jobs. Past discrimination is a significant factor in a person's present social position. As discussed previously and illustrated in Figure 3.1, past discrimination continues to take its toll on modern victims. Taxpayers, predominantly White, were unwilling to subsidize the public education of African Americans and Hispanics at the same levels as White pupils. Even as these actions have changed, today's schools show the continuing results of this uneven spending pattern from the past. Education clearly is an appropriate variable to control.

In Table 3.1, median income is compared, holding education constant, which means that we can compare Blacks and Whites and men and women with approximately the same amount of formal schooling. More education means more money, but the disparity remains. The gap between races does narrow somewhat as education increases. However, both African Americans and women lag behind their more affluent counterparts. The contrast remains dramatic: Women with a master's degree typically receive $52,438, which means they earn almost $7,478 less than men who complete only a bachelor's degree.

Thinking over the long term, a woman with a bachelor's degree will work full-time four years to earn $180,000. The typical male can work just three years, take the fourth year off without pay, and match the woman's earnings.

Note what happens to Asian American households. Although the highly educated Asian Americans earn a lot of money, they trail well behind their White counterparts. With a doctorate holder in the family, the typical Asian American household earns an estimated $141,337 compared to $165,850 in a White household. To put this another way, these highly educated Asian Americans will work six years to earn what Whites do in less than five years.

What do these individual differences look like if we consider them on a national level? Economist Andrew Brimmer (1995), citing numerous government studies, estimates that about 3 or 4 percent of the gross domestic product (GDP, or the value of goods and services) is lost annually by the failure to use African Americans' existing education. There had been little change in this economic cost from the mid-1960s to the mid-1990s. This estimate would be even

Table 3.1 Median Income by Race and Sex, Holding Education Constant

Even at the very highest levels of schooling, the income gap remains between Whites and Blacks. Education also has little apparent effect on the income gap between male and female workers. (Income values in dollars)

	Race				Sex	
	White Families	Black Families	Asian Families	Hispanic Families	Male	Female
Total	67,130	40,299	75,654	40,774	45,759	35,095
High School						
Nongraduate	35,986	21,616	42,679	30,734	27,653	20,130
Graduate	51,954	32,275	45,292	41,048	37,031	26,737
College						
Some college	62,206	42,468	67,152	50,605	47,072	31,954
Bachelor's degree	114,968	82,343	107,258	86,480	60,906	45,408
Master's degree	130,807	99,129	143,801	109,954	75,432	52,438
Doctorate degree	165,850	125,658	141,337	95,6400	100,000	70,519

Notes: Data released in 2007 for income earned in 2006. Figures are median income from all sources except capital gains. Included are public assistance payments, dividends, pensions, unemployment compensation, and so on. Incomes are for all workers over 25 years of age. High school graduates include those with GEDs. Data for Whites are for White non-Hispanics. "Some college" excludes associate degree holders. Family data above bachelor's degree are averages (not median) incomes and data for doctorate-holder's families are author's estimate.

Source: DeNavas-Walt, Carmen, Bernadette D. Proctor, and Jessica Smith 2007.

higher if we took into account economic losses caused by the underuse of the academic talents of women and other minorities.

Now that education has been held constant, is the remaining gap caused by discrimination? No, not necessarily. Table 3.1 uses only the amount of schooling, not its quality. Racial minorities are more likely to attend inadequately financed schools. Some efforts have been made to eliminate disparities between school districts in the amount of wealth available to tax for school support but have met with little success.

The inequality of educational opportunity may seem less important in explaining sex discrimination. Although women usually are not segregated from men, educational institutions encourage talented women to enter fields that pay less (nursing or elementary education) than other occupations requiring similar amounts of training. Even when they do enter the same occupation, the earnings disparity persists. Even controlling for age, a study of census data showed that female physicians and surgeons earned 69 percent of what their male counterparts did (Weinberg 2007).

Eliminating Discrimination

Two main agents of social change work to reduce discrimination: voluntary associations organized to solve racial and ethnic problems and the federal government, including the courts. The two are closely related: Most efforts initiated by the government were urged by associations or organizations representing minority groups, following vigorous protests by African Americans against racism. Resistance to social inequality by subordinate groups has been the key to change. Rarely has any government of its own initiative sought to end discrimination based on such criteria as race, ethnicity, and gender.

All racial and ethnic groups of any size are represented by private organizations that are, to some degree, trying to end discrimination. Some groups originated in the first half of the twentieth century, but most have been founded since World War II or have become significant forces in bringing about change only since then. These include church organizations, fraternal social groups, minor political parties, and legal defense funds, as well as more militant organizations operating under the scrutiny of law enforcement agencies. The purposes, membership, successes, and failures of these resistance organizations dedicated to eliminating discrimination are discussed throughout this book.

Government action toward eliminating discrimination is also recent. Each branch of the government has taken antidiscrimination actions: the executive, the judicial, and the legislative.

The first antidiscrimination action at the executive level was President Franklin D. Roosevelt's 1943 creation of the Fair Employment Practices Commission (FEPC), which handled thousands of complaints of discrimination, mostly from African Americans, despite strong opposition by powerful economic and political leaders and many southern Whites. The FEPC had little actual power. It had no authority to compel employers to stop discriminating but could only ask for voluntary compliance. Its jurisdiction was limited to federal government employees, federal contractors, and labor unions. State and local governments and any business without a federal contract were not covered. Furthermore, the FEPC never enjoyed vigorous support from the White House, was denied adequate funds, and was part of larger agencies that were hostile to the commission's existence. This weak antidiscrimination agency was finally dropped in 1946, only to be succeeded by an even weaker one in 1948.

The judiciary, charged with interpreting laws and the U.S. Constitution, has a much longer history of involvement in the rights of racial, ethnic, and religious minorities. However, its early decisions protected the rights of the dominant group, as in the 1857 U.S. Supreme Court's Dred Scott decision, which ruled that slaves remained slaves even when living or traveling in states where slavery was illegal. Not until the 1940s did the Supreme Court revise earlier decisions and begin to grant African Americans the same rights as those held by Whites. The 1954 *Brown v. Board of Education* decision, which stated that

What do you think? Do people in a workplace sometimes question the credentials of a minority hire? Do you think minority workers are sometimes viewed by their colleagues at work as taking the place of someone "more qualified?"

"separate but equal" facilities—including education—were unconstitutional, heralded a new series of rulings, arguing that distinguishing between races in order to segregate was inherently unconstitutional.

It was assumed incorrectly by many that Brown and other judicial actions would lead quickly to sweeping change. In fact, little change occurred initially, and resistance to ending racism continued.

The most important legislative effort to eradicate discrimination was the Civil Rights Act of 1964. This act led to the establishment of the Equal Employment Opportunity Commission (EEOC), which had the power to investigate complaints against employers and to recommend action to the Department of Justice. If the Justice Department sued and discrimination was found, the court could order appropriate compensation. The act covered employment practices of all businesses with more than twenty-five employees and nearly all employment agencies and labor unions. A 1972 amendment broadened the coverage to employers with as few as fifteen employees.

The Civil Rights Act of 1964 prohibited different voting registration standards for White and Black voting applicants. It also prohibited discrimination in public accommodations—that is, hotels, motels, restaurants, gasoline stations, and amusement parks. Publicly owned facilities, such as parks, stadiums, and swimming pools, were also prohibited from discriminating. Another important provision forbade discrimination in all federally supported programs and institutions, such as hospitals, colleges, and road construction projects.

The Civil Rights Act of 1964 covered discrimination based on race, color, creed, national origin, and sex. Although the inclusion of gender in employment criteria had been prohibited in the federal civil service since 1949, most laws and most groups pushing for change showed little concern about sex discrimination. There was little precedent for attention to sex discrimination even at the state level. Only Hawaii and Wisconsin had enacted laws against sex discrimination before 1964. As first proposed, the Civil Rights Act did not include mention of gender. One day before the final vote, opponents of the measure offered an amendment on gender bias in an effort to defeat the entire act. The act did pass with prohibition against sex bias included, an event that can only be regarded as a milestone for women seeking equal employment rights with men.

The Civil Rights Act of 1964 was not perfect. Since 1964, several acts and amendments to the original act have been added to cover the many areas of discrimination it left untouched, such as criminal justice and housing. Even in areas singled out for enforcement in the Civil Rights Act of 1964, discrimination still occurs. Federal agencies charged with enforcement of the act complain that they are underfunded or are denied wholehearted support by the White House. Also, regardless of how much the EEOC may want to act in a particular case, the person who alleges discrimination has to pursue the complaint over a long time, marked by long periods of inaction. Despite these efforts, devastating forms of discrimination persist. African Americans, Latinos, and others fall victim to redlining. **Redlining** is the pattern of discrimination against people trying to buy homes in minority and racially changing neighborhoods. Research finds that in twenty-five metropolitan areas, housing agents showed fewer housing units to Blacks and Latinos, steered them to minority neighborhoods, and gave them far less assistance in finding housing that met their needs. The concept of redlining is now being applied to areas other than home buying.

People living in predominantly minority neighborhoods have found that service deliverers refuse to go to their area. In one case that attracted national attention in 1997, Kansas City's Pizza Hut refused to deliver forty pizzas to an honor program at a high school in an all-Black neighborhood. A Pizza Hut spokesperson called the neighborhood unsafe and said that almost every city has "restricted areas" to which the company will not deliver. This admission was particularly embarrassing because the high school already had a $170,000-a-year contract with Pizza Hut to deliver pizzas as a part of its school lunch program. Service redlining covers everything from parcel deliveries to repair people as well as food deliveries. The red-pencil appears not to have been set aside in cities throughout the United States (Fuller 1998; Rusk 2001; Schwartz 2001; Turner et al. 2002; Yinger 1995).

Although civil rights laws often have established rights for other minorities, the Supreme Court made them explicit in two 1987 decisions involving groups other than African Americans. In the first of the two cases, an Iraqi American professor asserted that he had been denied tenure because of his Arab origins; in the second, a Jewish congregation brought suit for damages in response to the defacement of its synagogue with derogatory symbols. The Supreme Court ruled unanimously that, in effect, any member of an ethnic minority may sue under federal prohibitions against discrimination. These decisions paved the way for almost all racial and ethnic groups to invoke the Civil Rights Act of 1964 (Taylor 1987).

A particularly insulting form of discrimination seemed finally to be on its way out in the late 1980s. Many social clubs had limitations forbidding membership to minorities, Jews, and women. For years, exclusive clubs argued that they were merely selecting friends, but, in fact, a principal function of these clubs is as a forum to transact business. Denial of membership meant more than the inability to attend a luncheon; it also seemed to exclude certain groups from part of the marketplace, as Lawrence Otis Graham observed at the beginning of this chapter. The Supreme Court ruled unanimously, in *New York State Clubs Association v. City of New York* in 1988, that states and cities may ban sex discrimination by large private clubs where business lunches and similar activities take place. Although the ruling does not apply to all clubs and leaves the issue of racial and ethnic barriers unresolved, it did chip away at the arbitrary exclusiveness of private groups (Steinhauer 2006; Taylor 1988).

Memberships and restrictive organizations remain perfectly legal. The rise to national attention of professional golfer Tiger Woods, of mixed Native American, African, and Asian ancestry, made the public aware that there were at least twenty-three golf courses where he would be prohibited from playing by virtue of race. In 2002, women's groups tried unsuccessfully to have the golf

Although more and more Latinos and African Americans are buying their own homes, the assets of accumulation run well behind that of White households—a legacy, in part, of past, and present discrimination.

champion speak out as the Master's and British Open were played on courses closed to women as members (Scott 2003).

Proving discrimination even as outlined for generations in legislation continues to be difficult. In the 2007 *Ledbetter v. Goodyear Tire and Rubber Co.* ruling, the Supreme Court affirmed that victims had to file a formal complaint within 180 days of the alleged discrimination. This set aside thousands of cases where employees learned their initial pay was lower to comparably employed White or male workers only after they had been in a job for years. Given the usual secrecy in workplaces around salaries, it is now all the more difficult for potential cases of pay disparity to be effectively advanced (Greenhouse 2007).

The inability of the Civil Rights Act, similar legislation, and court decisions to end discrimination does not result entirely from poor financial and political support, although it does play a role. The number of federal employees assigned to investigate and prosecute bias cases is insufficient. Many discriminatory practices, such as those described as institutional discrimination, are seldom subject to legal action.

Wealth Inequality:
Discrimination's Legacy

Discrimination that has occurred in the past carries into the present and future. As noted in Figure 3.1, a lack of inherited wealth is one element of the past. African American and other minority groups have had less opportunity to accumulate assets such as homes, land, and savings that can insulate them and later their children from economic setbacks.

Income refers to salaries and wages, and **wealth** is a more inclusive term encompassing all a person's material assets, including land, stocks, and other types of property. Wealth allows one to live better; even modest assets provide insurance against the effects of job layoffs, natural disasters, and long-term illness and afford individuals much better interest rates when they need to borrow money. It allows children to graduate from college relatively debt free or perhaps with no college loans to pay back at all. This reminds us that for many it is not a question of wealth in the sense of assets but wealth as measured by indebtedness.

Studies document that the kinds of disparities in income we have seen are even greater when wealth is considered. In 2004, only 4 percent of homebuyers were African Americans—at least one-third of what we would expect. This makes sense, however, because if individuals experience lower incomes throughout their lives, they are less likely to be able to put anything aside. They are more likely to have to pay interest rather than save for their future or their children's future.

Little wonder then that White children are more likely to surpass parents' income than Black children are. Furthermore, White children are more likely to move up the economic social class ladder than are Black children who are also more likely to actually fall back in absolute terms.

A close analysis of wealth shows that typically African American families have $86,000 less wealth than their White counterparts even when comparing members of comparably educated, employed households. Evidence indicates that this inequality in wealth has been growing over the last ten years rather than staying the same or declining (Bureau of the Census 2005a, 623; Economic Mobility Project 2007a; Oliver and Shapiro 2006).

Environmental Justice

Discrimination takes many forms and is not necessarily apparent, even when its impact can be far reaching. Take the example of Kennedy Heights, a well-kept working-class neighborhood nestled in southeastern Houston. This community faces a real threat, and it is not from crime or drugs. The threat that community residents fear is right under their feet in the form of three oil pits abandoned by Gulf Oil in 1927. The residents, mostly African American, argue that they have suffered high rates of cancer, lupus, and other illnesses because the chemicals from the oil fields poison their water supply. The residents first sued Chevron USA in 1985, and the case is still making its way through the courtrooms of not less than six states and the federal judiciary.

Lawyers and other representatives for the residents say that the oil company is guilty of environmental racism because it knowingly allowed a predominantly Black housing development to be built on the contaminated land. They are able to support this charge with documents, including a 1954 memorandum from an appraiser who suggested that the oil pits be drained of any toxic substances and the land filled for "low-cost houses for White occupancy." When the land did not sell right away, an oil company official in a 1967 memorandum suggested a tax-free land exchange with a developer who intended to use the land for "Negro residents and commercial development." For this latter intended use by African Americans, there was no mention of any required environmental cleanup of the land. The oil company counters that it just assumed the developer would do the necessary cleanup of the pits (Maning 1997; Verhovek 1997).

The conflict perspective sees the case of the Houston suburb as one in which pollution harms minority groups disproportionately. **Environmental justice** refers to the efforts to ensure that hazardous substances are controlled so that all communities receive protection regardless of race or socioeconomic circumstance. After the Environmental Protection Agency (EPA) and other organizations documented discrimination in the locating of hazardous waste sites, an executive order was issued in 1994 that requires all federal agencies to ensure that low-income and minority communities have access to better information about their environment and have an opportunity to participate in shaping government policies that affect their community's health. Initial efforts to implement the policy have met widespread opposition, including criticism from some proponents of economic development who argue that the guidelines unnecessarily delay or altogether block locating new industrial sites.

Low-income communities and areas with significant minority populations are more likely to be adjacent to waste sites than are affluent White communities. Studies in California show the higher probability that people of color live closer to sources of air pollution. Another study concluded that grade schools in Florida nearer environmental hazards are disproportionately Black or Latino. People of color jeopardized by environmental problems also lack the resources and political muscle to do something about it (Pastor, Morello-Frosch, and Saad 2005; Pellow and Brulle 2007; Stretesky and Lynch 2002).

Issues of environmental justice are not limited to metropolitan areas. Another continuing problem is abuse of Native American reservation land. Many American Indian leaders are concerned that tribal lands are too often regarded as dumping grounds for toxic waste that go to the highest bidder. On the other hand, the economic devastation faced by some tribes in isolated areas has led one tribe in Utah to actually seek out becoming a depot for discarded nuclear waste (*New York Times* 2005a; Skull Valley Goshutes 2006).

As with other aspects of discrimination, experts disagree. There is controversy within the scientific community over the potential hazards of some of the problems, and there is even some opposition within the subordinate communities being affected. This complexity of the issues in terms of social class and race is apparent, as some observers question the wisdom of an executive order that slows economic development coming to areas in dire need of employment opportunities. On the other hand, some counter that such businesses typically employ few less-skilled workers and only make the environment less livable for those left behind. Despite such varying viewpoints, environmental

So desperate are the economic conditions of isolated Indian tribes that they often seek out questionable forms of economic development. The Skull Valley Goshute Indian Reservation in Utah is trying to attract a nuclear waste dump, and local and state officials are trying to block this possibility.

justice is an excellent example of resistance and change in the 1990s that could not have been foreseen by the civil rights workers of the 1950s.

Affirmative Action

Affirmative action is the positive effort to recruit subordinate-group members, including women, for jobs, promotions, and educational opportunities. The phrase affirmative action first appeared in an executive order issued by President Kennedy in 1961. The order called for contractors to "take affirmative action to ensure that applicants are employed, and that employees are treated during employment, without regard to their race, creed, color, or national origin." However, at that time, no enforcement procedures were specified. Six years later, the order was amended to prohibit discrimination on the basis of sex, but affirmative action was still defined vaguely.

Today, affirmative action has become a catchall term for racial preference programs and goals. It has also become a lightning rod for opposition to any programs that suggest special consideration of women or racial minorities.

Affirmative Action Explained

Affirmative action has been viewed as an important tool for reducing institutional discrimination. Whereas previous efforts were aimed at eliminating individual acts of discrimination, federal measures under the heading of affirmative action have been aimed at procedures that deny equal opportunities, even if they are not intended to be overtly discriminatory. This policy has been implemented to deal with both current discrimination and past discrimination outlined earlier in this chapter.

Affirmative action has been aimed at institutional discrimination in such areas as the following:

- Height and weight requirements that are unnecessarily geared to the physical proportions of White men without regard to the actual characteristics needed to perform the job and, therefore, exclude women and some minorities

- Seniority rules, when applied to jobs historically held only by White men, that make more recently hired minorities and females more subject to layoff—the "last hired, first fired" employee—and less eligible for advancement

- Nepotism-based membership policies of some unions that exclude those who are not relatives of members who, because of past employment practices, are usually White

- Restrictive employment leave policies, coupled with prohibitions on part-time work or denials of fringe benefits to part-time workers, that make it difficult for the heads of single-parent families, most of whom are women, to get and keep jobs and also meet the needs of their families

- Rules requiring that only English be spoken at the workplace, even when not a business necessity, which result in discriminatory employment practices toward people whose primary language is not English
- Standardized academic tests or criteria geared to the cultural and educational norms of middle-class or White men when these are not relevant predictors of successful job performance
- Preferences shown by law and medical schools in admitting children of wealthy and influential alumni, nearly all of whom are White
- Credit policies of banks and lending institutions that prevent the granting of mortgages and loans in minority neighborhoods or that prevent the granting of credit to married women and others who have previously been denied the opportunity to build good credit histories in their own names

Employers have also been cautioned against asking leading questions in interviews, such as "Did you know you would be the first Black to supervise all Whites in that factory?" or "Does your husband mind your working on weekends?" Furthermore, the lack of minority-group or female employees may in itself represent evidence for a case of unlawful exclusion (Commission on Civil Rights 1981; also see Bohmer and Oka 2007).

The Legal Debate

How far can an employer go in encouraging women and minorities to apply for a job before it becomes unlawful discrimination against White men? Since the late 1970s, a number of bitterly debated cases on this difficult aspect of affirmative action have reached the U.S. Supreme Court. The most significant cases are summarized in Table 3.2. Furthermore, as we will see, the debate has moved into party politics.

In the 1978 Bakke case (*Regents of the University of California v. Bakke*), by a narrow 5:4 vote, the Court ordered the medical school of the University of California at Davis to admit Allan Bakke, a qualified White engineer who had originally been denied admission solely on the basis of his race. The justices ruled that the school had violated Bakke's constitutional rights by establishing a fixed quota system for minority students. However, the Court added that it was constitutional for universities to adopt flexible admission programs that use race as one factor in making decisions.

Colleges and universities responded with new policies designed to meet the Bakke ruling while broadening opportunities for traditionally underrepresented minority students. However, in 1996, the Supreme Court allowed a lower court decision to stand: that affirmative action programs for African American and Mexican American students at the University of Texas law school were unconstitutional. The ruling effectively prohibited schools in the

Table 3.2 Key Decisions on Affirmative Action

In a series of split and often very close decisions, the Supreme Court has expressed a variety of reservations in specific situations.

Year	Favorable/ Unfavorable to Policy	Case	Vote	Ruling
1971	+	Griggs v. Duke Power Co.	9:0	Private employers must provide a remedy where minorities were denied opportunities, even if unintentional.
1978	–	Regents of the University of California v. Bakke	5:4	Prohibited holding specific number of places for minorities in college admissions.
1979	+	United Steelworkers of America v. Weber	5:2	Okay for union to favor minorities in special training programs.
1984	–	Firefighters Local Union No 1784 (Memphis, TN) v. Stotts	6:1	Seniority means recently hired minorities may be laid off first in staff reductions.
1986	+	International Association of Firefighters v. City of Cleveland	6:3	May promote minorities over more senior Whites.
1986	+	New York City v. Sheet Metal	5:4	Approved specific quota of minority workers for union.
1987	+	United States v. Paradise	5:4	Endorsed quotas for promotions of state troopers.
1987	+	Johnson v. Transportation Agency, Santa Clara, CA	6:3	Approved preference in hiring for minorities and women over better-qualified men and Whites.
1989	–	Richmond v. Croson Company	6:3	Ruled a 30 percent set-aside program for minority contractors unconstitutional.
1989	–	Martin v. Wilks	5:4	Ruled Whites may bring reverse discrimination claims against Court-approved affirmative action plans.
1990	+	Metro Broadcasting v. FCC	5:4	Supported federal programs aimed at increasing minority ownership of broadcast licenses.

Year	Favorable/ Unfavorable to Policy	Case	Vote	Ruling
1995	−	*Adarand Constructors Inc. v. Peña*	5:4	Benefits based on race are constitutional only if narrowly defined to accomplish a compelling interest.
1996	−	*Texas v. Hopwood*	*	Let stand a lower court decision covering Louisiana, Mississippi, and Texas that race could not be used in college admissions.
2003	+	*Grutter v. Bollinger*	5:4	Race can be a factor in admissions at the University of Michigan Law School.
2003	−	*Gratz v. Bollinger*	6:3	Cannot use a strict formula awarding advantage based on race for admissions to the University of Michigan.

*5th U.S. Circuit Court of Appeals decision.

lower court's jurisdiction of Louisiana, Mississippi, and Texas from taking race into account in admissions. In 2003, the Supreme Court made two rulings concerning the admissions policies at the University of Michigan. In one case involving the law school, the Court upheld the right of the school to use applicants' race as criteria for admission decisions but ruled against a strict admissions formula awarding points to minority applicants who applied to the university's undergraduate school. Given the various legal actions, further challenges to affirmative action can be expected (Greenhouse 2003).

Has affirmative action actually helped alleviate employment inequality on the basis of race and gender? This is a difficult question to answer, given the complexity of the labor market and the fact that there are other antidiscrimination measures, but it does appear that affirmative action has had a significant impact in the sectors where it has been applied. Sociologist Barbara Reskin (1998) reviewed available studies looking at workforce composition in terms of race and gender in light of affirmative action policies. She found that gains in minority employment can be attributed to affirmative action policies. This includes both firms mandated to follow affirmative action guidelines and those that took them on voluntarily. There is also evidence that some earnings gains can be attributed to affirmative action. Economists M. V. Lee Badgett and Heidi Hartmann (1995), reviewing twenty-six other research studies, came to similar conclusions: Affirmative action and other federal compliance programs have had a modest impact, but it is difficult to assess, given larger economic changes such as recessions or the rapid increase in women in the paid labor force.

Reverse Discrimination

Although researchers debated the merit of affirmative action, the public— particularly Whites, but also some affluent African Americans and Hispanics— questioned the wisdom of the program. Particularly strident were the charges of reverse discrimination: that government actions cause better-qualified White men to be bypassed in favor of women and minority men. **Reverse discrimination** is an emotional term, because it conjures up the notion that somehow women and minorities will subject White men in the United States to the same treatment received by minorities during the last three centuries. Such cases are not unknown, but they are uncommon—less than ten of the race-related complaints to the federal government were filed by Whites and only 18 percent of gender-related complains and 4 percent of the course cases were filed by men.

Increasingly, critics of affirmative action call for color-blind policies that would end affirmative action and, they argue, allow all people to be judged fairly. However, will that mean an end to the institutional practices that favored

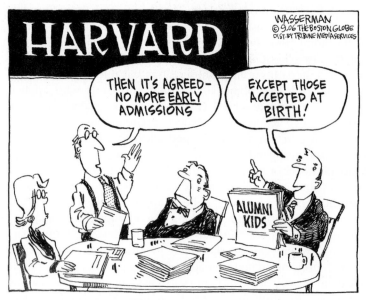

Affirmative action is criticized for giving preferential treatment, but colleges have a long history of giving admissions preferences to relatives of past graduates who are much more likely to be White rather than Black or Latino.

Whites? For example, according to the latest data, 40 percent of applicants who are children of Harvard's alumni, who are almost all White, are admitted to the university compared to 11 percent of nonalumni children. Ironically, studies show that these children of alumni typically are far more likely than either minority students or athletes to run into academic trouble (*Economist* 2004b; Massey and Mooney 2007; Pincus 2003, 2008).

Is it possible to have color-blind policies prevail in the United States in the twenty-first century? Supporters of affirmative action contend that as long as businesses rely on informal social networks, personal recommendations, and family ties, White men will have a distinct advantage built on generations of being in positions of power. Furthermore, an end to affirmative action should also mean an end to the many programs that give advantages to certain businesses, homeowners, veterans, farmers, and others. Most of these preference holders are White (Kilson 1995; Mack 1996).

Consequently, by the 1990s and into the twenty-first century, affirmative action had emerged as an increasingly important issue in state and national political campaigns. In 2003, the Supreme Court reviewed the admission policies at the University of Michigan, which may favor racial minorities (see Table 3.2). In 2006, Michigan citizens, by a 58 percent margin, voted to restrict all their state universities from using affirmative action in their admissions policies. Generally, discussions have focused on the use of quotas in hiring practices. Supporters of affirmative action argue that hiring goals establish "floors" for minority inclusion but do not exclude truly qualified candidates from any group. Opponents insist that these "targets" are, in fact, quotas that lead to reverse discrimination (Lewin 2006).

The state of California, in particular, was a battleground for this controversial issue. The California Civil Rights Initiative was placed on the ballot in 1996 as a referendum to amend the state constitution and prohibit any programs that give preference to women and minorities for college admission, employment, promotion, or government contracts. Overall, 54 percent of the voters backed the state proposition, with 61 percent of men in favor compared with only 48 percent of women. Whites, who represented 74 percent of the voters, voted in favor of the measure overwhelmingly, with 63 percent backing Proposition 209. This compares with 26 percent of African Americans, 24 percent of Hispanics, and 39 percent of Asian Americans favoring the end of affirmative action in state-operated institutions. Obviously, the voters—Whites and men—who perceived themselves as least likely to benefit from affirmative action overwhelmingly favored Proposition 209.

Legal challenges continue concerning Proposition 209, which is being implemented unevenly throughout the state. Much of the attention has focused on the impact that reducing racial preference programs will have in law and medical schools, in which competition for admission is very high. The courts have upheld the measures, and by 2008, several other states were considering such measures in statewide referendums (Dolan 2000; Schmidt 2007).

The Glass Ceiling

We have been talking primarily about racial and ethnic groups as if they have uniformly failed to keep pace with Whites. Although this notion is accurate, there are tens of thousands of people of color who have matched and even exceeded Whites in terms of income. For example, in 2006, more than 1.1 million Black households and another 1.1 million Hispanic families earned more than $100,000. What can we say about financially better-off members of subordinate groups in the United States (DeNavas-Walt, Proctor, and Lee 2007)?

Prejudice does not necessarily end with wealth. Black newspaper columnist De Wayne Wickham (1993) wrote of the subtle racism he had experienced. He heard a White clerk in a supermarket ask a White customer whether she knew the price of an item the computer would not scan; when the problem occurred while the clerk was ringing up Wickham's groceries, she called for a price check. Affluent subordinate-group members routinely report being blocked as they move toward the first-class section aboard airplanes or seek service in upscale stores. Another journalist, Ellis Cose (1993), has called these insults the soul-destroying slights to affluent minorities that lead to the "rage of a privileged class."

Discrimination persists for even the educated and qualified from the best family backgrounds. As subordinate-group members are able to compete successfully, they sometimes encounter attitudinal or organizational bias that prevents them from reaching their full potential. They have confronted what has come to be called the **glass ceiling.** This refers to the barrier that blocks the promotion of a qualified worker because of gender or minority membership (Figure 3.4). Often, people entering nontraditional areas of employment become marginalized and are made to feel uncomfortable, much like the situation of immigrants who feel a part of two cultures, as we have discussed in Chapter 1.

The reasons for glass ceilings are as many as the occurrences. It may be that one Black or one woman vice president is regarded as enough, so the second potential candidate faces a block to movement up through management. Decision makers may be concerned that their clientele will not trust them if they have too many people of color or may worry that a talented woman could become overwhelmed with her duties as a mother and wife and thus perform poorly in the workplace.

Concern about women and minorities climbing a broken ladder led to the formation in 1991 of the Glass Ceiling Commission, with the U.S. secretary of labor chairing the twenty-one-member group. Initially, it regarded the following as some of the glass ceiling barriers:

- Lack of management commitment to establishing systems, policies, and practices for achieving workplace diversity and upward mobility
- Pay inequities for work of equal or comparable value

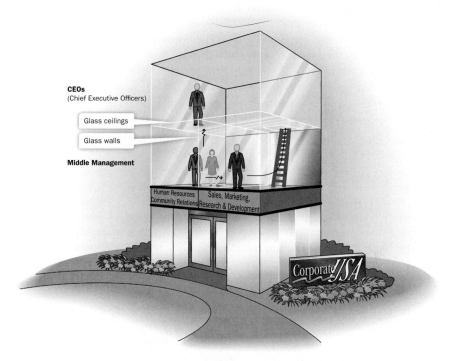

Figure 3.4 Glass Ceilings and Glass Walls
Women and minority men are moving up in corporations but encounter glass ceilings that block entry to top positions. In addition, they face glass walls that block lateral moves to areas from which executives are promoted. These barriers contribute to women and minority men not moving into the ultimate decision-making positions in the nation's corporate giants.

- Sex-, race-, and ethnicity-based stereotyping and harassment
- Unfair recruitment practices
- Lack of family-friendly workplace policies
- "Parent-track" policies that discourage parental leave policies
- Limited opportunities for advancement to decision-making positions

This significant underrepresentation of women and minority males in managerial positions results in large part from the presence of glass ceilings. Sociologist Max Weber wrote over a hundred years ago that the privileged class monopolizes the purchase of high-priced consumer goods and wields the power to grant or withhold opportunity from others. To grasp just how White and male the membership of this elite group is, consider the following: Eighty-two percent of the 11,500 people who serve on the boards of directors of Fortune 1,000 corporations are non-Hispanic White males. For every 82 White men on these boards, there are 2 Latinos, 2 Asian Americans, 3 African Americans, and 11 White women (Strauss 2002; Weber [1913–1922] 1947).

Glass ceilings are not the only barrier. There are also glass walls. Catalyst, a nonprofit research organization, conducted interviews in 1992 and, again, in 2001 with senior and middle managers from larger corporations. The study found that even before glass ceilings are encountered, women and racial and ethnic minorities face **glass walls** that keep them from moving laterally. Specifically, the study found that women tend to be placed in staff or support positions in areas such as public relations and human resources and are often directed away from jobs in core areas such as marketing, production, and sales. Women are assigned to and, therefore, trapped in jobs that reflect their stereotypical helping nature and encounter glass walls that cut off access to jobs that might lead to broader experience and advancement (Catalyst 2001; Lopez 1992).

Researchers have documented a differential impact that the glass ceiling has on White males. It appears that men who enter traditionally female occupations are more likely to rise to the top. Male elementary teachers become principals and male nurses become supervisors. The **glass escalator** refers to the male advantage experienced in occupations dominated by women. Whereas females may become tokens when they enter traditionally male occupations, men are more likely to be advantaged when they move out of sex-typical jobs. In summary, women and minority men confront a glass ceiling that limits upward mobility and glass walls that reduce their ability to move into fast-track jobs leading to the highest reaches of the corporate executive suite. Meanwhile, men who do choose to enter female-dominated occupations are often rewarded with promotions and positions of responsibility coveted by their fellow female workers (Budig 2002; Cognard-Black 2004).

Conclusion

The job advertisement read "African Americans and Arabians tend to clash with me so that won't work out." Sounds like it was from your grandfather's era? Actually, it appeared on the popular CraigsList Web site in 2006 and is just one example of how explicit discrimination thrives even in the digital age (Hughlett 2006).

Discrimination takes its toll, whether or not a person who is discriminated against is part of the informal economy or looking for a job on the Internet. Even members of minority groups who are not today being overtly discriminated against continue to fall victim to past discrimination. We have also identified the costs of discrimination to members of the privileged group. The

attitudes of Whites and even members of minority groups themselves are influenced by the images they have of racial and ethnic groups. These images come from what has been called *statistical discrimination,* which causes people to act based on stereotypes they hold and the actions of a few subordinate-group members.

From the conflict perspective, it is not surprising to find the widespread presence of the informal economy proposed by the dual labor market model and even an underclass. Derrick Bell (1994), an African American law professor, has made the sobering assertion that "racism is permanent." He contends that the attitudes of dominant Whites prevail, and society is willing to advance programs on behalf of subordinate groups only when they coincide with needs as perceived by those Whites.

The surveys presented in Chapter 2 show gradual acceptance of the earliest efforts to eliminate discrimination, but that support is failing as color-blind racism takes hold, especially as it relates to affirmative action. Indeed, concerns about doing something about alleged reverse discrimination are as likely to be voiced as concerns about racial or gender discrimination or glass ceilings and glass walls.

Institutional discrimination remains a formidable challenge in the United States. Attempts to reduce discrimination by attacking institutional discrimination have met with staunch resistance. Partly as a result of this outcry from some of the public, especially White Americans, the federal government gradually deemphasized its affirmative action efforts, beginning in the 1980s and into the twenty-first century. Most of the material in this chapter has been about racial groups, especially Black and White Americans. It would be easy to see intergroup hostility as a racial phenomenon, but that would be incorrect. Throughout the history of the United States, relations between some White groups have been characterized by resentment and violence. The next two chapters examine the ongoing legacy of immigration and the nature and relations of White ethnic groups.

Key Terms

absolute deprivation   87
affirmative action   108
discrimination   87
dual or split labor market   95
environmental justice   106
glass ceiling   114
glass escalator   116

glass wall   116
income   105
informal economy   94
institutional discrimination   92
irregular or underground economy   94

redlining   103
relative deprivation   87
reverse discrimination   112
total discrimination   90
wealth   105

Review Questions

1. Why might people still feel disadvantaged, even though their incomes are rising and their housing circumstances have improved?
2. Why does institutional discrimination sometimes seem less objectionable than individual discrimination?
3. In what way does the economy of the United States operate on several economic levels?
4. Why are questions raised about affirmative action although inequality persists?
5. Distinguish among glass ceilings, glass walls, and glass escalators. How do they differ from more obvious forms of discrimination in employment?

Critical Thinking

1. Discrimination can take many forms. Select a case of discrimination that you think just about everyone would agree is wrong. Then describe

another incident in which the alleged discrimination was of a more subtle form. Who is likely to condemn and who is likely to overlook such situations?

2. Resistance is a continuing theme of intergroup race relations. Discrimination implies the oppression of a group, but how can discrimination also unify the oppressed group to resist such unequal treatment? How can acceptance, or integration, for example, weaken the sense of solidarity within a group?

3. Voluntary associations such as the National Association for the Advancement of Colored People (NAACP) and government units such as the courts have been important vehicles for bringing about a measure of social justice. In what ways can the private sector—corporations and businesses—also work to bring about an end to discrimination?

Internet Connections—Research Navigator™

Follow the instructions given in "Internet Connections—Research Navigator™" in Chapter 1 of this text to access the features of Research Navigator™. Once at the Web site, enter your login name and password. Then, to use the ContentSelect database, enter keywords such as "informal economy," "affirmative action," and "glass ceiling," and the research engine will supply relevant and recent scholarly and popular press publications. Use the New York Times Search-by-Subject Archive to find recent news articles related to sociology and the Link Library feature to locate relevant Web links organized by the key terms associated with this chapter.

4 Immigration and the United States

CHAPTER OUTLINE

119

─────────────────⟨ HIGHLIGHTS ⟩─────────────────

The diversity of the American people is unmistakable evidence of the variety of places from which immigrants have come. Yet each succeeding generation of immigrants found itself being reluctantly accepted, at best, by the descendants of earlier arrivals. The Chinese were the first immigrant group to be singled out for restriction with the passage of the 1882 Exclusion Act. The initial Chinese immigrants became scapegoats for America's sagging economy in the last half of the nineteenth century. Growing fears that too many non-American types were immigrating motivated the creation of the national origin system and the quota acts of the 1920s. These acts gave preference to certain nationalities until the passage of the Immigration and Nationality Act in 1965 ended that practice. Many immigrants today in the United States are transnationals who still maintain close ties to their country of origin, sending money back, keeping current with political events, and making frequent return trips. Concern about both illegal and legal immigration continues with renewed attention in the aftermath of the September 11, 2001, terrorist attacks. Restrictionist sentiment has grown, and debates rage over whether immigrants, even legal ones, should receive services such as education, government-subsidized health care, and welfare. The challenges to an immigrant household upon arrival are not evenly felt as women play the central role in facilitating the transition. Controversy also continues to surround the policy of the United States toward refugees.

Two very different experiences of coming of age in the United States point to the different lives of immigrants in the United States.

Yuki Lin, born virtually at midnight at New York Downtown Hospital in Manhattan was identified as the first baby born in the United States in 2007.

Toys "Я" Us proudly announced that she would receive the promised $25,000 U.S. Savings Bond as a part of a special holiday promotion. One problem— Yuki's parents, both 23-year-old restaurant workers—were not legal United States residents. Immediately, the toy store giant rescinded its offer and said it was going to a baby born 19 seconds later in Georgia after documenting the legality of the parents. When the change became public, an outcry against Toys "Я" Us grew, and finally, the corporation agreed to give savings bonds to both babies declaring, "We love all babies" (Williams and Bernstein 2007).

Faeza Jaber is a 48-year-old single mother in her first months in the United States with her 7-year-old son Khatab. When she arrived in Phoenix, it was 114 degrees hot, which is hotter than her home in Baghdad. She was granted her refugee status after her husband, who was an office manager and interpreter for *Time* magazine, was murdered in 2004 on the way to work at a time when interpreters for foreign companies were being targeted. Previously a computer programmer at the Baghdad airport, she has found the transition difficult as she works as a part-time teacher's assistant at Khatab's elementary school. She strives to learn English and is encouraged to know that of the 600 Iraqi refugees who pass annually through Phoenix, 91 percent find a job and go off all state and federal subsidies within five months of arrival (Bennett 2008).

The armed immigration agents arrived at the Petit Jean Poultry Plant in Arkadelphia, Arkansas, just before the 7:30 a.m. early morning shift break for

Refugee Faeza Jaber and her son Khatab pause outside a mall in Phoenix, Arizona, where they relocated after the killing of her husband, Omar, who was shot by an unknown assailant in Baghdad in March 2004.

breakfast. Half the shift, 119 workers, was taken away in plastic handcuffs to a detention center where all but six were sent back to Mexico. In the weeks following, the 10,000 residents of Arkadelphia were upset that their community had been disrupted. People they had known as classmates at the local community college, neighbors, customers, fellow churchgoers, and clients had disappeared. Although the people of this Arkansas town usually embrace law enforcement, they did not like what had happened. Some even went so far as to reach the deported workers in Mexico and try to arrange to bring them back to town by crossing the border illegally (Chu and Mustafa 2006; Hennessy-Fiske 2006).

These dramas being played out in New York City and Phoenix illustrate the themes in immigration today. Immigrant labor is needed, but concerns over illegal immigration persist and, even for those who arrive legally, the transition can be difficult. For the next generation it gets a little easier and, for some, perhaps too easy as they begin to forget their family's heritage. Many come legally, applying for immigrant visas, but others enter illegally. In the United States we may not like lawbreakers, but often we seek services and low-priced products made by people who come here illegally. How do we control this immigration without violating the principle of free movement within the nation? How do we decide who enters? And how do we treat those who come here either legally or illegally?

The diversity of ethnic and racial backgrounds of Americans today is the living legacy of immigration. Except for descendants of Native Americans or of Africans brought here enslaved, today's population is entirely the product of people who chose to leave familiar places to come to a new country.

The social forces that cause people to emigrate are complex. The most important have been economic: financial failure in the old country and expectations of higher incomes and standards of living in the new land. Other factors include dislike of new regimes in their native lands, racial or religious bigotry, and a desire to reunite families. All these factors push people from their homelands and pull them to other nations such as the United States. Immigration into the United States, in particular, has been facilitated by cheap ocean transportation and by other countries' removal of restrictions on emigration.

Immigration: A Global Phenomenon

Immigration, as we noted in Chapter 1, is a worldwide phenomenon and contributes to globalization as more and more people see the world as their "home" rather than one specific country. People move across national borders throughout the world. Generally, immigration is from countries with lower standards of living to those that offer better wages. However, wars and famine may precipitate hundreds of thousands of people moving into neighboring countries and sometimes resettling permanently.

Scholars of immigration often point to push and pull factors. For example, economic difficulties, religious or ethnic persecution, and political unrest may push individuals from their homelands. Immigration to a particular nation, the pull factors, may be a result of perceptions of a better life ahead or to join a community of their fellow nationals already established abroad.

A potent factor contributing to immigration anywhere in the world is chain immigration. **Chain immigration** refers to an immigrant who sponsors several other immigrants who, upon their arrival, may sponsor still more. Laws that favor people desiring to enter a given country who already have relatives there or someone who can vouch for them financially may facilitate this sponsorship. But probably, the most important aspect of chain immigration is that immigrants anticipate knowing someone who can help them adjust to their new surroundings and find a new job, place to live, and even where to find the kind of foods that are familiar to them. Later in this chapter, we will revisit the social impact that immigration has worldwide.

Patterns of Immigration to the United States

There have been three unmistakable patterns of immigration to the United States: The number of immigrants has fluctuated dramatically over time largely owing to government policy changes, settlement has not been uniform across the country but centered in certain regions and cities, and the source of immigrants has changed over time. We will first look at the historical picture of immigrant numbers.

Vast numbers of immigrants have come to the United States. Figure 4.1 indicates the high but fluctuating number of immigrants who arrived during every decade from the 1820s through the beginning of the twenty-first century. The United States received the largest number of legal immigrants during the 1990s, which is likely to be surprised in the first decade of twenty-first century, but because the country was much smaller in the period from 1900 through 1910, the numerical impact was even greater then.

The reception given to immigrants in this country has not always been friendly. Open bloodshed, restrictive laws, and the eventual return of almost one-third of immigrants and their children to their home countries attest to the uneasy feeling toward strangers who want to settle here.

Opinion polls in the United States from 2000 through 2008 have never shown more than 10 percent of the public in favor of more immigration, and usually about 45 to 55 percent want less. Even a 2007 survey of Latinos found a sizable 30 percent advocated having immigration levels decreased. We want the door open until we get through, and then we want to close it (Gallup 2008).

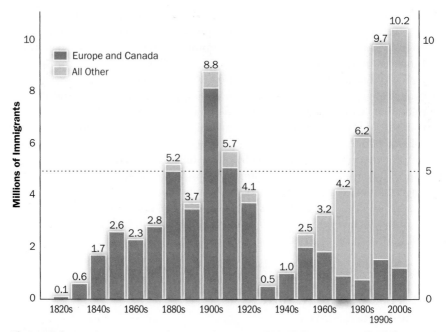

Figure 4.1 Legal Migration in the United States, 1820–2010

Source: Office of Immigartion Statistics 2007 and estimates by the author for the period 2000–2010.

Today's Foreign-Born Population

Before considering the sweep of past immigration policies, let us consider today's immigrant population. About 12 percent of the nation's people are foreign born; this proportion is between the high figure of about 15 percent in 1890 and a low of 4.7 percent in 1970. By global comparisons, the foreign-born population in the United States is large but not unusual. Whereas most industrial countries have a foreign population of around 5 percent, Canada's foreign population is 19 percent and Australia's is 25 percent.

As noted earlier, immigrants have not settled evenly across the nation. As shown in the map in Figure 4.2, the six states of California, New York, Florida, Texas, New Jersey, and Illinois account for 70 percent of the nation's total foreign-born population but less than 40 percent of the nation's total population.

Cities in these states are the focus of the foreign-born population. Almost half (43.3 percent) live in the central city of a metropolitan area, compared with about one-quarter (27 percent) of the nation's population. More than one-third of residents in the cities of Miami, Los Angeles, San Francisco, San Jose, and New York City are now foreign born (Camarota 2007b).

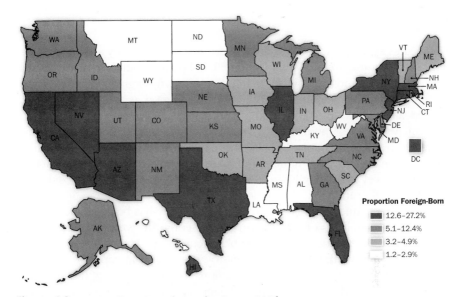

Figure 4.2 Foreign-Born Population for States, 2006

Source: Author's estimate based on Census Bureau data in the American Community Survey 2006. Bureau of the Census 2007b.

The third pattern of immigration is that the source of immigrants has changed. As shown in Figure 4.3, the majority of today's 37.9 million foreign-born people are from Latin America. Primarily, they are from Central America and, more specifically, Mexico. By contrast, Europeans, who dominated the early settlement of the United States, now account for less than one in seven of the foreign born today.

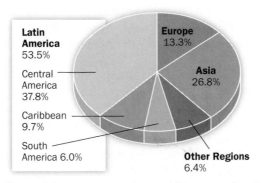

Figure 4.3 Foreign Born by World Regions of Birth

Source: Data for 2004 reported in 2005 in Bureau of the Census 2005c.

Early Immigration

European explorers of North America were soon followed by settlers, the first immigrants to the Western Hemisphere. The Spanish founded St. Augustine, Florida, in 1565, and the English founded Jamestown, Virginia, in 1607. Protestants from England emerged from the colonial period as the dominant force numerically, politically, and socially. The English accounted for 60 percent of the 3 million White Americans in 1790. Although exact statistics are lacking for the early years of the United States, the English were soon outnumbered by other nationalities, as the numbers of Scots-Irish and Germans, in particular, swelled. However, the English colonists maintained their dominant position, as Chapter 5 will examine.

Throughout American history, immigration policy has been politically controversial. The policies of the English king, George III, were criticized in the U.S. Declaration of Independence for obstructing immigration to the colonies. Toward the end of the nineteenth century, the American republic itself was criticized for enacting immigration restrictions. In the beginning, however, the country encouraged immigration. At first, legislation fixed the residence requirement for naturalization at five years, although briefly, under the Alien Act of 1798, it was fourteen years, and so-called dangerous people could be expelled. Despite this brief harshness, immigration was unregulated through most of the 1800s, and naturalization was easily available.

Besides holding the mistaken belief that concerns about immigration are something new, we also assume that immigrants to the United States rarely reconsider their decision to come to a new country. Analysis of available records, beginning in the early 1900s, suggests that about 35 percent of all immigrants to the United States eventually emigrated back to their home country. The proportion varies, with the figures for some countries being much higher, but the overall pattern is clear: About one in three immigrants to this nation eventually chooses to return home (Wyman 1993).

The relative absence of federal legislation from 1790 to 1881 does not mean that all new arrivals were welcomed. **Xenophobia** (the fear or hatred of strangers or foreigners) led naturally to **nativism** (beliefs and policies favoring native-born citizens over immigrants). Although the term *nativism* has largely been used to describe nineteenth century sentiments, anti-immigration views and organized movements have continued into the twenty-first century. Political scientist Samuel P. Huntington (1993, 1996) articulated the continuing immigration as a "clash of civilizations," which could only be remedied by significantly reducing legal immigration, not to mention to close the border to illegal arrivals. His view, which enjoys support, was that the fundamental world conflicts of the new century are cultural in nature rather than ideological or even economic (Citrin et al. 2007; Schaefer 2008).

Historically, Roman Catholics in general and the Irish in particular were among the first Europeans to be ill-treated. We will look at how organized

"IT SAYS THIS ORANGE JUICE IS MADE WITH FRUIT PICKED ENTIRELY BY AMERICAN WORKERS. IT'S 43 DOLLARS."

Immigrant labor plays a significant role and one of them is that because many of them are paid with low wages, which, in turn, keeps prices lower for the consumer.

hostility toward Irish immigrants eventually gave way to their acceptance into the larger society in our next chapter.

However, the most dramatic outbreak of nativism in the nineteenth century was aimed at the Chinese. If there had been any doubt by the mid-1800s that the United States could harmoniously accommodate all and was indeed some sort of melting pot, debate on the Chinese Exclusion Act would negatively settle the question once and for all.

The Anti-Chinese Movement

Before 1851, official records show that only forty-six Chinese had immigrated to the United States. Over the next thirty years, more than 200,000 came to this country, lured by the discovery of gold and the opening of job opportunities in the West. Overcrowding, drought, and warfare in China also encouraged them to take a chance in the United States. Another important factor was improved oceanic transportation; it was actually cheaper to travel from Hong Kong to San Francisco than from Chicago to San Francisco. The frontier communities of the West, particularly in California, looked on the Chinese as a valuable resource to fill manual jobs. As early as 1854, so many Chinese wanted to emigrate that ships had difficulty handling the volume.

In the 1860s, railroad work provided the greatest demand for Chinese labor, until the Union Pacific and Central Pacific railroads were joined at Promontory, Utah, in 1869. The Union Pacific relied primarily on Irish laborers, but 90 percent of the Central Pacific labor force was Chinese because Whites generally refused to do the backbreaking work over the western terrain. Despite the contribution of the Chinese, White workers physically prevented them from attending the driving of the golden spike to mark the joining of the two railroads.

With the dangerous railroad work largely completed, people began to rethink the wisdom of encouraging Chinese to immigrate to do the work no one else would do. Reflecting their xenophobia, White settlers found the Chinese immigrants and their customs and religion difficult to understand. Indeed, few people actually tried to understand these immigrants from Asia. Although they had had no firsthand contact with Chinese Americans, Easterners and legislators were soon on the anti-Chinese bandwagon as they read sensationalized accounts of the lifestyle of the new arrivals.

Even before the Chinese immigrated, stereotypes of them and their customs were prevalent. American traders returning from China, European diplomats, and Protestant missionaries consistently emphasized the exotic and sinister aspects of life in China. The **sinophobes,** people with a fear of anything associated with China, appealed to the racist theory developed during the slavery controversy that non-Europeans were subhuman. Similarly, Americans were beginning to be more conscious of biological inheritance and disease, so it was not hard to conjure up fears of alien genes and germs. The only real challenge the anti-Chinese movement had was to convince people that the negative consequences of unrestricted Chinese immigration outweighed any possible economic gain. Perhaps briefly, racial prejudice had earlier been subordinated to industrial dependence on Chinese labor for the work that Whites shunned, but acceptance of the Chinese was short-lived. The fear of the "yellow peril" overwhelmed any desire to know more about Asian people and their customs (Takaki 1989).

Another nativist fear of Chinese immigrants was based on the threat they posed as laborers. Californians, whose labor force felt the effects of the Chinese immigration first, found support throughout the nation as organized labor feared that the Chinese would be used as strikebreakers. By 1870, Chinese workers had been used for that purpose as far east as Massachusetts. When Chinese workers did unionize, they were not recognized by major labor organizations. Samuel Gompers, founder of the American Federation of Labor (AFL), consistently opposed any effort to assist Chinese workers and refused to consider having a union of Chinese restaurant employees admitted into the AFL. Gompers worked effectively to see future Chinese immigration ended and produced a pamphlet titled "Chinese Exclusion: Meat vs. Rice: American Manhood Against Asiatic Coolieism—Which Shall Survive?" (Gompers and Gustadt 1908; Hill 1967).

Employers were glad to pay the Chinese low wages, but laborers came to direct their resentment against the Chinese rather than against their compatriots' willingness to exploit the Chinese. Only a generation earlier, the same concerns had been felt about the Irish, but with the Chinese, the hostility reached new heights because of another factor.

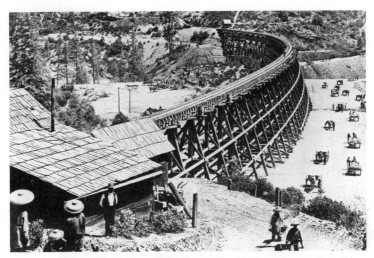

Chinese workers, such as these pictured in 1844, played a major role in building railroads in the West.

Although many arguments were voiced, racial fears motivated the anti-Chinese movement. Race was the critical issue. The labor market fears were largely unfounded, and most advocates of restrictions at that time knew that. There was no possibility that the Chinese would immigrate in numbers that would match those of Europeans at that time, so it is difficult to find any explanation other than racism for their fears (Winant 1994).

From the sociological perspective of conflict theory, we can explain how the Chinese immigrants were welcomed only when their labor was necessary to fuel growth in the United States. When that labor was no longer necessary, the welcome mat for the immigrants was withdrawn. Furthermore, as conflict theorists would point out, restrictions were not applied evenly: Americans focused on a specific nationality (the Chinese) to reduce the overall number of foreign workers in the nation. Because decision making at that time rested in the hands of the descendants of European immigrants, the steps to be taken were most likely to be directed against the least powerful: immigrants from China who, unlike Europeans seeking entry, had few allies among legislators and other policy makers.

In 1882, Congress enacted the Chinese Exclusion Act, which outlawed Chinese immigration for ten years. It also explicitly denied naturalization rights to the Chinese in the United States; that is, they were not allowed to become citizens. There was little debate in Congress, and discussion concentrated on how suspension of Chinese immigration could best be handled. No allowance was made for spouses and children to be reunited with their husbands and fathers in the United States. Only brief visits of Chinese government officials, teachers, tourists, and merchants were exempted.

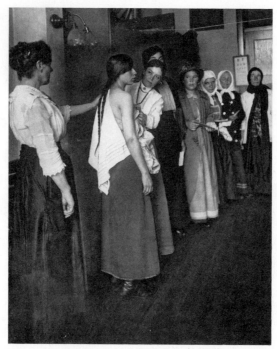

Here women immigrants are undergoing a physical examination before being permitted to enter in 1910.

The rest of the nineteenth century saw the remaining loopholes allowing Chinese immigration being closed. Beginning in 1884, Chinese laborers were not allowed to enter the United States from any foreign place, a ban that lasted ten years. Two years later, the Statue of Liberty was dedicated, with a poem by Emma Lazarus inscribed on its base. To the Chinese, the poem welcoming the tired, the poor, and the huddled masses must have seemed a hollow mockery.

In 1892, Congress extended the Exclusion Act for another ten years and added that Chinese laborers had to obtain certificates of residence within a year or face deportation. After the turn of the century, the Exclusion Act was extended again. Two decades later, the Chinese were not alone; the list of people restricted by immigration policy had expanded many times.

Restrictionist Sentiment Increases

As Congress closed the door to Chinese immigration, the debate on restricting immigration turned in new directions. Prodded by growing anti-Japanese feelings, the United States entered into the so-called Gentlemen's Agreement, completed in 1908. Japan agreed to halt further immigration to the United

States, and the United States agreed to end discrimination against the Japanese who had already arrived. The immigration ended, but anti-Japanese feelings continued. Americans were growing uneasy that the "new immigrants" would overwhelm the culture established by the "old immigrants." The earlier immigrants, if not Anglo-Saxon, were from similar groups such as the Scandinavians, the Swiss, and the French Huguenots. These people were more experienced in democratic political practices and had a greater affinity with the dominant Anglo-Saxon culture. By the end of the nineteenth century, however, more and more immigrants were neither English speaking nor Protestant and came from dramatically different cultures.

In 1917, Congress finally overrode President Wilson's veto and enacted an immigration bill that included the controversial literacy test. Critics of the bill, including Wilson, argued that illiteracy does not signify inherent incompetence but reflects lack of opportunity for instruction. Such arguments were not heeded, however. The act seemed innocent at first glance—it merely required immigrants to read thirty words in any language—but it was the first attempt to restrict immigration from Western Europe. The act also prohibited immigration from the South Sea islands and other parts of Asia not already excluded. Curiously, this law that closed the door on non–Anglo-Saxons permitted a waiver of the test if the immigrants came because of their home government's discrimination against their race (*New York Times* 1917a, 1917b).

The National Origin System

Beginning in 1921, a series of measures were enacted that marked a new era in American immigration policy. Whatever the legal language, the measures were drawn up to block the growing immigration from southern Europe, such as from Italy and Greece.

Anti-immigration sentiment, combined with the isolationism that followed World War I, caused Congress to severely restrict entry privileges not only of the Chinese and Japanese but also of Europeans as well. The national origin system was begun in 1921 and remained the basis of immigration policy until 1965. This system used the nationality to determine whether a person could enter as a legal alien, and the number of previous immigrants and their descendants was used to set the group's annual immigration cap.

To understand the effect of the national origin system on immigration, it is necessary to clarify the quota system. The quotas were deliberately weighted in favor of immigration from northern Europe. Because of the ethnic composition of the country in 1920, the quotas placed severe restrictions on immigration from the rest of Europe and from other parts of the world. Immigration from the Western Hemisphere (i.e., Canada, Mexico, Central and South America, and the Caribbean) continued unrestricted. The quota for each nation was set at 3 percent of the number of people descended from each nationality recorded in the 1920 census. Once the statistical manipulations were completed, almost 70 percent of the quota for the Eastern Hemisphere went to just three countries: Great Britain, Ireland, and Germany.

The absurdities of the system soon became obvious, but it was nevertheless continued. British immigration had fallen sharply, so most of its quota of 65,000 went unfilled. However, the openings could not be transferred, even though countries such as Italy, with a quota of only 6,000, had 200,000 people who wanted to enter. However one rationalizes the purpose behind the act, the result was obvious: Any English person, regardless of skill and whether related to anyone already here, could enter the country more easily than, say, a Greek doctor whose children were American citizens. The quota for Greece was 305, with the backlog of people wanting to come reaching 100,000.

By the end of the 1920s, annual immigration had dropped to one-fourth of its pre–World War I level. The worldwide economic depression of the 1930s decreased immigration still further. A brief upsurge in immigration just before World War II reflected the flight of Europeans from the oppression of expanding Nazi Germany. The war virtually ended transatlantic immigration. The era of the great European migration to the United States had been legislated out of existence.

The 1965 Immigration and Nationality Act

The national origin system was abandoned with the passage of the 1965 Immigration and Nationality Act, signed into law by President Lyndon B. Johnson at the foot of the Statue of Liberty. The primary goals of the act were to reunite families and to protect the American labor market. The act also initiated restrictions on immigration from Latin America. After the act, immigration increased by one-third, but the act's influence was primarily on the composition rather than the size of immigration. The sources of immigrants now included Italy, Greece, Portugal, Mexico, the Philippines, the West Indies, and South America. The effect is apparent when we compare the changing sources of immigration over the last 180 years, as shown in Figure 4.4. The most recent period shows that Asian and Latin American immigrants combined to account for 81 percent of the people who were permitted entry. This contrasts sharply with early immigration, which was dominated by arrivals from Europe.

The nature of immigration laws is exceedingly complex and is subjected to frequent, often minor, adjustments. In 2000 and 2006, between 840,000 and 1,270,000 people were legally admitted annually. For the most recent year, people were admitted for the following reasons:

Relatives of citizens	55%
Relatives of legal residents	9%
Employment based	13%
Refugees/people seeking political asylum	17%
Diversity (lottery among applications from nations historically sending few immigrants)	3%
Other	3%

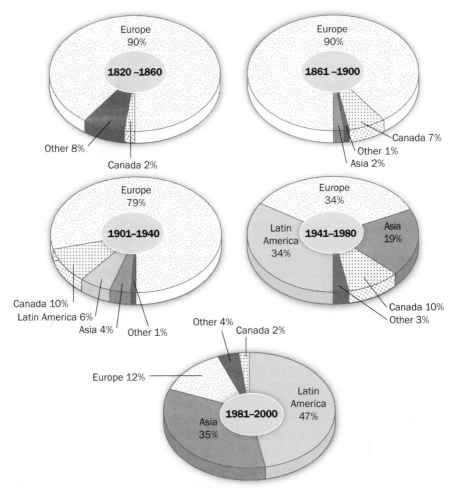

Figure 4.4 Legal Immigrants Admitted to the United States by Region of Last Residence, 1820–2000

Source: Office of Immigration Statistics. 2006, pp. 10–13.

Overall, two-thirds of the immigrants come to join their families, one-seventh because of skills needed in the United States and another one-seventh because of special refugee status (Office of Immigration Statistics 2007: Table 7).

Contemporary Social Concerns

Although our current immigration policies are less restrictive than other nations' restrictions, they are the subject of great debate. In Table 4.1, we summarize the benefits and concerns regarding immigration to the United States. We will consider four continuing criticisms of our immigration policy: the brain

Table 4.1 Immigration Benefits and Concerns

Potential Benefits	Areas of Concern
Provide needed skills	Drain needed resources from home country
Contribute to taxes	Send remittances (or migradollars) home
May come with substantial capital to start business	Less-skilled immigrants compete with those already disadvantaged
Diversify the population (intangible gain)	Population growth
Maintain ties with countries throughout the world	May complicate foreign policy by lobbying the government
	Illegal immigration

drain, population growth, mixed status, and illegal immigration. All four, but particularly illegal immigration, have provoked heated debates on the national level and continuing efforts to resolve them with new policies. We will then consider the economic impact of immigration, followed by the nation's policy toward refugees, a group distinct from immigrants.

The Brain Drain

How often have you identified your science or mathematics teacher or your physician as someone who was not born in the United States? This nation has clearly benefited from attracting human resources from throughout the world, but this phenomenon has had its price for the nations of origin.

Brain drain is the immigration to the United States of skilled workers, professionals, and technicians who are desperately needed by their home countries. In the mid-twentieth century, many scientists and other professionals from industrial nations, principally Germany and Great Britain, came to the United States. More recently, however, the brain drain has pulled emigrants from developing nations, including India, Pakistan, the Philippines, and several African nations. They are eligible for what are referred to as H-1B visas qualifying for permanent work permits.

One out of four physicians in the United States is foreign born and plays a critical role in serving areas with too few doctors. Thousands of skilled, educated Indians now seek to enter the United States, pulled by the economic opportunity. The pay differential is so great that beginning in 2004, when foreign physicians were no longer favored with entry to the United States, physicians in the Philippines were retraining as nurses so that they could immigrate to the United States where, employed as nurses, they would make four times what they would as doctors in the Philippines (Mullen 2005; *New York Times* 2005b).

The brain drain controversy was evident long before the passage of the 1965 Immigration Act. However, the 1965 act seemed to encourage such immigration

Even during times of strongest sentiment against immigration, provisions exist to allow legal entry to overseas technical workers who are in short supply in the United States.

by placing the professions in one of the categories of preference. Various corporations, including Motorola and Intel, now find that one-third of their high-tech jobs are held by people born abroad, although many received their advanced education in the United States. Furthermore, these immigrants have links to their old countries and are boosting U.S. exports to the fast-growing economic regions of Asia and Latin America.

Many foreign students say they plan to return home. Fortunately for the United States, many do not and make their talents available in the United States. One study showed that the majority of foreign students receiving their doctorates in the sciences and engineering are still here four years later. Yet, critics note that this supply allows the country to overlook its minority scholars. Presently, for every two minority doctorates, there are five foreign citizens receiving this degree. In the physical sciences, for every doctorate issued to a minority citizen, foreign citizens receive eleven. More attention needs to be given to encourage African Americans and Latinos to enter high-tech career paths.

Conflict theorists see the current brain drain as yet another symptom of the unequal distribution of world resources. In their view, it is ironic that the United States gives foreign aid to improve the technical resources of African and Asian countries while maintaining an immigration policy that encourages professionals in such nations to migrate to our shores. These are the very countries that have unacceptable public health conditions and need native scientists, educators, technicians, and other professionals. In addition, by relying on foreign talent, the United States does not need to take the steps necessary to encourage native members of subordinate groups to enter these desirable fields of employment (Hoffer et al. 2001; Pearson 2006; Wessel 2001).

Population Growth

The United States, like a few other industrial nations, continues to accept large numbers of permanent immigrants and refugees. Although such immigration has increased since the passage of the 1965 Immigration and Nationality Act, the nation's birthrate has decreased. Consequently, the contribution of immigration to population growth has become more significant.

Immigration, legal and illegal, accounted for about 45 to 60 percent of the nation's growth in the early years of the twenty-first century. To some observers, the United States is already overpopulated. The respected environmentalist group Sierra Club debated for several years on taking an official position favoring restricting immigration, recognizing that more people puts greater strain on the nation's natural resources. Thus far, the majority of the members have indicated a desire to keep a neutral position rather than enter the politically charged immigration debate (Barringer 2004; Camarota 2007b; Passel and Cohn 2008).

The patterns of uneven settlement by immigrants in the United States are expected to continue so that future immigrants' impact on population growth will be felt much more in certain areas: say, California and New York, rather than Wyoming or West Virginia. Although immigration and population growth may be viewed as national concerns, their impact is localized in certain areas such as southern California and large urban centers nationwide (Bean et al. 2004).

Mixed-Status Families

Very little is simple when it comes to immigration, and this is particularly true to the challenge of "mixed status." **Mixed status** refers to families where one or more is a citizen and the one or more is a noncitizen. This especially becomes problematic when the noncitizens are illegal or undocumented immigrants.

The problem of mixed status clearly emerges on two levels. On the macro level, when policy debates are made about issues that seem clear to many people such as should illegal immigrants be eligible to attend state colleges or should illegal immigrants be immediately deported, the complicating factor of mixed status families quickly emerges. On the micro level, the daily toll on members of mixed status households is very difficult. Often the legal resident or even the U.S. citizen in a household finds their daily life limited for fear of revealing the undocumented status of a parent or brother or even a son.

A growing problem is families that are "mixed status." One or more members of an immediate family may be legal residents or even citizens but there also may be a member who is in the country illegally. There are almost 7 million families in which the head of the household or spouse is an illegal immigrant. Yet in about one-third of these families one or more of the children are U.S. citizens. This means that some of the issues facing illegal immigrants, whom we will discuss later, will also affect the citizens in the families because they are reluctant to bring attention to themselves for fear of revealing the legal status of their mother or father (Brewington 2008; Fix and Zimmerman 1999; Passel 2005).

Illegal Immigration

The most bitterly debated aspect of U.S. immigration policy has been the control of illegal or undocumented immigrants. These immigrants and their families come to the United States in search of higher-paying jobs than their home countries can provide.

In "Listen to Our Voices," sociologist Douglas Massey ponders the border militarization that has occurred amidst concerns over illegal immigration.

LISTEN TO OUR VOICES

The Wall that Keeps Illegal Workers In

Douglas S. Massey

The Mexican–American border is not now and never has been out of control. The rate of undocumented migration, adjusted for population growth, to the United States has not increased in 20 years. That is, from 1980 to 2004 the annual likelihood that a Mexican will make his first illegal trip to the United States has remained at about 1 in 100.

What has changed are the locations and visibility of border crossings. And that shift, more than anything, has given the public undue fears about waves of Mexican workers trying to flood into America.

Until the 1990s, the vast majority of undocumented Mexicans entered through either El Paso or San Diego. El Paso has around 700,000 residents and is 78 percent Hispanic, whereas San Diego County has three million residents and is 27 percent Hispanic. Thus, the daily passage of even thousands of Mexicans through these metropolitan areas was not very visible or disruptive.

This all changed in 1992 when the Border Patrol built a steel fence south of San Diego from the Pacific Ocean to the port of entry at San Ysidro, California, where Interstate 5 crosses into Mexico. This fence, and the stationing of officers and equipment behind it, blocked one of the busiest illicit crossing routes and channeled migrants toward the San Ysidro entry station, where their numbers rapidly built up to impossible levels.

Every day the same episode unfolded: the crowd swelled to a critical threshold, whereupon many migrants made what the local press called "banzai runs" into the United States, darting through traffic on the Interstate and clambering over cars.

Waiting nearby were Border Patrol officers, they're not to arrest the migrants but to capture the mayhem on video, which was later edited into an agency documentary. Although nothing had changed except the site of border crossings, the video gave the impression that the border was overwhelmed by a rising tide of undocumented migrants.

In response to the ensuing public uproar, the policy of tougher order enforcement was expanded to all of the San Diego and El Paso area in 1993 and 1994. So migrants began going to more remote locations along the border in Arizona. In 1989, two-thirds of undocumented migrants came in through El Paso or San Diego; but by 2004, two-thirds crossed somewhere else. (My statistics on Mexican immigration come from a study I have been undertaking with financing from the National Institutes of Health since 1982.)

Unlike the old crossing sites, these new locations were sparsely settled, so the sudden appearance of thousands of Mexicans attracted considerable attention and understandably generated much agitation locally. Perceptions of a breakdown at the border were heightened by news reports of rising deaths among migrants; by redistricting flows into harsh, remote terrain, the United States tripled the death rate during border crossing.

Less well known is that American policies also reduced the rate of apprehension, because those remote sectors of the border had fewer Border Patrol officers. My research found that during the 1980s, the probability that an undocumented migrant would be apprehended while crossing stood at around 33 percent; by 2000 it was at 10 percent, despite increases in federal spending on border enforcement.

Naturally, public perceptions of chaos on the border prompted more calls for enforcement and the hardening strategy was extended to other sectors. The number of Border Patrol officers increased from around 2,500 in the early 1980s to around 12,000 today, and the agency's annual budget rose to $1.6 billion from $200 million. The boundary between Mexico and the United States has become perhaps the most militarized frontier between two nations at peace anywhere in the world.

Although border militarization had little effect on the probability of Mexicans migrating illegally, it did reduce the likelihood that they would return to their homeland. America's tougher line roughly tripled the average cost of getting across the border illegally; thus Mexicans who had run the gauntlet at the border were more likely to hunker down and stay in the United States. My study has shown that in the early 1980's, about half of all undocumented Mexicans returned home within 12 months of entry, but by 2000, the rate of return migration stood at just 25 percent.

The United States is now locked into a perverse cycle whereby additional border enforcement further decreases the rate of return migration, which accelerates undocumented population growth, which brings calls for harsher enforcement.

The only thing we have to show for two decades of border militarization is a larger undocumented population than we would otherwise have, a rising number of Mexicans dying while trying to cross, and a growing burden on taxpayers for enforcement that is counterproductive.

We need an immigration policy that seeks to manage the cross-border flows of people that are inevitable in a global economy, not to repress them through unilateral police actions.

Source: From "The Wall that Keeps Illegal Workers In" by Douglas Massey, *New York Times,* April 4, 2006, p. A13. Reprinted by permission.

Since, by definition, illegal immigrants are in the country illegally, the exact number of these undocumented or unauthorized workers is subject to estimates and disputes. Based on the best available information, there are more than 11 million illegal immigrants in the United States and probably closer to

12 million. This compares to about 4 million in 1992. Today about 7.2 million are employed, accounting for about 5 percent of the entire civilian labor force (Camarota 2007b; Passel 2006).

Illegal immigrants, and even legal immigrants, have become tied by the public to almost every social problem in the nation. They become the scapegoats for unemployment; they are labeled as "drug runners" and, especially since September 11, 2001, "terrorists." Their vital economic and cultural contribution to the United States is generally overlooked, as it has been for more than a hundred years.

The cost of the federal government's attempt to police the nation's borders and locate illegal immigrants is sizable. There are significant costs for aliens, that is, foreign-born noncitizens, and for other citizens as well. Civil rights advocates have expressed concern that the procedures used to apprehend and deport people are discriminatory and deprive many aliens of their legal rights. American citizens of Hispanic or Asian origin, some of whom were born in the United States, may be greeted with prejudice and distrust, as if their names automatically imply that they are illegal immigrants. Furthermore, these citizens and legal residents of the United States may be unable to find work because employers wrongly believe that their documents are forged.

In the context of this illegal immigration, Congress approved the Immigration Reform and Control Act of 1986 (IRCA) after debating it for nearly a decade. The act marked a historic change in immigration policy compared with earlier laws, as summarized in Table 4.2. Amnesty was granted to 1.7 million illegal immigrants who could document that they had established long-term residency in the United States. Under the IRCA, hiring illegal aliens became illegal,

Table 4.2 Major Immigration Policies

Policy	Target Group	Impact
Chinese Exclusion Act, 1882	Chinese	Effectively ended all Chinese immigration for more than 60 years
National origin system, 1921	Southern Europeans	Reduced overall immigration and significantly reduced likely immigration from Greece and Italy
Immigration and Nationality Act, 1965	Western Hemisphere and the less skilled	Facilitated entry of skilled workers and relatives of U.S. residents
Immigration Reform and Control Act of 1986	Illegal immigration	Modest reduction of illegal immigration
Illegal Immigration Reform and Immigrant Responsibility Act of 1996	Illegal immigration	Greater border surveillance and increased scrutiny of legal immigrants seeking benefits

so that employers are subject to fines and even prison sentences. It appears that the act has had mixed results in terms of illegal immigration. According to data compiled by the U.S. Border Patrol, arrests along the border declined substantially in the first three years after the law took effect. However, illegal immigration eventually returned to the levels of the early 1980s (Pear 2007).

Many illegal immigrants continue to live in fear and hiding, subject to even more severe harassment and discrimination than before. From a conflict perspective, these immigrants, primarily poor and Hispanic or Asian, are being firmly lodged at the bottom of the nation's social and economic hierarchies. However, from a functionalist perspective, employers, by paying low wages, are able to produce goods and services that are profitable for industry and more affordable to consumers. Despite the poor working conditions often experienced by illegal immigrants here, they continue to come because it is still in their best economic interest to work here in disadvantaged positions rather than to seek wage labor unsuccessfully in their home countries.

Little workplace enforcement occurs for the hiring of undocumented workers. Although never a priority, it has fallen to the point where only about five employers are fined annually involving 400 workers nationwide (Echaveste 2005).

Amidst heated debate, Congress reached a compromise and passed the Illegal Immigration Reform and Immigrant Responsibility Act of 1996, which emphasized making more effort to keep immigrants from entering the country illegally. Illegal immigrants will not have access to benefit programs such as Social Security and welfare. For now, legal immigrants will be entitled to such benefits, although social service agencies are required to verify their legal status. Another significant element was to increase border control and surveillance.

The illegal aliens or undocumented workers are not necessarily transient. A 2006 estimate indicated 60 percent had been here for at least five years. Many have established homes, families, and networks with relatives and friends in the United States whose legal status might differ. These are the "mixed-status" households noted earlier. For the most part their lives are not much different from legal residents except when they seek services that require citizenship status to be documented (Passel 2006).

Policy makers continue to avoid the only real way to stop illegal immigration, which is to discourage employment opportunities. The public often thinks in terms of greater surveillance at the border. After the terrorist attacks of September 11, 2001, greater control of border traffic took on a new sense of urgency, even though almost all the men who took over the planes had entered the United States legally. It is very difficult to secure the vast boundaries that mark the United States on land and sea.

Reflecting the emphasis on heightened security, a potentially major shake-up recently took place. Since 1940, the Immigration and Naturalization Service (INS) had been in the Department of Justice, but in 2003, it was transferred to the newly formed Department of Homeland Security (see Table 4.3). The

Table 4.3 Transformation of Immigration Management

Following 9/11, management of immigration in the United States was reorganized, as of March 1, 2003, from INS in the Department of Justice to three new agencies in the new Department of Homeland Security.

Before	After
Located in Department of Justice	Located in Department of Homeland Security
Immigration and Naturalization Services (INS)	INS dissolved
Immigration services	U.S. Citizen and Immigration Services (USCIS or CIS)
Naturalization (citizenship)	
Applications	
Visas	
U.S. Border Patrol	U.S. Customs and Borders Protection (CBP)
Inspections at border	
Deportations at border	
Immigration enforcement—interior (includes removals and detentions)	U.S. Immigration and Customs Enforcement (ICE)

various functions of the INS were split into three agencies with a new Bureau of Citizenship and Immigration Services and two other units separately concerned with customs and border protection. For years, immigrant advocates had argued to separate border enforcement from immigration, but the placement of immigrant services in the office responsible for protecting the United States from terrorists sends a chilling message to immigrants.

Numerous civil rights groups and migrant advocacy organizations have expressed alarm over the large number of people now crossing into the United States illegally who perish in their attempt. Death occurs to some in deserts, in isolated canyons, and while concealed in containers or locked in trucks during smuggling attempts. Several hundred die annually in the Southwest, seeking more and more dangerous crossing points, as border control has increased. However, this death toll has received little attention, causing one journalist to liken it to a jumbo jet crashing between Los Angeles and Phoenix every year without anyone giving it much notice (Del Olmo 2003; Sullivan 2005).

What certainly was noticed was the public debate in 2006 over how to stop further illegal immigration and what to do about illegal immigrants already inside the United States. Debate over hardening the border by erecting a 700-mile-long double concrete wall brought concerns that desperate immigrants would take even more chances with their lives in order to work in the United States. A Congressional proposal to make assisting an illegal immigrant

Ask Yourself

Ever thought about how the nation's extensive jail and prison system related to immigration today? Everyday about 26,000 immigrants await determination of their fate in correctional facilities. Here is a different example of "Texas hold 'em" in southern Texas. This $65 million tent city was constructed in the summer of 2006 to accommodate 2,000 immigrants identified as illegal who are most likely to be sent back to their home countries.

already here a felony led to strong counterdemonstrations drawing tens of thousands of marchers in cities across the Untied States. Meanwhile the federal government, as it has for a century, struggled between the need to attract workers to do jobs many people here legally would not want to do and the desire to enforce the laws governing legal immigration (Tumulty 2006).

Path to Citizenship: Naturalization

Naturalization is the conferring of citizenship on a person after birth. This is achieved through a process outlined by Congress and extends to foreigners the same benefits given to native-born U.S. citizens with the exception that naturalized citizens cannot serve as president.

Until the 1970s, the majority of persons naturalizing were born in Europe, but reflecting changing patterns of immigration, Asia and Latin America are the largest source of new citizens. In fact in 2006, the number of naturalized citizens from Mexico came close to matching those from all of Europe. In recent years, the number of new citizens going through the naturalization process has been between a half and one million a year (Simanski 2007).

Table 4.4 So You Want to Be a Citizen?

Try these sample questions from the naturalization test (answers below).

1. What do the stripes on the flag represent?
2. How many changes, or amendments, are there to the Constitution?
3. Who is the chief justice of the Supreme Court?
4. What are some of the requirements to be eligible to become president?
5. What are inalienable rights?
6. What is the introduction to the Constitution called and what year was it written?
7. Name one right or freedom guaranteed by the First Amendment.
8. What group of essays supported passage of the U.S. Constitution?

Source: Citizen and Immigration Services (CIS) 2008. Sample reflects changes proposed by CIS as of January 2008.

Answers: 1. The first 13 states; 2. 27; 3. John Roberts; 4. Candidates for president must be natural-born citizens, be at least 35 years old, and have lived in the United States for at least 14 years; 5. Individual rights that people are born with; 6. The Preamble and 1787; 7. The rights are freedom of speech, of religion, of assembly, of press, and to petition the government; 8. The Federalist Papers.

The general conditions for becoming naturalized in the United States are the following:

- Eighteen years of age
- Continuous residence for at least five years (three years for the spouses of U.S. citizens)
- Good moral character as determined by the absence of conviction of selected criminal offenses
- Ability to read, write, speak, and understand words of ordinary usage in the English language
- Ability to pass a test in U.S. government and history

In Table 4.4 we offer a sample of the type of questions immigrants face on the citizenship test.

Although we often picture the United States as having a very insular, nativistic attitude toward foreigners living here, the country has a rather liberal policy toward people maintaining the citizenship of their old country. Although most countries do not allow people to maintain dual (or even multiple) citizenships, the United States does not forbid it. Dual citizenship is most common when a person goes through naturalization after already being a citizen of another country or is a U.S.-born citizen and goes through the process of becoming a citizen of another country, for example, after marrying a foreigner.

Most other countries will demand you renounce citizenship of another country but, in practice, the United States rarely takes that step even if you do officially renounce your citizenship as required by that country. In practice, the

United States will still consider you a citizen, with the right to vote, and allow you to carry a U.S. passport—all of which may be prohibited by the foreign country. Generally, it is only when one chooses to make a major statement by personally informing the federal government of their intent or through other public actions that the United States would not continue to recognize you as a citizen (Department of State 2008).

The Economic Impact of Immigration

There is much public and scholarly debate about the economic effects of immigration, both legal and illegal. Varied, conflicting conclusions have resulted from research ranging from case studies of Korean immigrants' dominance among New York City greengrocers to mobility studies charting the progress of all immigrants and their children. The confusion results in part from the different methods of analysis. For example, the studies do not always include political refugees, who generally are less prepared than other refugees to become assimilated. Sometimes the research focuses only on economic effects, such as whether people are employed or on welfare; in other cases it also considers cultural factors such as knowledge of English.

Perhaps the most significant factor is whether a study examines the national impact of immigration or only its effects on a local area. Overall, we can conclude from the research that immigrants adapt well and are an asset to the local economy. In some areas, heavy immigration may drain a community's resources. However, it can also revitalize a local economy. Marginally employed workers, most of whom are either themselves immigrants or African Americans, often experience a negative impact by new arrivals. With or without immigration, competition for low-paying jobs in the United States is high, and those who gain the most from this competition are the employers and the consumers who want to keep prices down (Steinberg 2005).

The impact of immigration on African Americans deserves special attention. Given that African Americans are a large minority and many continue to be in the underclass, many people including some Blacks themselves perceive immigrants as advancing at the expense of the African American community. There is evidence that in the very lowest paid jobs, for example, workers in chicken processing plants, wages have dropped with the availability of unskilled immigrants to perform them and Blacks have left these jobs for good. Many of these African Americans do not necessarily move to better or even equivalent jobs. This pattern is repeated in other relatively low-paying undesirable employment sectors, so Blacks are not alone in being impacted but given other job opportunities; the impact is longer lasting (Borjas et al. 2006; Kochhar 2006; Sum, Harrington, and Khatiwda 2006).

According to survey data, many people in the United States hold the stereotypical belief that immigrants often end up on welfare and thereby cause increases in taxes. Economist David Card studied the 1980 "Mariel" boatlift that brought 125,000 Cubans into Miami and found that even this substantial addition of mainly low-skilled workers had no measurable impact on the wages or unemployment rates of low-skilled White and African American workers in the Miami area (Card, DiNardo, and Estes 1998; Lowenstein 2006).

About 70 percent of illegal immigrant workers pay taxes of one type or another. Many of them do not file to receive entitled refunds or benefits. For example, in 2005, the Social Security Administration identified thousands of unauthorized workers contributing to the fund about $7 billion that could not be credited properly (Porter 2005).

Social science studies generally contradict many of the negative stereotypes about the economic impact of immigration. A variety of recent studies found that immigrants are a net economic gain for the population both in times of economic boom and even in periods of recession. But despite national gains, in some areas and for some groups, immigration may be an economic burden or create unwanted competition for jobs (Kochhar 2006).

What about the immigrants themselves? Considering contemporary immigrants as a group, we can make some conclusions, which show a mix of some success and evidence that adaptation typically is very difficult.

Less Encouraging

- Although immigrants have lower divorce rates and are less likely to form single-parent households than natives, their rates equal or exceed these rates by the second generation.
- Children in immigrant families tend to be healthier than U.S.-born children, but the advantage declines. We will consider this in greater detail later in this chapter.
- Immigrant children attend schools that are disproportionately attended by other poor children and students with limited English proficiency, so they are ethnically, economically, and linguistically isolated.

Positive Signs

- Immigrant families and, more broadly, noncitizen households are more likely to be on public assistance, but their time on public assistance is less and they receive fewer benefits. This is even true when considering special restrictions that may apply to noncitizens.
- Second-generation immigrants (i.e., children of immigrants) are overall doing as well as or better than White non-Hispanic natives in educational attainment, labor force participation, wages, and household income.
- Immigrants overwhelmingly (65 percent) continue to see learning English as an ethical obligation of all immigrants.

These positive trends diverge between specific immigrant groups, with Asian immigrants doing better than European immigrants, who do better than Latino immigrants (Capps et al. 2002; Economic Mobility Project 2007b; Farkas 2003; Fix and Passel 2001; Myers et al. 2004).

One economic aspect of immigration that has received increasing attention is the role of remittances. **Remittances (or migradollars)** are the monies that immigrants return to their country of origin. The amounts are significant and measure in the hundreds of millions of dollars flowing from the United States to a number of countries where they are a very substantial source of support for families and even venture capital for new businesses. Although some observers express concern over this outflow of money, others counter that it probably represents a small price to pay for the human capital that the United States is able to use in the form of the immigrants themselves. Immigrants in the United States send billions to their home countries and worldwide remittances bring about $300 billion to developing countries, easily surpassing all other forms of foreign aid (International Fund for Agricultural Development 2007).

Remittances are widely recognized as critical to the survival of millions of households worldwide. One estimate concluded that one out of every five people in Mexico regularly receives a payment from abroad. The monies also play a significant role in the financial health of many economies (Hagenbaugh 2006).

The concern about immigration today is both understandable and perplexing. The nation has always been uneasy about new arrivals, especially those who are different from the more affluent and the policy makers. Yet most of the last two decades have been marked by low unemployment, low inflation, and much-diminished anxiety about our economic future. This paradoxical situation—a strong economy and concerns about immigration framed in

Remittances from immigrants and overseas relatives are a powerful economic force. As shown here in Mexico, these migradollars help to finance people's businesses and even assist them in buying homes.

Immigration is a challenge to all family members, but immigrant women must not only navigate a new culture and a new country for themselves but also for their children; such as in this household in Colorado.

economic arguments—suggests that other concerns, such as ethnic and racial tensions, are more important in explaining current attitudes toward immigration in the United States.

Women and Immigration

Immigration is presented as if all immigrants are similar with the only distinctions being made concerning point of origin, education, and employment prospects. Another significant distinction is whether immigrants travel with or without their families. We often think that historical immigrants to the United States were males in search of work. Men dominate much of the labor migration worldwide, but because of the diversified labor force in the United States and some policies that facilitate relatives coming, immigration to the United States generally has been fairly balanced. Actually, most immigration historically appears to be families. For example, from 1870 through 1940 men entering the United States exceeded women by only about 10 to 20 percent. Since 1950 to the present, women immigrants have actually exceeded men by a modest amount (Gibson and Jung 2006).

The second-class status women normally experience in society is reflected in immigration. Most dramatically, women citizens who married immigrants who were not citizens actually lost their U.S. citizenship from 1907 through 1922 with few exceptions. However, this policy did not apply to men (Johnson 2004).

Immigrant women face all the challenges faced by immigrant men plus some additional ones. Typically, they have the responsibility of navigating the new society when it comes to services for their family and, in particular, children. Many new immigrants view the United States as a dangerous place to raise a family and, therefore, remain particularly vigilant of what happens in their children's lives.

Caring for the health of their households falls mainly on women in their social roles as mother, wife, and caregiver for aging parents. In "Research Focus," we consider the most recent research on how immigrants are doing in the United States in terms of health and that the outcome may not be what one expects.

Male immigrants are more likely to be consumed with work, leaving the women to navigate the bureaucratic morass of city services, schools, medical facilities, and even everyday concerns such as stores and markets. Immigrant women in need of special services for medical purposes or because they are

---

RESEARCH FOCUS

Assimilation May Be Hazardous to Your Health

Immigrants come to the United States seeking a better life, but the transition can be very difficult. We are familiar with the problems new arrivals experience in finding good jobs, but we may be less aware of how pervasive the challenges are.

Researchers continuously show that immigrants often encounter health problems as they leave behind old health networks and confront the private pay system of medical care in the United States. The outcome is that the health of immigrants often deteriorates. Interestingly, this occurs with Puerto Ricans, who are citizens upon arrival and obviously do not experience as much culture shock as other new arrivals. Scholars Nancy Landale, R. S. Orapesa, and Bridget Gorman looked at the implications for infant mortality of migration from Puerto Rico to the United States. Their analysis showed that children of migrants have lower rates of infant mortality than do children of mainland-born Puerto Rican women. This means that babies of Puerto Rican mothers who are born in the United States are more likely to die than those of mothers who migrated from Puerto Rico.

Why does this happen? Immigrants generally are still under the protection of their fellow travelers. They are still networked with other immigrants, who assist them in adapting to life in the United States. However, as life in a new country continues, these important social networks break down as people learn to navigate the new social system—in this example, the health care system. They are more likely to be uninsured and unable to afford medical care except in emergencies. The researchers do note that Puerto Ricans in the United States, regardless of recency of arrival, still experience better health than those in Puerto Rico. Of course, this finding only further indicates the legacy of the colonial relationship of Puerto Rico to the United States and the health care system there on the island.

Source: King 2007; Landale et al. 2000; Lara et al. 2005; Read and Emerson 2005.

victims of domestic violence are often reluctant to seek outside help. Yet immigrant women are more likely to be the liaison for the household including adult men to community associations and religious organizations (Hondagneu-Sotelo 2003).

Women play a critical role in overseeing the household, and for immigrant women, the added pressures of being in a new country and trying to move ahead in a different culture heighten this social role.

The Global Economy and Immigration

Immigration exists because of political boundaries that bring the movement of peoples to the attention of national authorities. Within the United States, people may move their residence, but they are not immigrating. For residents in the member nations of the European Union, free movement of people within the union is also protected.

Yet, increasingly, people recognize the need to think beyond national borders and national identity. As was noted in Chapter 1, **globalization** is the worldwide integration of government policies, cultures, social movements, and financial markets through trade, movement of people, and the exchange of ideas. In this global framework, even immigrants are less likely to think of themselves as residents of only one country. For generations, immigrants have used foreign-language newspapers to keep in touch with events in their home country. Today, cable channels carry news and variety programs from their home country, and the Internet offers immediate access to the homeland and kinfolk thousands of miles away.

While bringing the world together, globalization has also sharpened the focus on the dramatic economic inequalities between nations. Today, people in North America, Europe, and Japan consume thirty-two times more resources than the billions of people in developing nations. Thanks to tourism, the media, and other aspects of globalization, the people of less-affluent countries know of this affluent lifestyle and, of course, often aspire for it (Diamond 2003).

Transnationals are immigrants who sustain multiple social relationships linking their societies of origin and settlement. Immigrants from the Dominican Republic not only identify themselves with Americans but also maintain very close ties to their Caribbean homeland. They return for visits, send remittances (migradollars), and host extended stays of relatives and friends. Back in the Dominican Republic, villages reflect these close ties, as shown in billboards promoting special long-distance services to the United States and by the presence of household appliances sent by relatives. The volume of remittances worldwide is easily the most reliable source of foreign money going to poor countries, far outstripping foreign aid programs.

The growing number of transnationals, as well as immigration in general, directly reflects the world systems analysis we considered in Chapter 1.

Transnationals are not new, but the ability to communicate and transfer resources makes it different today from the immigration experience of the nineteenth century. The global economic system today that has such sharp contrasts between the industrial haves and the developing have-not nations only serves to encourage movement across borders. The industrial haves gain benefits from it even when they seem to discourage it. The movement back and forth only serves to increase globalization and the creation of informal social networks between people seeking a better life and those already enjoying increased prosperity.

The transnationals themselves maintain a multithreaded relationship between friends and relatives in the United Sates, their home country, and perhaps other countries were relatives and friends have resettled. Besides the economic impact of remittances described above, scholars are increasingly giving attention to "social remittances" that include ideas, social norms,and practices (religious and secular) throughout this global social network (Levitt and Jaworsky 2007).

Refugees

Refugees are people living outside their country of citizenship for fear of political or religious persecution. Enough refugees exist to populate an entire "nation." There are approximately 12 to 14 million refugees worldwide. That makes the nation of refugees larger than Belgium, Sweden, or Cuba. The United States has touted itself as a haven for political refugees. However, as we shall see, the welcome to political refugees has not always been unqualified.

The United States makes the largest financial contribution of any nation to worldwide assistance programs. The United States resettles about 70,000 refugees annually and served as the host to a cumulative 1 million refugees between 1990 and 2003. The post-9/11 years have seen the procedures become much more cumbersome for foreigners to acquire refugee status and gain entry to the United States. Many other nations much smaller and much poorer than the United States have many more refugees than the United States, with Jordan, Iran, and Pakistan hosting over a million refugees each (Jefferys 2007).

The United States, insulated by distance from wars and famines in Europe and Asia, has been able to be selective about which and how many refugees are welcomed. Since the arrival of refugees uprooted by World War II, the United States through the 1980s had allowed three groups of refugees to enter in numbers greater than regulations would ordinarily permit: Hungarians, Cubans, and Southeast Asians. Compared with the other two groups, the nearly 40,000 Hungarians who arrived after the unsuccessful revolt against the Soviet Union of November 1956 were few indeed. At that time, however, theirs was the fastest mass immigration to this country since before 1922. With little delay, the United States amended the laws so that the Hungarian refugees could enter. Because of their small numbers and their dispersion throughout this country, the Hungarians as a distinct ethnic group are in little evidence

caglecartoons.com

FLORIDA TODAY JEFF PARKER ©2006

PLYMOUTH ROCK

"THEY SAY THEY'RE BUILDING A WALL BECAUSE TOO MANY OF US ENTER ILLEGALLY AND WON'T LEARN THEIR LANGUAGE OR ASSIMILATE INTO THEIR CULTURE..."

In 2006, despite public pressure to crack down on illegal immigrants and counterdemonstrations to make it easier for long-term undocumented workers to become legal, the only major proposal to make it through Congress was to create a wall of several hundred miles between the United States and Mexico. Here a cartoonist ponders the irony if native peoples had done as much for the onslaught of European immigrants.

today. The much larger and longer period of movement of Cuban and Southeast Asian refugees into the United States continues to have a profound social and economic impact.

Despite periodic public opposition, the U.S. government is officially committed to accepting refugees from other nations. According to the United Nations treaty on refugees, which our government ratified in 1968, countries are obliged to refrain from forcibly returning people to territories where their lives or liberty might be endangered. However, it is not always clear whether a person is fleeing for his or her personal safety or to escape poverty. Although people in the latter category may be of humanitarian interest, they do not meet the official definition of refugees and are subject to deportation.

Refugees are people who are granted the right to enter a country while still residing abroad. **Asylees** are foreigners who have already entered the United States and now seek protection because of persecution or a well-founded fear of persecution. This persecution may be based on the individual's race, religion, nationality, membership in a particular social group, or political opinion. Asylees are eligible to adjust to lawful permanent resident status after one year of continuous presence in the United States. Asylum is granted to about 13,000 people annually.

Because asylees, by definition, are already here, the outcome is either to grant them legal entry or to return them to their home country. It is the practice of deporting people fleeing poverty that has been the subject of criticism. There is a long tradition in the United States of facilitating the arrival of people leaving Communist nations, such as the Cubans. Mexicans who are refugees from poverty, Liberians fleeing civil war, and Haitians running from despotic rule are not similarly welcomed. The plight of Haitians has become one of particular concern.

Haitians began fleeing their country, often on small boats, in the 1980s. The U.S. Coast Guard intercepted many Haitians at sea, saving some of these boat people from death in their rickety and overcrowded wooden vessels. The Haitians said they feared detentions, torture, and execution if they remained in Haiti. Yet both Republican and Democratic administrations viewed most of the Haitian exiles as economic migrants rather than political refugees and opposed granting them asylum and permission to enter the United States. Once apprehended, the Haitians are returned. In 1993, the U.S. Supreme Court, by an 8:1 vote, upheld the government's right to intercept Haitian refugees at sea and return them to their homeland without asylum hearings.

African Americans and others denounce the Haitian refugee policy as racist. They contrast it to the "wet foot, dry foot" policy toward Cuban refugees. If the government intercepts Cubans at sea, they are returned; but if they escape detection and make it to the mainland, they may apply for asylum. About 75 percent of Cubans seeking asylum are granted refugee status, compared with only 22 percent of Haitians.

Even with only about a thousand Haitians successfully making it into the United States each year, there is an emerging Haitian American presence, especially in southern Florida. As of 2000, about 70,000 immigrants and their descendants live in metropolitan Miami. Despite continuing obstacles, the community exhibits pride in those who have succeeded, from a Haitian American Florida state legislator to hip-hop musician Wyclef Jean (Alvarez 2008; Dahlburg 2001; U.S. Committee for Refugees 2003).

New foreign military campaigns often bring new refugee issues. The occupation of Iraq, beginning in 2003, had been accompanied by large movements of Iraqis throughout the country and the region. Hopefully most will return home, but some clearly are seeking to relocate to the United States. As was true in Vietnam, many Iraqis who have aided the U.S.-led mission have increasingly sought refuge in the West fearing for their safety if they were to remain in Iraq or even in the Middle East. Gradually, the United States has begun to offer refugee status to Iraqis, some 2,700 have arrived in 2008 where they join an Iraqi American community of 90,000. The diverse landscape of the United States takes on yet another nationality group in large numbers (Bennett 2008; Klein 2008).

Conclusion

For its first hundred years, the United States allowed all immigrants to enter and become permanent residents. However, the federal policy of welcome did not mean that immigrants would not encounter discrimination and prejudice. With the passage of the Chinese Exclusion Act, discrimination against one group of potential immigrants became law. The Chinese were soon joined by the Japanese as peoples forbidden by law to enter and prohibited from becoming naturalized citizens. The development of the national origin system in the 1920s created a hierarchy of nationalities with people from northern Europe encouraged to enter, whereas other Europeans and Asians encountered long delays. The possibility of a melting pot, which had always been a fiction, was legislated out of existence.

In the 1960s and again in 1990, the policy was liberalized so that the importance of nationality was minimized, and a person's work skills and relationship to an American were emphasized. This liberalization came at a time when most Europeans no longer wanted to immigrate to the United States.

One out of ten people in the United States is foreign born; many are technical, professional, and craft workers. Also, 34 percent are household workers, and 33 percent of our farm laborers are foreign born. The U.S. economy and society are built on immigrant labor from farm fields to science laboratories (Camarota 2007b).

Throughout the history of the United States, as we have seen, there has been intense debate over the nation's immigration and refugee policies. In a sense, this debate reflects the deep value conflicts in the U.S. culture and parallels the "American dilemma" identified by Swedish social economist Gunnar Myrdal (1944). One strand of our culture, epitomized by the words "Give us your tired, your poor, your huddled masses," has emphasized egalitarian principles and a desire to help people in their time of need. At the same time, however, hostility to potential immigrants and refugees, whether the Chinese in the 1880s, European Jews in the 1930s and 1940s, or Mexicans, Haitians, and Arabs today, reflects not only racial, ethnic, and religious prejudice but also a desire to maintain the dominant culture of the in-group by keeping out those viewed as outsiders. The conflict between these cultural values is central to the American dilemma of the twenty-first century.

At present the debate about immigration is highly charged and emotional. Some people see it in economic terms, whereas others see the new arrivals as a challenge to the very culture of our society. Clearly, the general perception is that immigration presents a problem rather than a promise for the future.

Today's concern about immigrants follows generations of people coming to settle in the United States. This immigration in the past produced a very diverse country in terms of both nationality and religion, even before the immigration of the last fifty years. Therefore, the majority of Americans today are not descended from the English, and Protestants are just over half of all worshipers. This diversity of religious and ethnic groups is examined in Chapter 5.

Key Terms

Review Questions

1. What are the functions and dysfunctions of immigration?
2. What were the social and economic issues when public opinion mounted against Chinese immigration to the United States?
3. Ultimately, what do you think is the major concern people have about contemporary immigration to the United States: the numbers of immigrants, their legal status, or their nationality?
4. What principles appear to guide U.S. refugee policy?

Critical Thinking

1. What is the immigrant root story of your family? Consider how your ancestors arrived in the United States and also how your family's past has been shaped by other immigrant groups.
2. Can you find evidence of the brain drain in terms of the professionals with whom you come in contact? Do you regard this as a benefit? What groups in the United States may not have been encouraged to fill such positions by the availability of such professionals?
3. Develop a socioeconomic picture of the economy of immigration was one-third of what social or political policies it is today. Outline the short-term (thru the next two years) and long term (next 75 years) implications economically, politically, and culturally.

Internet Connections—Research Navigator™

Follow the instructions found in "Internet Connections—Research Navigator™" in Chapter 1 of this text to access the features of Research Navigator™. Once at the Web site, enter your login name and password. Then, to use the ContentSelect database, enter keywords such as "remittances," "asylum," and "refugees," and the research engine will supply relevant and recent scholarly and popular press publications. Use the *New York Times* Search-by-Subject Archive to find recent news articles related to sociology and the Link Library feature to locate relevant Web links organized by the key terms associated with this chapter.

5 Ethnicity and Religion

CHAPTER OUTLINE

—————————————⟨ HIGHLIGHTS ⟩—————————————

The United States includes a multitude of ethnic and religious groups. Do they coexist in harmony or in conflict? How significant are they as sources of identity for their members? Because White is a race, significant attention has been given to the social construction of race as it applies to White people. Many White ethnic groups have transformed their ethnic status into Whiteness. In the 1960s and 1970s, there was a resurgence of interest in White ethnicity, partly in response to the renewed pride in the ethnicity of Blacks, Latinos, and Native Americans. We have an ethnicity paradox in which White ethnics seem to enjoy their heritage but at the same time seek to assimilate into the larger society. Major White ethnic groups such as Irish, Italian, and Polish Americans have experienced similar, yet distinctive, social circumstances in the United States. We can make some tentative comparisons from their experiences and what we could expect among today's immigrants. Religious diversity continues and expands with immigration and growth in the followings of non-Christian faiths. Religious minorities experience intolerance in the present as they have in the past. Constitutional issues such as school prayer, secessionist minorities, creationism, and public religious displays are regularly taken to the Supreme Court. The Amish are presented as a case study of the experience of a specific religious group in the United States.

Betty O'Keefe is a 60-year-old Californian who is a fifth-generation Irish American, meaning that her grandmother's grandmother came to the United States from Ireland. Sociologist Mary Waters (1990, 97) asked her what it was like growing up in the United States.

When I was in high school my maiden name was Tynan. This was 1940. I was dating some boys from school, and two different times when the parents found out I was an Irish Catholic, they told him he couldn't go out with me. The Protestants were like that. . . . One of his brothers later married someone named O'Flannery and I was so thrilled. I said I hope your mother is turning in her grave. So I am happy that my children have the name O'Keefe. So that people know right away what their background is. I think it is better. They would never be put in the position I was in.

Do you think something like that could happen now?

I don't think so openly. But I think it is definitely still there. You are not as bad (being an Irish Catholic) as a Black, but you are not Protestant. You are not Jewish either, which would be worse, but still you are not of their church.

The names of the descendants of immigrants may be Badovich, Khan, Jablonski, Reggio, or Williams. They may follow any one of thousands of faiths and gather at any of the 360,000 churches, mosques, synagogues, and temples. Our nation's motto is E Pluribus Unum, and although there may be doubt that we are truly united into one common culture following a single ideology, there is little doubt about our continuing diversity as a nation of peoples.

Indeed, the very complexity of relations between dominant and subordinate groups in the United States today is partly the result of its heterogeneous population. No one ethnic origin or religious faith encompasses all the inhabitants of the United States. Even though our largest period of sustained immigration is three generations past, an American today is surrounded by remnants of cultures and practitioners of religions whose origins are foreign to this country. Religion and ethnicity continue to be significant in defining a person's identity.

Ethnic Diversity

The ethnic diversity of the United States at the beginning of the twenty-first century is apparent to almost everyone. Passersby in New York City were undoubtedly surprised once when two street festivals met head-to-head. The procession of San Gennaro, the patron saint of Naples, marched through Little Italy, only to run directly into a Chinese festival originating in Chinatown. Teachers in many public schools often encounter students who speak only one language, and it is not English. Students in Chicago are taught in Spanish, Greek, Italian, Polish, German, Creole, Japanese, Cantonese, or the language of a Native American tribe. In the Detroit metropolitan area, classroom instruction is conveyed in twenty-one languages, including Arabic, Portuguese, Ukrainian, Latvian, Lithuanian, and Serbian. In many areas of the United States, you can refer to a special yellow pages and find a driving instructor who speaks Portuguese or a psychotherapist who will talk to you in Hebrew.

Germans are the largest ancestral group in the United States; the 2000 census showed almost one-sixth of Americans saying they had at least some German ancestry. Although most German Americans are assimilated, it is possible to see the ethnic tradition in some areas, particularly in Milwaukee, whose population has 48 percent German ancestry. There, three Saturday schools teach German, and one can affiliate with thirty-four German American clubs and visit a German library that operates within the public library system. Just a bit to the south in River Forest, a Chicago suburb, kinderwerkstatt meets weekly to help parents and children alike to maintain German culture (Carvajal 1995; Freedman 2004; Johnson 1992; Usdansky 1992).

Germany is one of twenty European nations from which at least 1 million people claim to have ancestry. The numbers are striking when one considers the size of some of the sending countries. For example, there are over 36 million Irish Americans, and the Republic of Ireland had a population of 4 million in 2008. Similarly, over 4 million people claim Swedish ancestry, and there are 9 million people living in Sweden today. Of course, many Irish Americans and Swedish Americans are of mixed ancestry, but not everyone in Ireland is Irish, nor is everyone in Sweden Swedish.

Why Don't We Study Whiteness?

Race is socially constructed, as we learned in Chapter 1. Sometimes we come to define race in a clear-cut manner. A descendant of a Pilgrim is White, for example. But sometimes race is more ambiguous: People who are the children of an African American and Vietnamese American union are biracial or "mixed," or whatever they come to be seen as by others. Our recognition that race is socially constructed has sparked a renewed interest in what it means to be White in the United States. Two aspects of White as a race are useful to consider: the historical creation of whiteness and how contemporary White people reflect on their racial identity.

When the English immigrants established themselves as the political founders of the United States, they also came to define what it meant to be White. Other groups that today are regarded as White, such as Irish, Germans, Norwegians, or Swedes, were not always considered White in the eyes of the English. Differences in language and religious worship, as well as past allegiance to a king in Europe different from the English monarch, all caused these groups to be seen not so much as Whites in the Western Hemisphere but more as nationals of their home country who happened to be residing in North America.

The old distrust in Europe, where, for example, the Irish were viewed by the English as socially and culturally inferior, continued on this side of the Atlantic Ocean. Karl Marx, writing from England, reported that the average English worker looked down on the Irish the way poor Whites in the U.S. South looked down on Black people (Ignatiev 1994, 1995; Roediger 1994).

Whiteness

As European immigrants and their descendants assimilated to the English and distanced themselves from other oppressed groups such as American Indians and African Americans, they came to be viewed as White rather than as part of a particular culture. Writer Noel Ignatiev (1994, 84), contrasting being White with being Polish, argues that "Whiteness is nothing but an expression of race privilege." This strong statement argues that being White, as opposed to being Black or Asian, is characterized by being a member of the dominant group.

Whites as people do not think of themselves as a race or have a conscious racial identity. The only occasion when a White racial identity emerges is momentarily when Whites fill out a form asking for self-designation of race or one of those occasions when they are culturally or socially surrounded by people who are not White.

Many immigrants who were not "White on arrival" had to "become White" in a process long forgotten by today's White Americans. The long documented transparent racial divide that engulfed the South during slavery allowed us to ignore how Whiteness was constructed.

Therefore, contemporary White Americans generally give little thought to "being White." Consequently, there is little interest in studying "Whiteness" or considering "being White" except that it is "not being Black." Unlike non-Whites, who are much more likely to interact with Whites, take orders from Whites, and see Whites as the leading figures in the mass media, Whites enjoy the privilege of not being reminded of their Whiteness.

Unlike racial minorities, Whites downplay the importance of their racial identity although they are willing to receive the advantages that come from being

White privilege, as described by Peggy McIntosh, includes holding a position in a company without coworkers suspecting it came about because of your race.

White. This means that advocacy of a "color-blind" or "race-neutral" outlook permits the privilege of Whiteness to prevail (Bonilla-Silva 2002; Yancey 2003).

The new interest seeks to look at Whiteness but not from the vantage point of a White supremacist. Rather, focusing on White people as a race or on what it means today to be White goes beyond any definition that implies superiority over non-Whites. It is also recognized that "being White" is not the same experience for all Whites any more than "being Asian American" or "being Black" is the same for all Asian Americans or all Blacks. Historian Noel Ignatiev observes that studying Whiteness is a necessary stage to the "abolition of whiteness"— just as, in Marxist analysis, class consciousness is a necessary stage to the abolition of class. By confronting Whiteness, society grasps the all-encompassing power that accompanies socially constructed race (Lewis 2004; McKinney 2003; Roediger 2006).

White Privilege

Whiteness carries with it a sense of identity of being White as opposed to being, for example, Asian or African. For many people it may not be easy to establish a social identity of Whiteness, as in the case of biracial children. However, one can argue that the social identity of Whiteness exists if one enjoys the privilege of being White.

White privilege refers to the rights or immunities granted as a particular benefit or favor for being White. This advantage exists unconsciously and is often invisible to the very White people who enjoy it (Ferber 2008).

Scholar Peggy McIntosh of the Wellesley College Center for Research on Women looked at the privilege that comes from being White and the added privilege of being male. The other side of racial oppression is the privilege enjoyed by dominant groups. Being White or being successful in establishing a White identity carries with it distinct advantages. Among those that McIntosh (1988) identified were the following:

- Being considered financially reliable when using checks, credit cards, or cash
- Taking a job without having coworkers suspect it came about because of your race
- Never having to speak for all the people of your race
- Watching television or reading a newspaper and seeing people of your own race widely represented
- Speaking effectively in a large group without being called a credit to your race
- Assuming that if legal or medical help is needed, your race will not work against you

Whiteness does carry privileges, but most White people do not consciously think of them except on the rare occasions when they are questioned. We will return to the concepts of Whiteness and White privilege, but let us also consider the rich diversity of religion in the United States, which parallels the ethnic diversity of this nation.

The Rediscovery of Ethnicity

Robert Park (1950, 205), a prominent early sociologist, wrote in 1913 that "a Pole, Lithuanian, or Norwegian cannot be distinguished, in the second generation, from an American, born of native parents." At one time, sociologists saw the end of ethnicity as nearly a foregone conclusion. W. Lloyd Warner and Leo Srole (1945) wrote in their often-cited *Yankee City* series that the future of ethnic groups seemed to be limited in the United States and that they would be quickly absorbed. Oscar Handlin's *Uprooted* (1951) told of the destruction of immigrant values and their replacement by American culture. Although Handlin was among the pioneers in investigating ethnicity, assimilation was the dominant theme in his work.

Many writers have shown almost a fervent hope that ethnicity would vanish. The persistence of ethnicity was for some time treated by sociologists as dysfunctional because it meant a continuation of old values that interfered with the allegedly superior new values. For example, to hold on to one's language delayed entry into the larger labor market and the upward social mobility it afforded. Ethnicity was expected to disappear not only because of assimilation but also because aspirations to higher social class and status demanded that it vanish. Somehow, it was assumed that one could not be ethnic and middle class, much less affluent.

The Third-Generation Principle

Historian Marcus Hansen's (1952) **principle of third-generation interest** was an early exception to the assimilationist approach to White ethnic groups. Simply stated, Hansen maintained that in the third generation—the grandchildren of the original immigrants—ethnic interest and awareness would actually increase. According to Hansen, "What the son wishes to forget, the grandson wishes to remember."

Hansen's principle has been tested several times since it was first put forth. John Goering (1971), in interviewing Irish and Italian Catholics, found that ethnicity was more important to members of the third generation than it was to the immigrants themselves. Similarly, Mary Waters (1990), in her interviews of White ethnics living in suburban San Jose, California, and suburban Philadelphia, Pennsylvania, observed that many grandchildren wanted to study their ancestors' language, even though it would be a foreign language to them. They also expressed interest in learning more of their ethnic group's history and a desire to visit the homeland.

Social scientists in the past were quick to minimize the ethnic awareness of blue-collar workers. In fact, ethnicity was viewed as merely another aspect of White ethnics' alleged racist nature, an allegation that will be examined later in

For many Irish American participants in a St. Patrick's Day Parade, this is their most visible expression of symbolic ethnicity during an entire year.

this chapter. Curiously, the very same intellectuals and journalists who bent over backward to understand the growing solidarity of Blacks, Hispanics, and Native Americans refused to give White ethnics the academic attention they deserved (Kivisto 2008; Wrong 1972).

The new assertiveness of Blacks and other non-Whites of their rights in the 1960s unquestionably presented White ethnics with the opportunity to reexamine their own position. "If solidarity and unapologetic self-consciousness might hasten Blacks' upward mobility, why not ours?" asked the White ethnics, who were often only a half step above Blacks in social status. The African American movement pushed other groups to reflect on their past. The increased consciousness of Blacks and their positive attitude toward African culture and the contributions worldwide of African Americans are embraced in what we called the Afrocentric perspective (Chapter 1). Therefore, the mood was set in the 1960s for the country to be receptive to ethnicity. By legitimizing Black cultural differences from White culture, along with those of Native Americans and Hispanics, the country's opinion leaders legitimized other types of cultural diversity.

Symbolic Ethnicity

Observers comment both on the evidence of assimilation and on the signs of ethnic identity that seem to support a pluralistic view of society. How can both be possible?

First, there is the visible evidence of **symbolic ethnicity,** which may lead us to exaggerate the persistence of ethnic ties among White Americans. According to sociologist Herbert Gans (1979), ethnicity today increasingly involves the symbols of ethnicity, such as eating ethnic food, acknowledging ceremonial holidays such as St. Patrick's Day, and supporting specific political issues or the issues confronting the old country. One example was the push in 1998 by Irish Americans to convince state legislatures to make it compulsory in public schools to teach about the Irish potato famine, which was a significant factor in immigration to the United States. This symbolic ethnicity may be more visible, but this type of ethnic heritage does not interfere with what people do, read, or say or even whom they befriend or marry.

The ethnicity of the twenty-first century, embraced by English-speaking Whites, is largely symbolic. It does not include active involvement in ethnic activities or participation in ethnic-related organizations. In fact, sizable proportions of White ethnics have gained large-scale entry into almost all clubs, cliques, and fraternal groups. Such acceptance is a key indicator of assimilation. Ethnicity has become increasingly peripheral to the lives of the members of the ethnic group. Although they may not relinquish their ethnic identity, other identities become more important.

Second, the ethnicity that does exist may be more a result of living in the United States than actual importing of practices from the past or the old country. Many so-called ethnic foods or celebrations, for example, began in the United States. The persistence of ethnic consciousness, then, may not depend on foreign birth, a distinctive language, and a unique way of life. Instead, it may reflect the experiences in the United States of a unique group that developed a cultural tradition distinct from that of the mainstream. For example, in Poland, the szlachta, or landed gentry, rarely mixed socially with the peasant class. In the United States, however, even with those associations still fresh, they interacted together in social organizations as they settled in concentrated communities segregated physically and socially from others (Lopata 1994; Winter 2008).

Third, maintaining ethnicity can be a critical step toward successful assimilation. This ethnicity paradox facilitates full entry into the dominant culture. The ethnic community may give its members not only a useful financial boost but also the psychological strength and positive self-esteem that will allow them to compete effectively in a larger society. Thus, we may witness people participating actively in their ethnic enclave while trying to cross the bridge into the wider community (Lal 1995).

Therefore, ethnicity gives continuity with the past in the form of an effective or emotional tie. The significance of this sense of belonging cannot be emphasized enough. Whether reinforced by distinctive behavior or by what Milton Gordon (1964) called a sense of "peoplehood," ethnicity is an effective, functional source of cohesion. Proximity to fellow ethnics is not necessary for a person to maintain social cohesion and in-group identity. Fraternal organizations or sports-related groups can preserve associations between ethnics who are separated geographically. Members of ethnic groups may even maintain their feelings of in-group solidarity after leaving ethnic communities in the central cities for the suburban fringe.

The Irish Americans

The Irish presence in the United States stretches back to the 1600s and reflects a diversity based on time of entry, settlement area, and religion. Irish Americans have been visible both in a positive way in terms of playing a central role in American life and in a negative way at certain historical periods being victimized like so many other immigrant groups.

Early Irish Immigration (before 1845)

The Protestants dominated the early Irish immigration to the colonies even though these Presbyterians from Ireland of Scotch descent accounted for only one out of ten, at most one out of seven, of the island of Ireland's residents in the eighteenth century. Motivating the early immigrants was the lure of free land in North America, which was in sharp contrast to Ireland where more and more tenants had to compete for land. The powerful landlords there took full advantage by squeezing more and more profits out of the tenants, making migration to colonial America attractive.

The Roman Catholics among the early immigrants were a diverse group. Some were extensions of the privileged classes seeking even greater prosperity. Protestant settlers of all national backgrounds were united in their hatred of Catholicism. In most of the colonies, Catholics could not practice their faith openly and either struggled inwardly or converted to Anglicanism. Other Roman Catholics and some Protestants came as an alternative to prison or after signing articles of indenture arriving bound to labor for periods of customarily three to five years but sometimes as long as seven years (Meagher 2005).

The American Revolution temporarily stopped the flow of immigration, but soon, deteriorating economic conditions in Ireland spurred even greater movement to North America. British officials, by making passage to the newly formed republic of the United States expensive, diverted many immigrants to British North America (Canada). Yet the numbers to the United States remained significant and, although still primarily Protestant, drew from a broader spectrum of Ireland both economically and geographically.

Many mistakenly overlook this early immigration and begin with Irish immigration during the Great Famine. Yet the Irish were the largest group after the English among immigrants during the colonial period. The historical emphasis on the famine immigrants is understandable, given the role it played in Ireland and its impetus for the massive transfer of population from Ireland to the United States.

The Famine Years

In 1845, a fungus wiped out the potato crop of Ireland, as well as much of western Europe and even coastal America. Potatoes were particularly central to the lives of the Irish and the devastating starvation did not begin to recede until 1851. Mortality was high, especially among the poor and in the more agricultural areas of the island. Predictably, to escape catastrophe, some 2 million fled mostly to England, but then many continued on to the United States. From 1841 through 1890, over 3.2 million Irish arrived in the United States (Figure 5.1).

This new migration fleeing the old country was much more likely to consist of families rather than single men. The arrival of entire households and extended kinship networks increased significantly the rapid formation of Irish social organizations in the United States. This large influx of immigrants led to the creation of ethnic neighborhoods complete with parochial schools and parish churches serving as focal points. Fraternal organizations such as the Ancient Order of Hibernians, corner saloons, local political organizations, and Irish nationalist groups seeking the ouster of Britain from Ireland rounded out neighborhood social life.

Even in the best of times, the lives of the famine Irish would have been challenging in the United States, but they arrived at a very difficult time. Nativist—that is, anti-Catholic and anti-immigrant—movements were already emerging and being embraced by politicians.

From independence until around 1820, little evidence appeared of the anti-Catholic sentiment of colonial days, but the cry against Roman Catholicism grew as Irish immigration increased. Prominent citizens encouraged hatred of these new arrivals. Samuel F. B. Morse, inventor of the telegraph and an accomplished painter, wrote a strongly worded anti-Catholic work in 1834

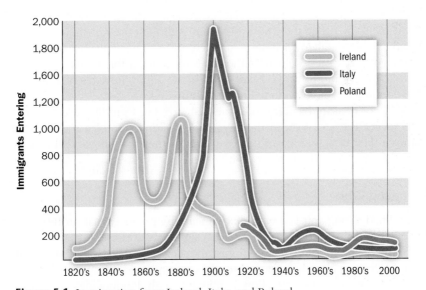

Figure 5.1 Immigration from Ireland, Italy, and Poland

Note: Immigration after 1925 from Northern Ireland not included. No separate data for Poland from 1900 to 1920.

Source: Office of Immigration Statistics, 2006, Table 2.

titled *A Foreign Conspiracy Against the Liberties of the United States.* Morse felt that the Irish were shamefully illiterate and deserved no respect. In the minds of prejudiced people, the Irish were particularly unwelcome because they were Catholic. Many readily believed Morse's warning that the Pope planned to move the Vatican to the Mississippi River Valley.

This antagonism was not limited to harsh words. From 1834 to 1854, mob violence against Catholics across the country led to death, the burning of a Boston convent, the destruction of a Catholic church and the homes of Catholics, and the use of Marines and state militia to bring peace to American cities as far west as St. Louis.

In retrospect, the reception given to the Irish is not difficult to understand. Many immigrated after the potato crop failure and famine in Ireland. They fled not so much to a better life as from almost certain death. The Irish Catholics brought with them a celibate clergy, who struck the New England aristocracy as strange and reawakened old religious hatreds. The Irish were worse than Blacks according to the dominant Whites, because unlike the slaves and even the freed Blacks, who "knew their place," the Irish did not suffer their maltreatment in silence. Employers balanced minorities by judiciously mixing immigrant groups to prevent unified action by the laborers. For the most part, nativist efforts only led the foreign borns to emphasize their ties to Europe.

By the 1850s, nativism became an open political movement pledged to vote only for "native" Americans, to fight Catholicism, and to demand a twenty-one-year naturalization period. Party members were instructed to divulge nothing about their program and to say that they knew nothing about it. As a result, they came to be called the Know-Nothings. Although the Know-Nothings soon vanished, the antialien mentality survived and occasionally became formally organized into societies such as the Ku Klux Klan in the 1860s and the anti-Catholic American Protective Association in the 1890s. Revivals of anti-Catholicism continued well into the twentieth century.

Mostly of peasant backgrounds, the Irish arriving were ill-prepared to compete successfully for jobs in the city. Their children found it much easier to improve their occupational status over that of their fathers as well as experienced upward mobility in their own lifetimes.

Becoming White

Ireland had a long antislavery tradition including practices that prohibited Irish trade in English slaves. Some 60,000 Irish signed an address in 1841 petitioning Irish Americans to join the abolitionist movement in the United States. Many Irish Americans already opposed to slavery applauded the appeal, but they were soon drowned out by fellow immigrants with denouncing or questioning the authenticity of the petition.

The Irish immigrants, subjected to derision and menial jobs, sought to separate themselves from the even lower classes and particularly Black Americans and especially the slaves. It was not altogether clear that the Irish were "white" during the antebellum period. Irish character was rigidly cast in negative racial typology. Although the shared experiences of oppression could have led Irish Americans to allay with Black Americans, they grasped for Whiteness at the margins of their life in the United States. Direct competition was not common between the two groups. For example, in 1855, Irish immigrants made up 87 percent of New York City's unskilled laborers whereas free Blacks accounted for only 3 percent (Greeley 1981; Ignatiev 1995; Roediger 1994).

In 1863, the Union government implemented a national conscription law to fight in the Civil War. Men could avoid service by presenting an acceptable substitute or paying $300. Irish Americans already experiencing heavy losses had grown tired of the war. Opposition to conscription was widespread but especially visible in Boston and New York City. The opposition grew violent in New York City with participants, mostly poor Irish Americans, striking out first against symbols of the government and then targeting African American organizations and even individual Blacks. The vandalism and violence were aimed at those even weaker than the working-class Irish who resented "a rich man's war and a poor man's fight." The "Draft Riots of 1863," as they came to be called, violently showed the dilemma many Irish Americans felt of fighting for the freedom of their Negro competitors in the labor market. Eventually, the rioters were quelled with the dispatch of troops fresh from Gettysburg including Irish American soldiers.

As Irish immigration continued in the latter part of the nineteenth century until Irish independence in 1921, they began to see themselves favorably in comparison to the initial waves of Italian, Polish, and Slovak Roman Catholic immigrants. The Irish Americans began to assume more leadership positions in politics and labor unions. Loyalty to the church still played a major role. By 1910, the priesthood was the professional occupation of choice for second-generation men. Irish women were more likely than their German and English immigrant counterparts to become schoolteachers. In time, Irish Americans' occupational profiles diversified, and they began to experience slow advancement and gradually were welcomed into the White working class as their identity as "White" overcame any status as "immigrant."

With mobility came social class distinctions within Irish America. The immigrants and their children who began to move into the more affluent urban areas were derogatorily referred to as the "lace-curtain Irish." The lower-class Irish immigrants they left behind, meanwhile, were referred to as the "shanty Irish." But as immigration from Ireland slowed and upward mobility quickened, fewer and fewer Irish qualified as the poor cousins of their predecessors.

In the 1950s, as in the nineteenth century, economic hard times in Ireland spurred immigration to the United States. However, a cap of 2,000 immigrants from any one European country led to the sporadic influx of illegal immigrants from the Republic of Ireland. Congressional action in 1987 included a provision that resulted in another 16,000 visas for Irish immigrants. This recent experience with immigration controls led several national and local Irish American organizations to stand with those, in 2007, who protested for procedures to allow illegal immigrants to apply for citizenship.

In the twentieth century, the most visible components of Irish American life had roots that are still visible in the twenty-first century. Extended formal schooling was stressed and entering professions, especially the law, was encouraged. The Irish, with their long struggle for political independence, comprehended the essentials of representative government. Politics and civic employment opportunities, such as law enforcement, became a critical path both to influence and to upward mobility. This pattern continues today. Indeed, of the 345 firefighters who perished in New York City's Twin Trade Towers collapse of September 11, 2001, 145 were members of the Emerald Society, the fire department's Irish American fraternal group (Meagher 2005, 610).

For the Irish American man, the priesthood was viewed as a desirable and respected occupation. Irish Americans furthermore played a leadership role in the Roman Catholic Church in the United States. The Irish dominance persisted long after other ethnic groups swelled the ranks of the faithful (Fallows 1979; Lee and Bean 2007; Lee and Casey 2006).

The Contemporary Picture

By 2006, 36 million people identified as having Irish ancestry—second only to German ancestry and nine times the present population of Ireland itself. Massachusetts has the largest concentration of Irish Americans with 24 percent of the state indicating Irish ancestry (American Community Survey 2006).

Contemporary Irish immigration is relatively slight, accounting for perhaps 1 out of 1,000 legal arrivals today compared to over a third of all immigrants in the 1840s and 1850s. About 202,000 people in the United States were born in Ireland—comparable to the number of Portuguese born in the United States. Today's Irish American typically enjoys the symbolic ethnicity of food, dance, and music. Gaelic language instruction is limited to less than thirty colleges. Visibility as a collective ethnic group is greatest with the annual St. Patrick's Day celebrations when everyone seems to be Irish or with the occasional fervent nationalism aimed at curtailing Great Britain's role in Northern Ireland. Yet some stereotypes remain concerning excessive drinking despite available data indicating that alcoholism rates are no higher and sometimes lower among people of Irish ancestry compared to descendants of other European immigrant groups.

St. Patrick's Day celebrations, as noted previously, offer an example of how ethnic identity evolves over time. The Feast of St. Patrick has a long history, but the public celebrations with parties, concerts, and parades originated in the United States, which were then exported to Ireland in the latter part of the twentieth century. Even today, the large Irish American population often defines what is authentic Irish globally. For example, participants in Irish step dancing in the United States have developed such a clout in international competitions that they have come to define many aspects of cultural expression, much to the consternation of the Irish in Ireland (Hassrick 2007; American Community Survey 2006).

Well-known Irish Americans span society including the celebrity chef Bobby Flay, actor Philip Seymour Hoffman, comedian Conan O'Brien, and author Frank McCourt as well as the political dynasties of Kennedy in Massachusetts and Daley in Chicago. Reflecting growing rates of intermarriage, Irish America also includes singer Mariah Carey (her mother Irish and her father African American and Venezuelan).

The Irish were the first immigrant group to encounter prolonged organized resistance. Strengthened by continued immigration, facility with the English language, building on strong community and family networks, and familiarity with representative politics, Irish Americans became an integral part of the United States.

The Italian Americans

Although each European country's immigration to the United States has created its own social history, the case of Italians, though not typical of every nationality, offers insight into the White ethnic experience. Italians immigrated even during the colonial period, coming from what was a highly differentiated land because Italy did not unify and escape foreign domination until 1848.

Early Immigration

Italian Americans from the beginning played prominent roles during the American Revolution and the early days of the republic. Mass immigration began in the 1880s, peaking in the first twenty years of the twentieth century, when Italians accounted for one-fourth of European immigration (refer to Figure 5.1).

Italian immigration was concentrated not only in time but also by geography. The majority of the immigrants were landless peasants from rural southern Italy, the Mezzogiorno. Although many people in the United States assume that Italians are a nationality with a single culture, this is not true either culturally or economically. The Italian people recognize multiple geographic divisions reflecting sharp cultural distinctions. These divisions were brought with the immigrants to the New World.

Many Italians, especially in the early years of mass immigration in the nineteenth century, received their jobs through an ethnic labor contractor, the padrone. Similar arrangements have been used by Asian, Hispanic, and Greek immigrants, where the labor contractors, most often immigrants, have mastered sufficient English to mediate for their compatriots. Exploitation was common within the padrone system through kickbacks, provision of inadequate

Italian Americans celebrate a religious festival in Cambridge, Massachusetts.

housing, and withholding of wages. By World War I, 90 percent of Italian girls and 99 percent of Italian boys in New York City were leaving school at age 14 to work, but by that time, Italian Americans were sufficiently fluent in English to seek out work on their own, and the padrone system had disappeared. Still, by comparison to the Irish, the Italians in the United States were slower to accept fund schooling as essential to success (Sassler 2006).

Along with manual labor, the Catholic Church was a very important part of Italian Americans' lives at that time. Yet they found little comfort in a Catholic church dominated by an earlier immigrant group: the Irish. The traditions were different; weekly attendance for Italian Americans was overshadowed by the religious aspects of the feste (or festivals) held throughout the year in honor of saints (the Irish viewed the feste as practically a form of paganism). These initial adjustment problems were overcome with the establishment of ethnic parishes, a pattern repeated by other non-Irish immigrant groups. Thus, parishes would be staffed by Italian priests, sometimes imported for that purpose. Although the hierarchy of the church adjusted more slowly, Italian Americans were increasingly able to feel at home in their local parish church. Today, more than 70 percent of Italian Americans identify themselves as Roman Catholics (Luconi 2001).

Constructing Identity

As assimilation proceeded, Italian Americans began to construct a social identity as a nationality group rather than viewing themselves in terms of their village or province. As shown in Figure 5.2, over time, Italian Americans shed old identities for a new one. As immigration from Italy declined, the descendants' ties became more nationalistic. This move from local or regional to national identity was followed by Irish and Greek Americans. The changing

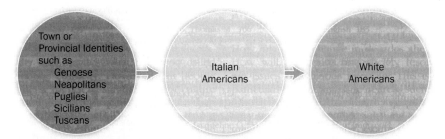

Figure 5.2 Constructing Social Identity Among Italian Immigrants
Over time Italian Americans moved from seeing themselves in terms of their provincial or
village identity to their national identity, and then they successfully became indistinguishable
from other Whites.

identity of Italian Americans reflected the treatment they received in the United
States, whereas non-Italians did not make those regional distinctions. However,
they were not treated well. For example, in turn-of-the-century New Orleans,
Italian Americans established special ties with the Black community because
both groups were marginalized in southern society. Gradually, Italian Americans became White and enjoyed all the privileges that come with it. Today, it
would be inconceivable to imagine that Italian Americans of New Orleans
would reach out to the African American community as their natural allies on
social and political issues (Guglielmo and Salerno 2003; Luconi 2001).

A controversial aspect of the Italian American experience involves organized crime, as typified by Al Capone (1899–1947). Arriving in U.S. society in
the bottom layers, Italians lived in decaying, crime-ridden neighborhoods that
became known as Little Italies. For a small segment of these immigrants, crime
was a significant means of upward social mobility. In effect, entering and leading criminal activity was one aspect of assimilation, though not a positive one.
Complaints linking ethnicity and crime actually began in colonial times with
talk about the criminally inclined Irish and Germans, and they continue with
contemporary stereotyping about groups such as Colombian drug dealers and
Vietnamese street gangs. Yet the image of Italians as criminals has persisted
from Prohibition-era gangsters to the view of Mob families today. As noted
earlier, it is not at all surprising that groups such as the Columbian Coalition
have been organized to counter such negative images.

The fact that Italians often are characterized as criminal, even in the mass
media, is another example of what we have called respectable bigotry toward
White ethnics. The persistence of linking Italians, or any other minority group,
with crime probably is attributable to attempts to explain a problem by citing a
single cause: the presence of perceived undesirables. Many Italian Americans
still see their image tied to old stereotypes. A 2001 survey of Italian American
teenagers found that 39 percent felt the media presented their ethnic group as
criminal or gang members and 34 percent as restaurant workers (Girardelli
2004; National Italian American Foundation 2006; Parrillo 2008).

The immigration of Italians was slowed by the national origin system, described in Chapter 4. As Italian Americans settled permanently, the mutual aid societies that had grown up in the 1920s to provide basic social services began to dissolve. More slowly, education came to be valued by Italian Americans as a means of upward mobility. Even becoming more educated did not ward off prejudice, however. In 1930, for example, President Herbert Hoover rebuked Fiorello La Guardia, then an Italian American member of Congress from New York City, stating that "the Italians are predominantly our murderers and bootleggers" and recommending that La Guardia "go back to where you belong" because, "like a lot of other foreign spawn, you do not appreciate this country which supports you and tolerates you" (Baltzell 1964, 30).

Although U.S. troops, including 500,000 Italian Americans, battled Italy during World War II, some hatred and sporadic violence emerged against Italian Americans and their property. However, they were not limited to actions against individuals. Italian Americans were even confined by the federal government in specific areas of California by virtue of their ethnicity alone, and 10,000 were relocated from coastal areas. In addition, 1,800 Italian Americans who were citizens of Italy were placed in an internment camp in Montana. The internees were eventually freed on Columbus Day 1942 as President Roosevelt lobbied the Italian American community to gain full support for the impending land invasion of Italy (Department of Justice 2001; Fox 1990).

In "Research Focus," we consider how social scientists examine the economic experience of these early Italian immigrants and their children in the United States and compare it to how Mexican immigrants are faring today.

RESEARCH FOCUS

Immigrants: Yesterday and Today

Anyone thinking about the future of today's immigrants reflects back upon the experiences of those that came a century ago. It is widely agreed that, despite difficult times and often harsh treatment by those already here, the immigrants of the late nineteenth and early twentieth century ultimately fared well. Certainly today their descendants are doing well. So can we generalize from this experience to today's immigrants?

Sociologist Joel Perlmann and other scholars have considered the experience of immigrants from south, central, and eastern Europe who were predominantly low-skilled workers. A significant component were Italian and Poles. Based on his analysis and that of other sociologists, we find that these earlier immigrant workers earned typically only between 60 and 88 percent in wages as that of non-immigrant Whites in the same occupational groups.

Contrary to the often commonly held belief, these immigrants did not end up in well-paying jobs in manufacturing that led them into the middle class in their own lifetime. Rather, they firmly remained working class until after World War II. Upward mobility occurred across generations typically, not within the lifetime of the arriving Italian, Polish, and other southern, central, and eastern European immigrants. This would mean economic parity took about three or four generations and not a decade as some romantically portray it.

Taking these data, he looks at contemporary Mexican immigrants. In may ways the deck is stacked against this, by far the largest, current immigrant group. Unlike their European counterparts of a century ago, many arrivals from Mexico (about 55 percent) are having to labor as illegal immigrants, which obviously curtails the opportunities available to them and their family members. Particularly harmful to rapid upward mobility is that today's second generation Mexicans in the United States are lagging further behind in education compared to most people than it was for the children of the turn-of-the-century European immigrants to the general population back then. This is particularly challenging given the much greater importance that formal schooling has today to economic success compared to a century ago.

Language acquisition does not appear an issue although given the large concentrations of Spanish-speaking neighborhoods that might seem to work against becoming fluent English speakers. Although 23 percent of the Hispanic immigrants as a group speak English very well, the percentage of these immigrants fluent in English rises to 88 percent among their U.S.-born children and then to 94 percent in the third generation.

It is early to make firm direct comparisons because the second-generation Mexican American is just coming of age, much less having full labor force experience and creating their own families. Although the complete entry of today's immigrants into economy is likely to come based on analysis of the situation today, comparisons to White ethnics suggests that it may take the immigrants longer by at least an additional generation.

Sources: Bean and Stevens 2003; Camarota 2007a; Dickson 2006; Hakimzadeh and Cohn 2007; Katz et al. 2007; Perlmann 2005; Portes 2006; Portes and Rumbaut 2006; Valdez 2006.

The Contemporary Picture

In politics, Italian Americans have been more successful, at least at the local level, where family and community ties can be translated into votes. However, political success did not come easily, because many Italian immigrants anticipated returning to their homeland and did not always take neighborhood politics seriously. It was even more difficult for Italian Americans to break into national politics.

Not until 1962 was an Italian American named to a cabinet-level position. Geraldine Ferraro's nomination as the Democratic vice presidential candidate in 1984 was every bit as much an achievement for Italian Americans as it was for women. The opposition to the nomination of Judge Samuel Alito to the Supreme Court in 2006 struck many as bordering on anti–Italian American sentiments in the manner the opposition was advanced. Numerous critics used the phrase "Judge Scalito" in obvious reference to the sitting Italian American on the Court, Justice Antonio Scalia (Cornacchia and Nelson 1992; National Italian American Foundation 2006).

A recent study of the members of the American Academy of Arts and Sciences, a group of nearly 4,000 members drawn from throughout the academic and scientific worlds, showed that Italian Americans are represented well below their representation on the nation's faculties. Ethnic disadvantage has not disappeared entirely (Alba and Abdel-Hady 2005).

There is no paucity of famous Italian Americans. They include athletes like Joe DiMaggio and Joe Paterno, politician Rudolph Giullani, director Francis Ford Coppola, singer Madonna, comedian Jay Leno, writer Mario Puzo, actor Nicholas Cage, chef Rachel Ray, and auto racing legend Mario Andretti.

In 2000, the 15.9 million people of Italian ancestry accounted for about 6 percent of the population, although only a small fraction of them had actually been born in Italy. Italian Americans still remain the seventh-largest immigrant group. Just how ethnically conscious is the Italian American community? Although the number is declining, 1 million Americans speak Italian at home; only six languages are spoken more frequently at home (Spanish, French, Chinese, Vietnamese, Tagalog [Philippines], and German). For another 14-plus million Italian Americans, however, the language tie to their culture is absent, and depending on their degree of assimilation, only traces of symbolic ethnicity may remain. In a later section, we will look at the role that language plays for many immigrants and their children (Shin and Bruno 2003).

Polish Americans

Immigrants from Poland have had experiences similar to that of the Irish and Italians. They had to overcome economic problems and personal hardships just to make the journey. Once in the United States, they found themselves often assigned to the jobs many citizens had not wanted to do. They had to adjust to a new language, a familiar yet different culture. And always they were looking back to the family members left behind who either wanted to join them in the United States or, in contrast, never wanted them to leave in the first place.

Like other arrivals, many Poles sought improvement in their lives in what came to called the Za Chlebem (For Bread) migration. The Poles who came were, at different times, more likely than many other European immigrants to see themselves as forced immigrants and were often described by, and themselves adopted, the terminology directly reflecting their social roles—exiles, refugees, displaced persons, or émigrés. The primary force for this exodus was the changing political status of Poland through most of the nineteenth and twentieth centuries, which was as turbulent as were the lives of the new arrivals.

Early Immigration

Polish immigrants were among the settlers at Jamestown, Virginia, in 1608, to help develop the colony's timber industry, but it was the Poles who came later in that century that made a lasting mark. The successful exploits of Polish immigrants such as cavalry officer Casimir Pulaski and military engineer Thaddeus Kosciuszko are still commemorated today in communities with large Polish American populations. As we can see in Figure 5-1, it was not until the 1890s that Polish immigration was significant in comparison to some other European arrivals. Admittedly, it is difficult to exactly document the size of this immigration because Poland or parts of the country became part, at various historical periods, of Austria-Hungary, Germany (Prussia), and the Soviet Union so that the migrants were not officially coming from a nation called "Poland."

Many of the Polish immigrants were adjusting not only to a new culture but also to a more urban way of life. Sociologists William I. Thomas and Florian Znaniecki in their classic study, *The Polish Peasant in Europe and America*, traced the path from rural Poland to urban America. Many of the peasants did not necessarily come directly to the United States but first traveled through other European countries. This pattern is not unique and reminds us that, even today, many immigrants have crossed several countries sometimes establishing themselves for a period of time before finally settling in the United States (Thomas and Znaniecki 1996).

Like the Italians and Irish, they arrived at the large port cities of the East Coast but, unlike them, the Polish immigrants were more likely to settle in cities further inland or work in mines in Pennsylvania. In such areas, they would join kinfolk or acquaintances through the process of chain migration described in the previous chapter.

The reference to coal mining as an occupation reflects the continuing tendency of immigrants to work in jobs avoided by U.S. citizens because they paid little or were dangerous or both. For example, in September 1897, a group of miners in Lattimer, Pennsylvania, marched to demand safer working conditions and an end to special taxes placed only on foreign-born workers. In the ensuing confrontation with local officials, police officers shot at the protesters killing nineteen people, most of whom were Polish, the others Lithuanians and Slovaks (Duszak 1997).

Polonia

With growing numbers, the emergence of Polonia (meaning Polish communities outside of Poland) became more common in cities throughout the Midwest. Male immigrants who came alone often took shelter through a system of inexpensive boarding houses called tryzmanie bortnków (brother-keeping), which allowed the new arrival to save and send money back to Poland to support his family. These funds eventually provided the financial means necessary to bring family members over, adding to the size of Polonia in cities such as Buffalo, Cleveland, Detroit, Milwaukee, Pittsburgh, and above all in Chicago where the population of Poles was second only to Warsaw, Poland.

Religion has played an important role among the Polish immigrants and their descendants. Most of the Polish immigrants who came to the United

States prior to World War I were Roman Catholic. They quickly established their own parishes where new arrivals could feel welcomed. Although religious services at that time were in the Latin language, as they had been in Poland, the many service organizations around the parish, not to mention the Catholic schools, kept the immigrants steeped in the Polish language and the latest happenings back home. Jewish Poles began immigrating during the first part of the twentieth century to escape the growing hostility they felt in Europe that culminated in the Holocaust. Their numbers swelled greatly until movement from Poland stopped with the invasion of Poland by Germany in 1939 and then resumed again after the war.

Although the Jewish–Catholic distinction may be the most obvious distinguishing factor among Polish Americans, there are other divisions as well. Regional subgroups such as the Kashubes, the Górali, and the Mazurians have often carried great significance. Some Poles emigrated from areas where German actually was the language of origin.

Feelings about Poland and its future have both served to unify Polonia and at times reflect the political, economic, and culture divisions of the Poles' ancestral homeland, which they have been able to follow through the dozens of Polish-language local and national newspapers, magazines, radio stations, and cable television news shows.

As with other immigrant groups, Polish Americans could make use of a rich structure of self-help voluntary associations that was already well established by the 1890s. Besides providing economic assistance and social networks, these organizations also directed attention to the political and ideological controversies that swirled around in Poland. Groups like the Polish National Alliance and the Polish Roman Catholic Union, both headquartered in Chicago, had well over a hundred thousand members for most of the twentieth century.

Not all organizations smoothly cut across different generations of Polish immigrants. For example, the Poles who came immediately after World War II as political refugees fleeing Soviet domination were quite different in their outlook than the descendants of the economic refugees from the turn of the century. These kinds of tensions in an immigrant community are not unusual even if they go unnoticed by the casual observer who lumps all immigrants of the same nationality together (Jaroszyńska-Kirchmann 2004).

Like many other newcomers, Poles have been not only stigmatized as outsiders but also stereotyped as simple and uncultured—the typical biased view of working-class White ethnics. Their struggles in manual occupations placed them in direct competition with other White ethnics and African Americans, which occasionally led to labor disputes and longer-term tense and emotional rivalries. "Polish jokes" continue now to have a remarkable shelf life in casual conversation well into the twenty-first century. Jewish Poles suffer the added indignities of anti-Semitism (Dolan and Stotsky 1997).

Richie Sambora, guitarist with the rock group Bon Jovi, is one of many well-known Polish Americans.

The Contemporary Picture

Today, Polonia in the United States exceeds 10 million. Although this may not seem significant in a country of over 300 million, we need to recall that today Poland itself has a population of only about 39 million. Whether it was to support the efforts of Lech Walesa, Solidarity movement leader confronting the Soviet Union in the 1980s, or to celebrate the elevation of Karol Józef Wojtyla as Pope John Paul II in 1978, Polish Americans are a central part of the global Polish community.

Aging Polish American communities have received an influx of new arrivals since 1989 as elections in Poland marked the end of Soviet dominance, allowing Poles to join their relatives and facilitating immigration of entire households. Poland's entry into NATO in 1999 and the European Union in 2004 smoothed the way even further for Poles to migrate to Western Europe and on to the United States.

Many Polish Americans have retained little of their rich cultural traditions and may barely acknowledge even symbolic ethnicity. Others are still immersed in Polonia and their lives still revolve around many of the same religious and social institutions that were the center of Polonia a century ago. For example, as of 2006, fifty-four Roman Catholic churches in the metropolitan Chicago area still offer Polish-language masses. Although in many of these parishes there may be only one service in Polish serving a declining number of celebrants, a few traditional "Polish" churches actually still have Polish-speaking priests in residence. Even with the decline in Polish-language service, Pole seminarians are actively recruited by the Roman Catholic church although now English language training is often emphasized.

Polish core neighborhoods and strips of stores proudly proclaiming their Polish connections still abound, but increasingly, Polish Americans have moved into suburban communities—first to inner-ring suburbs and then out to the further reaches of metropolitan centers. This migration outward from the traditional ethnic enclaves is evidence of upward mobility and growing diversity in occupations and leisure-time pursuits.

In the latter part of the twentieth century, some of the voluntary associations relocated or built satellite centers to serve the outlying Polish American populations. To sustain their activities financially, these social organizations also reached out of the central cities in order to tap into the financial resources of suburban Poles. Yet also increasingly, people of Polish descent have now made their way into the same social networks populated by Irish, Italian, and other ethnic Americans (Bukowcyk 1996; Erdmans 1998, 2006; Lopata 1994; Mocha 1998; Polzin 1973; Stone 2006).

Among the many Polish Americans well known or remembered today are actor Adrien Brody, home designer Martha (Kostyra) Stewart, comedian Jack Benny (Benjamin Kubelsky), guitarist Richie Sambora of the rock group Bon Jovi, actress Jane Kaczmarek of *Malcolm in the Middle,* entertainer Liberace, *Wheel of Fortune* host Pat Sajak, baseball star Stan Musial, football star Mike Ditka, novelist Joseph Conrad (Józef Korzeniowski), singer Bobby Vinton (Stanley Ventula, Jr.), polio vaccine pioneer Albert Sabin, and director Stanley Kubrick.

The Language Divide

One evening in Chicago, Audrey Cho, holding a handout listing federal holdings, faced her ten adult students and asked, "Who is Washington?" Confused looks came over the faces of the Korean, Mexican, Peruvian, and Mongolian immigrants. Finally, someone raised his hand and said, "February 16th?" Cho, herself having immigrated from South Korea, remained patient and stated "No, it's who, not when." Learning English may not be easy but many immigrants of all ages are trying (Kaneya 2004, 6).

In "Listen to Our Voices," Albanian immigrant Harallamb Terba speaks of his efforts to attend Truman College and the Chicago City College and become a part of American society. Language is both a barrier to assimilation and a means for upward mobility.

LISTEN TO OUR VOICES

I Was Born in Tirana

Harallamb Terba

My name is Harallamb Terba. I was born in Tirana, Albania, in November 21st, 1965. I came here exactly in March 25, 1996. It was afternoon, 5:00 Chicago time, but my watch say 12:00 in the night because it is seven hours different from my country to here. [Laughs.]

I'm in college now. My major is computer information system. I think after I will be graduating from school, I'm gonna start working, maybe for a company. I love working in computer, computer programming, designing and building programs, applications. I think my life is gonna be good. I always think about that. My wife is in school, too. She's taking sign language. She loves working with deaf people. So I think she is gonna get a good job....

Home is the place where you live. I think about my home in my country. It's the place where you born. But this is the life. The life change. You have to move. You have to try and when you try for the best, it's better for you. I like my country. I like the people there, but I feel this is my home now. I don't feel that about Albania now. I feel that when I was in Albania, I have this thought in my mind that, "I will go. One day I will go in the United States. Everything that I did here it's nothing. I have to get my education. I have to work. I have to do, but everything it's gonna start when I go in the United States." That's why I wish to came here younger.

I think to have my own home, years after. I think about that. It's not important, but I always loved having my own home, my yard. I always loved that because I have been grow up with big home with a yard in front, so that's why I love that. But now I'm living in apartment and everything is OK. I like that.

In the future I want plan for to have children. I'm going to tell my children in the future that they will be American because they will be born here, but I always am gonna tell them from where they are, their parents are. So they have to know about their country because this was the country that grow us, their father and their mother. So they have to know about their culture. Maybe I'm gonna advise them that when they go in Albanian, to be more Albanian than Albanians are, because Albanians are gonna see them just, "Hey, you are from America. You're American." You know what happens.

America to me means freedom, and the land where everyone can do what he dreams. Dreams come true. It's a hard work to do what you want, but finally you can do that. I came from one country that you want to do something, but no one lets you to do that. You can only do what they say to you. So here, if you want to do that, if you like to do that, you can do that. It's hard. I know it's hard. Nothing is easy in our life today, but you can do that. And this is more important for our life, to do what we want.

Source: Excerpt from Harallamb Terba in *An Immigrant Class: Oral Histories from Chicago's Newest Immigrants* by Jeff Libman, 2004, pp. 194–195.

Language is key to people's functioning in a society, and it is critical in relation to how they see themselves. But when that language is different from the dominant tongue, it can be the source of hardship and stigmatization. About 19 percent of the population speaks a language other than English, as shown in Figure 5.3. Indeed, thirty-two different languages are spoken at home by at least 200,000 residents (Shin and Bruno 2003).

As of 2006, about half of the 37 million people born abroad spoke English less than "very well." This rises to 75 percent among those born in Mexico. Nationally, about 70 percent of Latino schoolchildren report speaking Spanish at home (Brodie et al. 2002; Bureau of the Census 2003, 158, 2007c: Table S0506).

The myth of Anglo superiority has rested in part on language differences. (The term *Anglo* in the following text is used to mean all non-Hispanics but primarily Whites.) First, the criteria for economic and social achievement usually include proficiency in English. By such standards, Spanish-speaking pupils are judged less able to compete until they learn English. Second, many Anglos believe that Spanish is not an asset occupationally. Only recently, as government agencies have belatedly begun to serve Latino people and as businesses recognize the growing Latino consumer market, have Anglos recognized that knowing Spanish is not only useful but also necessary to carry out certain tasks. However, as we see in education, voting, and language practices, many people in the United States are concerned and suspicious about the public use of any language other than English.

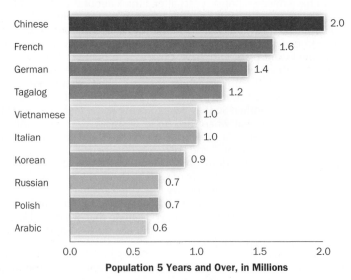

Figure 5.3 Ten Languages Most Frequently Spoken at Home Other Than English and Spanish
Source: Data for 2000 released in 2003 in Shin and Bruno 2003.

Bilingual Education

Until the last thirty years, there was a conscious effort to devalue Spanish and other languages and to discourage the use of foreign languages in schools. In the case of Spanish, this practice was built on a pattern of segregating Hispanic schoolchildren from Anglos. In the recent past in the Southwest, Mexican Americans were assigned to Mexican schools to keep Anglo schools all-White. These Mexican schools, created through de jure school segregation, were substantially underfunded compared with the regular public schools. Legal action against such schools dates back to 1945, but it was not until 1970 that the U.S. Supreme Court ruled, in *Cisneros v. Corpus Christi Independent School District,* that the de jure segregation of Mexican Americans was unconstitutional. Appeals delayed implementation of that decision, and not until September 1975 was the de jure plan forcibly overturned in Corpus Christi, Texas (Commission on Civil Rights 1976).

Even in integrated schools, Latino children were given separate, unequal treatment. "No Spanish" was a rule enforced throughout the Southwest, Florida, and New York City by school boards in the 1960s. Children speaking Spanish on school grounds, even on the playground, might be punished with detention after school, fines, physical reprimands, and even expulsion for repeated violations. From 1855 to as recently as 1968, teaching in any language other than English was illegal in California. Such laws existed despite a provision in the 1848 Treaty of Guadalupe Hidalgo between the United States and Mexico that guaranteed the right of Mexicans to maintain their culture. All official publications were to be bilingual, but "English only" became the social norm.

Is it essential that English be the sole language of instruction in schools in the United States? **Bilingualism** is the use of two or more languages in places of work or educational facilities, according each language equal legitimacy. Thus, a program of **bilingual education** may instruct children in their native language (such as Spanish) while gradually introducing them to the language of the dominant society (English). If such a program is also bicultural, it will teach children about the culture of both linguistic groups. Bilingual education allows students to learn academic material in their own language while they are learning a second language. Proponents believe that, ideally, bilingual education programs should also allow English-speaking pupils to be bilingual, but generally, they are directed only at making non-English speakers proficient in more than one language.

Programs to teach English as a second language (ESL) have been the cornerstones of bilingual education, but they are limited in approach. For example, ESL programs tend to emphasize bilingual but not bicultural education. As a result, the method can unintentionally contribute to ethnocentric attitudes, especially if it seems to imply that a minority group is not really worthy of attention. As conflict theorists are quick to note, the interests of the less powerful—in this case, millions of non–English-speaking children—are those least likely to be recognized and respected. One alternative to the ESL approach, viewed with much less favor by advocates of bilingualism, is **English immersion,** in which students are taught primarily in English, using their native languages only when they do not understand their lessons. In practice, such instruction usually becomes an English-only "crash program" (Hechinger 1987).

Since its introduction into U.S. schools, bilingual education has been beset by problems. Its early supporters were disillusioned by the small number of English-speaking children participating and by the absence of a bicultural component in most programs. However, the frustration has been most clearly visible in the lack of consensus among educators on how best to implement bilingual programs. Even when a school district decides what methods it prefers, superintendents find it difficult to hire qualified instructors, although this varies depending on the language and the part of the country. The problem is further complicated by the presence of children speaking languages other than the predominant second language, so superintendents may want to mount bilingual programs in many languages.

Do bilingual programs help children to learn English? It is difficult to reach firm conclusions on the effectiveness of the bilingual programs in general because they vary so widely in their approach to non-English-speaking children. The programs differ in the length of the transition to English and how long they allow students to remain in bilingual classrooms. A major study released in 2004 analyzed more than three decades of research, combining seventeen different studies, and found that bilingual education programs produce higher levels of student achievement in reading. The most successful are paired bilingual programs—those offering ongoing instruction in a native language and English at different times of the day (Slavin and Cheung 2003, Soltero 2008).

Drawing on the perspective of conflict theory, we can understand some of the attacks on bilingual programs. The criticisms do not necessarily result from careful educational research. Rather, they stem from the effort to assimilate children and to deprive them of language pluralism. This view, that any deviation from the majority is bad, is expressed by those who want to stamp out foreigners, especially in our schools. Research findings have little influence on those who, holding such ethnocentric views, try to persuade policy makers to follow their thinking. This perspective does not take into account that success in bilingual education may begin to address the problem of high school dropouts and the paucity of Hispanics in colleges and universities.

As one might expect, Latinos tend to be very supportive of bilingual programs. A 2003 national survey found that 72 percent of Hispanics (and a similar proportion of African Americans) favor school districts offering such programs compared to 53 percent of non-Hispanic Whites. Nonetheless, opposition to bilingualism can be quite strong among some Hispanics. A few are very active in organized efforts to stop such programs, and some Latino parents pressure schools to keep their children out of classrooms where Spanish may be spoken because of the misguided notion that English-only education,

The United States has a long history of receiving immigrants who do not speak English very well and the response recently has included both bilingual programs as well as calls for a constitutional amendment to make English the official language.

even for the youngest children, is the key to success (Freedman 2004; Mason 2003; Soltero 2004, 2008).

Official Language Movement

Attacks on bilingualism both in voting and in education have taken several forms and have even broadened to question the appropriateness of U.S. residents using any language other than English. Federal policy has become more restrictive. Local schools have been given more authority to determine appropriate methods of instruction; they have also been forced to provide more of their own funding for bilingual education.

In the United States, thirty states as of 2008 have made English their official language. Repeated efforts have been made to introduce a constitutional amendment declaring English as the nation's official language. Even such an action would not completely outlaw bilingual or multilingual government services. It would, however, require that such services be called for specifically as in the Voting Rights Act of 1965, which requires voting information to be available in multiple languages (U.S. English 2008).

As shown in Figure 5.4, non-English speakers cluster in certain states, but bilingualism attracts nationwide passions. The release in 2006 of "Nuestro Himmo," the Spanish-language version of "The Star-Spangled Banner," led to a strong reaction with 69 percent of people saying it was only appropriate to be

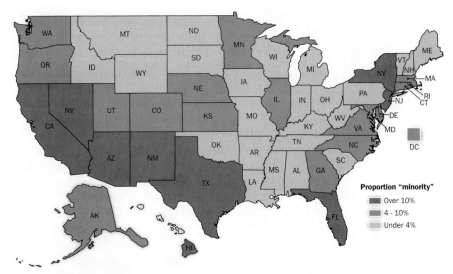

Figure 5.4 People Who Speak English Less than "Very Well"

Note: Data for 2006 is those people 5 years and over. National proportion is 8.7 percent.

Source: U.S. data for 2006 released in American Community Survey: Ranking Table R1603.

sung in English. Yet, at least one congressman decrying the Spanish version sang the anthem himself in English with incorrect lyrics. Similarly, a locally famous restaurant owner in Philadelphia posted signs at his Philly steak sandwich diner announcing he would only accept orders in English. Passions remain strong as policy makers debate how much support should be given to people who speak other languages (Carroll 2006; Koch 2006).

Religious Pluralism

In popular speech, the term *pluralism* has often been used in the United States to refer explicitly to religion. Although certain faiths figure more prominently in the worship scene, there has been a history of greater religious tolerance in the United States than in most other nations. Today there are more than 1,500 religious bodies in the United States, ranging from the more than 66 million members of the Roman Catholic Church to sects with fewer than 1,000 adherents. In virtually every region of the country, religion is being expressed in greater variety whether it be the Latinization of Catholicism and some Christian faiths or the de-Europeanizing of some established Protestant faiths as with Asian Americans or the "De-Christianizing" of the overall religious landscape with Muslims, Buddhists, Hindus, Sikhs, and others (Roof 2007).

How do we view the United States in terms of religion? There is an increasingly non-Christian presence in the United States. In 1900, an estimated

❓ Ask Yourself

How many different ways does religious expression emerge? Hillel Houses, such as this one at the University of Southern California, are both social and spiritual gathering places for Jewish students on college campuses.

96 percent of the nation was Christian, just over 1 percent nonreligious, and about 3 percent all other faiths. In 2007, it was estimated that the nation was 82 percent Christian, nearly 11 percent nonreligious, and another 7 percent all other faiths. The United States has a long Jewish tradition, and Muslims number close to 5 million. A smaller but also growing number of people adhere to such Eastern faiths as Hinduism, Buddhism, Confucianism, and Taoism (Newport 2007).

Sociologists use the word **denomination** for a large, organized religion that is not linked officially with the state or government. By far, the largest denomination in the United States is Catholicism, yet at least twenty-five other Christian religious denominations have 1 million or more members (Table 5.1).

There are also at least four non-Christian religious groups in the United States whose numbers are comparable to any of these large denominations. Jews, Muslims, Buddhists, and Hindus in the United States all number more than 1 million. Within each of these groups, there are branches or sects that distinguish themselves from each other. For example, as we examine in greater detail later in this chapter, in the United States and the rest of the world, some followers of Islam are Sunni Muslims and others are Shiites. There are further divisions within these groups, just as there are among Protestants, and in turn, among Baptists.

Even if religious faiths have broad representation, they tend to be fairly homogeneous at the local church level. This is especially ironic, given that many faiths have played critical roles in resisting racism and in trying to bring together the nation in the name of racial and ethnic harmony (Orfield and Liebowitz 1999).

Broadly defined faiths show representation of a variety of ethnic and racial groups. In Figure 5.5, we consider the interaction of White, Black, and Hispanic races with religions. Muslims, Pentecostals, and Jehovah's Witnesses are much more diverse than Presbyterians or Lutherans. Religion plays an even more central role for Blacks and Latinos than Whites. A 2004 national survey indicated that 65 percent of African Americans and 51 percent of Latinos attend a religious service every week, compared to 44 percent of non-Hispanic Whites (Winseman 2004).

It would also be incorrect to focus only on older religious organizations. Local churches that developed into national faiths in the 1990s, such as the

Table 5.1 Churches with More Than a Million Members

Denomination Name	Inclusive Membership
The Roman Catholic Church	67,515,016
Southern Baptist Convention	16,306,246
The United Methodist Church	7,995,456
The Church of Jesus Christ of Latter-day Saints	5,779,316
The Church of God in Christ	5,499,875
National Baptist Convention, U.S.A., Inc.	5,000,000
Evangelical Lutheran Church in America	4,774,203
National Baptist Convention of America, Inc.	3,500,000
Presbyterian Church (U.S.A.)	3,025,740
Assemblies of God	2,836,174
Progressive National Baptist Convention, Inc.	2,500,000
African Methodist Episcopal Church	2,500,000
National Missionary Baptist Convention of America	2,500,000
The Lutheran Church—Missouri Synod (LCMS)	2,414,997
Episcopal Church	2,154,572
Churches of Christ	1,639,495
Greek Orthodox Archdiocese of America	1,500,000
Pentecostal Assemblies of the World, Inc.	1,500,000
African Methodist Episcopal Zion Church	1,443,405
American Baptist Churches in the U.S.A.	1,371,278
United Church of Christ	1,218,541
Baptist Bible Fellowship International	1,200,000
Christian Churches and Churches of Christ	1,071,616
The Orthodox Church in America	1,064,000
Jehovah's Witness	1,069,533
Church of God	1,032,550

Note: Most recent data as of 2008. Membership reporting year ranges from 1992 to 2007.

Source: Reprinted by permission from *Yearbook of American and Canadian Churches 2006.* Copyright by National Council of Churches of Christ in the U.S.A.

Calvary Chapel, Vineyard, and Hope Chapel, have created a following among Pentecostal believers, who embrace a more charismatic form of worship devoid of many traditional ornaments, with pastors and congregations alike favoring informal attire. New faiths develop with increasing rapidity in what can only be called a very competitive market for individual religious faith. In addition, many people, with or without religious affiliation, become fascinated with spiritual concepts such as angels or become a part of loose-knit fellowships such as the Promise Keepers, an all-male movement of evangelical Christians

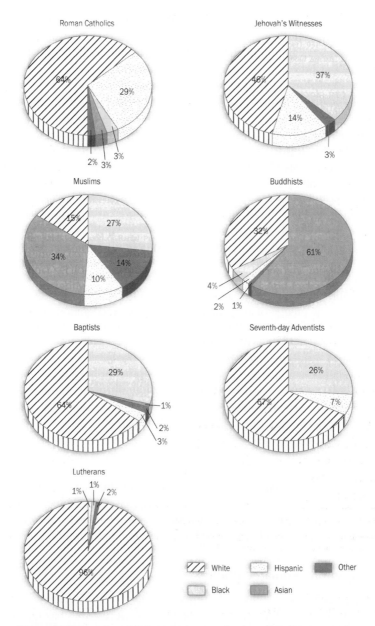

Figure 5.5 Racial and Ethnic Makeup of Selected Religions in the United States

Note: More recent study (Latino Coalition 2006) shows 44 percent of Roman Catholics to be Hispanic. Totals do not always sum up to 100 percent due to rounding.

Source: "Racial and Ethnic Make-Up of Selected Religions," in American Religious Identification Survey, 2001 by Egon Mayer. The Graduate Center of the City University of New York. Reprinted with permission.

founded in 1990. Religion in the United States is an ever-changing social phenomenon. Other non-mainstream faiths emerge in new arenas as evidenced by
Mormon Mitt Romney's effort for the Republican nomination for president in
2008 or the visible role of celebrities promoting the Church of Scientology
(Dudley and Roozen 2001; Schaefer and Zellner 2008).

Divisive conflicts along religious lines are muted in the United States compared with those in, say, the Middle East. Although not entirely absent, conflicts about religion in the United States seem to be overshadowed by civil
religion. **Civil religion** is the religious dimension in the United States that
merges the public life with sacred beliefs. It also reflects that no single faith is
privileged over all others.

Sociologist Robert Bellah (1967) borrowed the phrase *civil religion* from eigh-
teenth-century French philosopher Jean-Jacques Rousseau to describe a significant phenomenon in the contemporary United States. Civil religion exists
alongside established religious faiths, and it embodies a belief system incorporat-
ing all religions but not associated specifically with any one. It is the type of faith
to which presidents refer in inaugural speeches and to which American Legion
posts and Girl Scout troops swear allegiance. In 1954, Congress added the phrase
under God to the pledge of allegiance as a legislative recognition of religion's significance. Elected officials in the United States, beginning with Ronald Reagan,
often concluded even their most straightforward speeches with "God Bless the
United States of America," which in effect evokes the civil religion of the nation.

Functionalists see civil religion as reinforcing central American values that
may be more expressly patriotic than sacred in nature. Often, the mass media,
following major societal upheavals, from the 1995 Oklahoma City bombing to
the 2001 terrorist attacks, show church services with clergy praying and asking
for national healing. Bellah (1967) sees no sign that the importance of civil religion has diminished in promoting collective identity, but he does acknowledge that it is more conservative than during the 1970s.

In the following sections, we will explore the diversity among the major
Christian groups in the United States, such as Roman Catholics and Protestants,
as well as how Islam has emerged as a significant religious force in the United
States and can no longer be regarded as a marginal faith in terms of followers.

Diversity Among Roman Catholics

Social scientists have persistently tended to ignore the diversity within the
Roman Catholic Church in the United States. Recent research has not sustained
the conclusions that Roman Catholics are melding into a single group, following
the traditions of the American Irish Catholic model, or even that parishioners
are attending English-language churches. Religious behavior has been different for each ethnic group within the Roman Catholic Church. The Irish and the
French Canadians left societies that were highly competitive both culturally
and socially. Their religious involvement in the United States is more relaxed

than it was in Ireland and Quebec. However, the influence of life in the United States has increased German and Polish involvement in the Roman Catholic Church, whereas Italians have remained largely inactive. Variations by ethnic background continue to emerge in studies of contemporary religious involvement in the Roman Catholic Church (Eckstrom 2001).

Since the mid-1970s, the Roman Catholic Church in America has received a significant number of new members from the Philippines, Southeast Asia, and particularly Latin America. Although these new members have been a stabilizing force offsetting the loss of White ethnics, they have also challenged a church that for generations was dominated by Irish, Italian, and Polish parishes. Perhaps the most prominent subgroup in the Roman Catholic Church is the Latinos, who now account for one-third of all Roman Catholic parishioners. In the 2006 new class of priests ordained, nearly one-third were foreign born. Some Los Angeles churches in or near Latino neighborhoods must schedule fourteen masses each Sunday to accommodate the crowds of worshipers. By 2006, Latinos constituted 44 percent of Roman Catholics nationwide (*Chicago Tribune* 2006; Murphy and Banerjee 2005).

The Roman Catholic Church, despite its ethnic diversity, has clearly been a powerful force in reducing the ethnic ties of its members, making it also a significant assimilating force. The irony in this role of Catholicism is that so many nineteenth-century Americans heaped abuse on Catholics in this country for allegedly being un-American and having a dual allegiance. The history of the Catholic Church in the United States may be portrayed as a struggle within the membership between the Americanizers and the anti-Americanizers, with the former ultimately winning. Unlike the various Protestant churches that

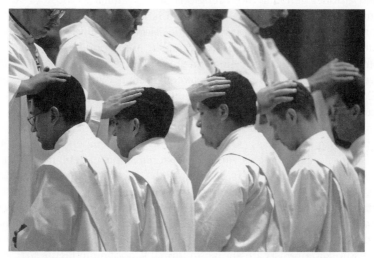

The Roman Catholic Church has experienced growth through immigration from Latin America but has had difficulty recruiting men into the priesthood. Here we see an ordination ceremony at the Holy Name Cathedral in Chicago, Illinois, in 2003.

accommodated immigrants of a single nationality, the Roman Catholic Church had to Americanize a variety of linguistic and ethnic groups. The Catholic Church may have been the most potent assimilating force after the public school system. Comparing the assimilationist goal of the Catholic Church and the present diversity in it leads us to the conclusion that ethnic diversity has continued in the Roman Catholic Church despite, not because of, this religious institution.

Diversity Among Protestants

Protestantism, like Catholicism, often is portrayed as a monolithic entity. Little attention is given to the doctrinal and attitudinal differences that sharply divide the various denominations in both laity and clergy. However, several studies document the diversity. Unfortunately, many opinion polls and surveys are content to learn whether a respondent is a Catholic, a Protestant, or a Jew. Stark and Glock (1968) found sharp differences in religious attitudes within Protestant churches. For example, 99 percent of Southern Baptists had no doubt that Jesus was the divine Son of God as contrasted to only 40 percent of Congregationalists. We can identify four "generic theological camps":

1. *Liberals:* United Church of Christ (Congregationalists) and Episcopalians
2. *Moderates:* Disciples of Christ, Methodists, and Presbyterians
3. *Conservatives:* American Lutherans and American Baptists
4. *Fundamentalists:* Missouri Synod Lutherans, Southern Baptists, and Assembly of God

Roman Catholics generally hold religious beliefs similar to those of conservative Protestants, except on essentially Catholic issues such as papal infallibility (the authority of the spiritual role in all decisions regarding faith and morals). Whether or not there are four distinct camps is not important: The point is that the familiar practice of contrasting Roman Catholics and Protestants is clearly not productive. Some differences between Roman Catholics and Protestants are inconsequential compared with the differences between Protestant sects.

Secular criteria as well as doctrinal issues may distinguish religious faiths. Research has consistently shown that denominations can be arranged in a hierarchy based on social class. As Figure 5.6 reveals, members of certain faiths, such as Episcopalians, Jews, and Presbyterians, have a higher proportion of affluent members. Members of other faiths, including Baptists, tend to be poorer. Of course, all Protestant groups draw members from each social stratum. Nonetheless, the social significance of these class differences is that religion becomes a mechanism for signaling social mobility. A person who is moving up in wealth and power may seek out a faith associated with a higher social ranking. Similar contrasts are shown in formal schooling in Figure 5.7.

Protestant faiths have been diversifying, and many of their members have been leaving them for churches that follow strict codes of behavior or

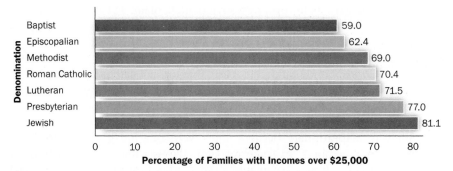

Figure 5.6 Income and Denominations
Denominations attract different income groups. All groups have both affluent and poor members, yet some have a higher proportion of members with high incomes and others are comparatively poor.
Source: General Social Survey, 1996 through 2006. See Davis et al. 2007.

fundamental interpretations of Biblical teachings. This trend is reflected in the gradual decline of the five mainline churches: Baptist, Episcopalian, Lutheran, Methodist, and Presbyterian. In 2006, these faiths accounted for about 58 percent of total Protestant membership, compared with 65 percent in the 1970s. With a broader acceptance of new faiths and continuing immigration, it is unlikely that these mainline churches will regain their dominance in the near future (Davis et al. 2007, 171–172).

Although Protestants may seem to define the civil religion and the accepted dominant orientation, some Christian faiths feel they, too, experience the discrimination usually associated with non-Christians such as Jews and Muslims. For example, representatives of the liberal and moderate faiths dominate the leadership of the military's chaplain corps. For example, there are

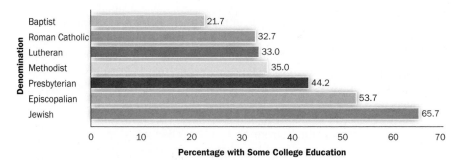

Figure 5.7 Education and Denominations
There are sharp differences in the proportion of those with some college education by denomination.
Source: General Social Survey, 1996 through 2006. See Davis et al. 2007.

16 Presbyterian soldiers for every Presbyterian chaplain, 121 Full Gospel worshippers for every Full Gospel chaplain, and 339 Muslim soldiers for every Muslim chaplain (Cooperman 2005).

As another example of denominational discrimination, in 1998, the Southern Baptist Convention amended its basic theological statements of beliefs to include a strong statement on family life. However, the statement included a declaration that a woman should "submit herself graciously" to her husband's leadership. There were widespread attacks on this position, which many Baptists felt was inappropriate because they were offering guidance for their denomination's members. In some respects, Baptists felt this was a form of respectable bigotry. It was acceptable to attack them for their views on social issues even though such criticism would be much more muted for many more liberal faiths that seem free to tolerate abortion (Bowman 1998; Niebuhr 1998).

Islam in the United States

Islam, with approximately 1.3 billion followers worldwide, is second to Christianity among the world's religions. Although news events and a worldview of Orientalism suggest an inherent conflict between Christians and Muslims, the two faiths are similar in many ways. Both are monotheistic (i.e., based on a single deity) and indeed worship the same God. Allah is the Arabic word for God and refers to the God of Moses, Jesus, and Muhammad. Both Christianity and Islam include a belief in prophets, an afterlife, and a judgment day. In fact, Islam recognizes Jesus as a prophet, though not the son of God. Islam reveres both the Old and New Testaments as integral parts of its tradition. Both faiths impose a moral code on believers, which varies from fairly rigid proscriptions for fundamentalists to relatively relaxed guidelines for liberals.

Islamic believers are divided into a variety of faiths and sects, such as Sunnis and Shi'is (or Shiites). These divisions sometimes result in antagonisms between the members, just as there are religious rivalries between Christian denominations. The large majority of Muslims in the United States are Sunni Muslims—literally those who follow the Sunnah, the way of the Prophet. Compared to other Muslims, they tend to be more moderate in their religious orthodoxy. The Shi'ia (primarily from Iraq, Iran, and southern Lebanon) are the second largest group. The two groups differ on who should have been the Caliph, or ruler, after the death of the Prophet Muhammad. This disagreement resulted in different understandings of beliefs and practices, concluding in the Sunni and Shi'ia worshipping separately from each other. They worship separately even if it means crossing national and linguistic lines to do so—provided there are sufficient numbers of Shi'ia to support their own mosque or masjid.

There are many other expressions of Islamic faith and even divisions among Sunnis and Shi'is, so to speak of Muslims as Sunni or Shi'i would be akin to speaking of Christians as Roman Catholic or Baptist, forgetting that there are

Although the Muslim presence in the United States has only been recognized by the general public very recently, it has a long history. Yarrow Marmout, an African Muslim and former slave, was painted in this portrait by famed artist Charles Wilson Peele in 1819.

Source: Charles Wilson Peale, "Yarrow Marmout." Courtesy of the Historical Society of Pennsylvania Collection, Atwater Kent Museum of Philadelphia.

other denominations as well as sharp divisions within the Roman Catholic and Baptist faiths. Furthermore, there are Muslim groups unique to the United States; later we will focus on the largest one—Islam among African Americans.

Based on the most recent studies, there are at least 2 million and perhaps as many as 5.7 million Muslims in the United States. About two-thirds are U.S.-born citizens. In terms of ethnic and racial background, the more acceptable estimates still vary widely. Estimates range as follows:

- 20–42 percent African American
- 24–33 percent South Asian (Afghan, Bangladeshi, Indian, and Pakistani)
- 12–32 percent Arab
- 10–22 percent "other" (Bosnian, Iranian, Turk, and White and Hispanic converts)

There appears to be total agreement that the Muslim population in the United States is growing rapidly through immigration and conversion (Ba-Yunus and

Kone 2004; Institute for Social Policy and Understanding 2004; King 2004; Paik 2001; Smith 2001).

Reflecting the growth of the Muslim population in the United States, the number of mosques has grown to more than 1,700. Mosques (more properly referred to as masjids) do not maintain identifiable membership rolls as do churches, but scholars have observed that mosques and the imam, the leader or spiritual guide of a mosque, are today taking some of the characteristics of a congregation. In order to maintain their tax-exempt status, mosques are forced to incorporate boards and bylaws. Imams in the United States are more likely to take on a pastoral role relating to nonreligious functions, such as helping immigrants adjust, and representing the Muslim community to other nonprofit groups serving the larger community.

However more common mosques are in the United States, these symbols of faith and houses of worship still attract a much different kind of attention than a steeple atop a Lutheran church. For many people in the United States, the mosque does not represent religious freedom and diversity or even a curiosity but a foreign threat in yet another example of Orientalism. Mosques are occasionally the focus of either government-initiated surveillance or police protection from anti-Muslim attacks. Muslim groups have found some communities blocking their efforts to build religious centers. Local authorities may require that the building be stripped of cultural symbols and even forgo the traditional dome.

Existing mosques have also experienced city councils blocking their efforts to publicly broadcast their call to prayer over loudspeakers even when neighboring churches just as loudly ring bells to signal the start of worship. Even after accepting some community-driven changes, mosques or Islamic centers often are victims of vandalism. However, there are also signs of acceptance. College campuses experiencing growing numbers of Muslims are adjusting by hiring part-time imams to minister to their needs, dedicating space for Muslims' prayer to be said five times a day, and providing for the restrictions of the Muslim diet (Ba-Yunus and Kone 2004; Leinwand 2004; Leonard 2003; Simon 2004; Wilgoren 2001).

In summary, Muslim Americans reflect a blended identity. **Blended identity** is the self-image and worldview that is a combination of religious faith, cultural background based on nationality, and the status of being a resident of the United States. As shown in Figure 5.8, Muslims often find their daily activities defined by their faith, their nationality, and their status as American, however, defined in terms of citizenship. Younger Muslims, especially, can move freely among the different identities. In Chicago, Muslim college students perform hip-hop in Arabic with lyrics like "La ilaha ila Allah" ("There is no God but Allah"). In Fremont, California, high school Muslim girls and some of their non-Muslim girlfriends hold an alternative prom decked out in silken gowns, dancing to both 50 Cent and Arabic music, dining on lasagna, but pausing at sunset to face toward Mecca and pray (Abdo 2004; Brown 2003; Mostofi 2003).

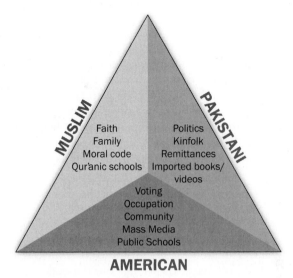

Figure 5.8 Blended Identity of Muslim Americans
Muslim Americans, as shown in this illustration of a Pakistani
Muslim living in the United States, form their identity by
bringing together three different identities: their faith, their
homeland, and the United States.

There is one remaining, basic question: What, if anything, is different about being Muslim in the United States as opposed to an Islamic country? In the United States, we have a Muslim population that numbers in the millions but reflects the diversity of the worldwide Islamic faith and practices their rituals and beliefs in a nation where the expression of Christianity dominates cultur-ally. Some scholars of Islam argue that the experience of democracy and the history of religious diversity and free expression have facilitated a stronger and even more correct Islamic practice—uninhibited by the more totalitarian regimes many find in their homelands. Certainly there is disagreement over what is correct, but there is little pressure outside the Muslim community in the United States about how to precisely follow the teachings of the Prophet Muhammad.

Other scholars contend that what makes the American Muslim experience unique is that followers must place an even stronger focus on Islam in order to survive in a culture that is so permissive and, indeed, encourages so much behavior that is prohibited by either Islamic law or cultural traditions. For many Muslims in the United States, pop culture looks like old-fashioned paganism, a cult that celebrates money and sex. In the United States, many Muslims experience both the freedom to be Muslim and the pressure to be Muslim (Belt 2002).

Religion and the Courts

Religious pluralism owes its existence in the United States to the First Amendment declaration that "Congress shall make no law respecting an establishment of religion, or prohibiting the free exercise thereof." The U.S. Supreme Court has consistently interpreted this wording to mean not that government should ignore religion but that it should follow a policy of neutrality to maximize religious freedom. For example, the government may not help religion by financing a new church building, but it also may not obstruct religion by denying a church adequate police and fire protection. We will examine four issues that continue to require clarification: school prayer, secessionist minorities, creationism (including intelligent design), and the public display of religious symbols.

Among the most controversial and continuing disputes has been whether prayer has a role in the schools. Many people were disturbed by the 1962 Supreme Court decision in *Engel v. Vitale* that disallowed a purportedly nondenominational prayer drafted for use in the New York public schools. The prayer was "Almighty God, we acknowledge our dependence upon Thee, and we beg Thy blessings upon us, our parents, our teachers, and our country." Subsequent decisions overturned state laws requiring Bible reading in public schools, laws requiring recitation of the Lord's Prayer, and laws permitting a daily one-minute period of silent meditation or prayer. Despite such judicial pronouncements, children in many public schools in the United States are led in regular prayer recitation or Bible reading.

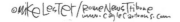

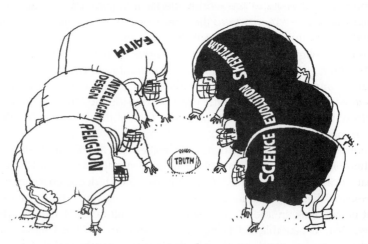

Competing interests argue over the inclusion of Intelligent Design as a valid aspect of science curriculum in public schools.

What about prayers at public gatherings? In 1992, the Supreme Court ruled 5:4 in *Lee v. Weisman* that prayer at a junior high school graduation in Providence, Rhode Island, violated the U.S. Constitution's mandate of separation of church and state. A rabbi had given thanks to God in his invocation. The district court suggested that the invocation would have been acceptable without that reference. The Supreme Court did not agree with the school board that a prayer at a graduation was not coercive. The Court did say in its opinion that it was acceptable for a student speaker voluntarily to say a prayer at such a program (Marshall 2001).

Public schools and even states have mandated a "moment of silence" at the start of the school day in what critics contend is a transparent attempt to get around *Lee v. Weisman*. The Supreme Court had struck down such actions earlier, but then prayer was clearly intended by legislators when they created these "moments." More recent mandates such as those in Illinois in 2007 have not had such explicit provisions, but more legal actions are expected to challenge such actions in public schools (Robelen 2007).

Several religious groups have been in legal and social conflict with the rest of society. Some can be called secessionist minorities in that they reject both assimilation and coexistence in some form of cultural pluralism. The Amish are one such group that comes into conflict with outside society because of its beliefs and way of life. The Old Order Amish shun most modern conveniences, and later in this chapter we will consider them as a case study of maintaining a lifestyle dramatically different from that of larger society.

Are there limits to the free exercise of religious rituals by secessionist minorities? Today, tens of thousands of members of Native American religions believe that ingesting the powerful drug peyote is a sacrament and that those who partake of peyote will enter into direct contact with God. In 1990, the Supreme Court ruled that prosecuting people who use illegal drugs as part of a religious ritual is not a violation of the First Amendment guarantee of religious freedom. The case arose because Native Americans were dismissed from their jobs for the religious use of peyote and were then refused unemployment benefits by the State of Oregon's employment division. In 1991, however, Oregon enacted a new law permitting the sacramental use of peyote by Native Americans (*New York Times* 1991).

In another ruling on religious rituals, in 1993, the Supreme Court unanimously overturned a local ordinance in Florida that banned ritual animal sacrifice. The High Court held that this law violated the free-exercise rights of adherents of the Santeria religion, in which the sacrifice of animals (including goats, chickens, and other birds) plays a central role. The same year, Congress passed the Religious Freedom Restoration Act, which said the government may not enforce laws that "substantially burden" the exercise of religion. Presumably, this action will give religious groups more flexibility in practicing their faiths. However, many local and state officials are concerned that the law has led to unintended consequences, such as forcing states to accommodate prisoners' requests for questionable religious activities or to permit a church to expand into a historic district in defiance of local laws (Greenhouse 1996).

The third area of contention has been whether the biblical account of creation should be or must be presented in school curricula and whether this account should receive the same emphasis as scientific theories. In the famous "monkey trial" of 1925, Tennessee schoolteacher John Scopes was found guilty of teaching the scientific theory of evolution in public schools. Since then, however, Darwin's evolutionary theories have been presented in public schools with little reference to the biblical account in Genesis. People who support the literal interpretation of the Bible, commonly known as **creationists,** have formed various organizations to crusade for creationist treatment in U.S. public schools and universities.

In a 1987 Louisiana case, *Edwards v. Aguillard,* the Supreme Court ruled that states may not require the teaching of creationism alongside evolution in public schools if the primary purpose of such legislation is to promote a religious viewpoint. Nevertheless, the teaching of evolution and creationism has remained a controversial issue in many communities across the United States (Applebome 1996).

Beginning in the 1980s, those who believe in a divine hand in the creation of life have advanced intelligent design (ID). Although not explicitly drawn on the biblical account, creationists feel comfortable with ID. **Intelligent design** is the idea that life is so complex it could only have been created by a higher intelligence. Supporters of ID advocate that it is a more accurate account than Darwinism or, at the very least, that it be taught as an alternative alongside the theory of evolution. In 2005, a federal judge in *Kitzmiller v. Dove Area School District* ended a Pennsylvania school district intention to require the presentation of ID. In essence, the judge found ID to be "a religious belief" that was only a subtler way of finding God's fingerprints in nature than traditional creationism. Because the issue continues to be hotly debated, future court cases are certain to come (Clemmitt 2005; Goodstein 2005).

The fourth area of contention has been a battle over public displays that depict symbols of or seem associated with a religion. Can manger scenes be erected on public property? Do people have a right to be protected from large displays such as a cross or a star atop a water tower overlooking an entire town? In a series of decisions in the 1980s through 1995, the Supreme Court ruled that tax-supported religious displays on public government property may be successfully challenged but are not permissible if they are made more secular. Displays that combine a crèche, the Christmas manger scene depicting the birth of Jesus, or the Hanukkah menorah and also include Frosty the Snowman or even Christmas trees have been ruled secular. These decisions have been dubbed "the plastic reindeer rules." In 1995, the Court clarified the issue by stating that privately sponsored religious displays may be allowed on public property if other forms of expression are permitted in the same location. The final judicial word has not been heard, and all these rulings should be viewed as tentative because the Court cases have been decided by close votes. Changes in the Supreme Court composition also may alter the outcome of future cases (Bork 1995; Hirsley 1991; Mauro 1995).

Limits of Religious Freedom: The Amish

The Amish began migrating to North America early in the eighteenth century and settled first in eastern Pennsylvania, where a large settlement is still found. Those who continued the characteristic lifestyle of the Amish are primarily members of the Old Order Amish Mennonite Church. By 2003, there were about 1,400 Old Order Amish settlements in the United States and Canada. Estimates place this faith and other Amish groups at about 200,000, with the majority living in three states: Ohio, Pennsylvania, and Indiana.

The Amish Way of Life

Amish practice self-segregation, living in settlements divided into church districts that are autonomous congregations composed of about seventy-five baptized members. If the district becomes much larger, it is again divided because the members meet in each other's homes. There are no church buildings. Amish homes are large, with the main floor often having removable walls so a household can take its periodic turn hosting the Sunday service.

Each Amish district has a bishop, two to four preachers, and an elder but there are no general conferences, mission groups, or cooperative agencies. The Amish differ little from the Mennonites in formal religious doctrine. Holy Communion is celebrated twice each year, and both groups practice washing of feet. Adults are baptized when they are admitted to formal membership in the church at about age 17–20. Old Order Amish services are conducted in German with a mixture of English, commonly known as Pennsylvania Dutch (from Deutsch, the German word for "German").

The Amish are best known for their plain clothing and their nonconformist way of life. Sociologists sometimes use the term **secessionist minorities** to refer to groups such as the Amish, who reject assimilation and practice coexistence or pluralism with the rest of society primarily on their own terms. The practice of Meidung, or shunning, persists, and sociologists view it as central to the Amish system of social control. The social norms of this secessionist minority that have evolved over the years are known as the Ordnung. These oral "expectations" or "understandings" specify the color and style of clothing, color and style of buggies, the use of horses for fieldwork, the use of the Pennsylvania Dutch dialect, worship services in the homes, unison singing without instruments, and marriage within the church, to name a few.

The Amish shun telephones and electric lights, and they drive horses and buggies rather than automobiles. The Ordnung also prohibits filing a lawsuit, entering military service, divorce, using air transportation, and even using wall-to-wall carpeting. They are generally considered excellent farmers, but they often refuse to use modern farm machinery. Concessions have been made but do vary from one Amish settlement to another. Among common exceptions to the Ordnung is the use of chemical fertilizers, insecticides, and pesticides, the use of indoor bathroom facilities, and modern medical and dental practice. Some Amish subgroups tolerate exceptions such as the use of bicycles, milking machines,and power lawn mowers, to name a few.

The Amish and Larger Society

The Amish have made some concessions to the dominant society, but larger society has made concessions to the Amish to facilitate their lifestyle. For example, in 1972, the U.S. Supreme Court, in *Yoder v. Wisconsin,* allowed Wisconsin Amish to escape prosecution from laws that required parents to send their children to school until age 18. Amish education ends at about age 13 because the community feels their members have received all the schooling necessary to prosper as Amish people. States waive certification requirements for Amish teaching staff (who are other Amish people), minimum wage requirements for the teachers, and school building requirements.

The Amish today do not totally reject social change. For example, until the late 1960s, church members could be excommunicated for being employed in other than agricultural pursuits. Now their work is much more diversified. Although you will not find Amish computer programmers, there are Amish engaged as blacksmiths, harness makers, buggy repairers, and carpenters. Non-Amish often hire these craftspeople as well.

The Amish, as shown in this group of young women on a farm in Kentucky, have made relatively few accommodations with the larger culture—the culture of outsiders referred collectively to by the Amish as the "English."

The movement by the Amish into other occupations is sometimes a source of tension with larger society, or the "English," as the Amish refer to non-Amish people. Conflict theorists observe that as long as the Amish remained totally apart from dominant society in the United States, they experienced little hostility. As they entered the larger economic sector, however, intergroup tensions developed in the form of growing prejudice. The Amish today may underbid their competitors.

The Amish entry into the commercial marketplace has also strained the church's traditional teaching on litigation and insurance, both of which are to be avoided. Mutual assistance has been the historical path taken, but that does not always mesh well with the modern businessperson. After legal action taken on their behalf, Amish businesses typically have been allowed to be exempt from paying Social Security and workers' compensation, another sore point with English competitors.

Children are not sent to high schools. This practice caused the Amish some difficulty because of compulsory school attendance laws, and some Amish parents have gone to jail rather than allow their children to go to high school. Eventually, as noted earlier, the Supreme Court, in *Yoder v. Wisconsin,* upheld a lower court's decision that a Wisconsin compulsory education law violated the Amish right to religious freedom. However, not all court rulings have been friendly to Amish efforts to avoid the practices and customs of the English. In another case, the effort by the Amish to avoid using the legally mandated orange triangles for marking slow-moving vehicles (such as their buggies) was rejected. If you travel through Amish areas, you can now see their horse-drawn buggies displaying this one symbol of modernity.

Living alongside this modernity, Amish youth often test their subculture's boundaries during a period of discovery called Rumspringa, a term that means "running around." Amish young people attend barn dances where taboos like drinking, smoking, and driving cars are commonly broken. Parents often react by looking the other way, sometimes literally. For example, when they hear radio sounds from a barn or motorcycle entering their property in the middle of the night, they do not immediately investigate and punish their offspring. Instead, they pretend not to notice, secure in the comfort that their children almost always return to the traditions of the Amish lifestyle. In 2004, UPN aired the "Amish in the City" reality program featuring five Amish youths, allegedly on Rumspringa, moving in with six city-wise young adults in Los Angeles. Critics on behalf of the Amish community noted that this exploitation showed how vulnerable the Amish are, since no program was developed to try to show the conversion of Muslim or Orthodox Jewish youth.

A growing area of Amish–English legal clashes is over the custom of young Amish children working as laborers. Amish families in western and central Pennsylvania in 1998 protested the federal government's enforcement of labor laws that are intended to protect children from workplace hazards. The Amish are turning to new businesses, such as sawmills and wood shops, as their available farmland begins to disappear. That means more children on the shop floor. The Amish contend that their religious and cultural traditions hold that children should work, but the U.S. Labor Department had taken a different view. The Amish argued that letting children work alongside their fathers instills core values of hard work, diligence, cooperation, and responsibility, values that they say are central to their faith. English businesses see this under-age employment as another form of unfair competition by the Amish. In 2004, Congress passed the law with the Amish in mind that exempted such child labor as long as machinery is not operated and adults are present.

The Old Order Amish have developed a pluralistic position that has become increasingly difficult to maintain as their numbers grow and as they enter the economy in competition with the English, or the non-Amish (Dart 1998; *Economist* 2004a; Kraybill 2001, 2003, 2008; Kraybill and Nolt 1995; Public Broadcasting System 1998; Schaefer and Zellner 2008).

Conclusion

Considering ethnicity and religion rein-forces our understanding of the patterns of intergroup relations first presented in Chapter 1. Figure 5.9 shows the rich variety of relationships as defined by people's eth-nic and religious identity. The profiles of Irish, Italian, and Polish Americans reflect the variety of White ethnic experiences.

Any study of life in the United States, especially one focusing on dominant and subordinate groups, cannot ignore religion and ethnicity. The two are closely related, as certain religious faiths predominate in certain nationalities. Both religious activity

and interest by White ethnics in their her-itage continue to be prominent features of the contemporary scene. People have been and continue to be ridiculed or deprived of opportunities solely because of their ethnic or religious affiliation. To get a true picture of people's place in society, we need to consider both ethnicity and social class (or what has been called ethclass) in associa-tion with their religious identification.

Religion is changing in the United States. As one commercial measure, Hall-mark created its first greeting card in 2003 for the Muslim holiday Eid-al-fitr, which

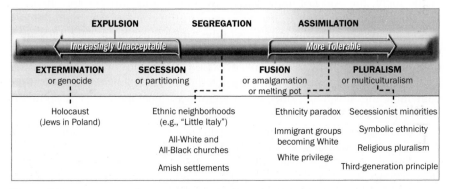

Figure 5.9 Intergroup Relations Continuum

marks the end of the month-long fast of Ramadan. The issue of the persistence of ethnicity is an intriguing one. Some people may only casually exhibit their ethnicity and practice what has been called symbolic ethnicity. However, can people immerse themselves in their ethnic culture without society punishing them for their will to be different? The tendency to put down White ethnics through respectable bigotry continues. Despite this intolerance, ethnicity remains a viable source of identity for many citizens today. There is also the **ethnicity paradox,** which finds that practicing one's ethnic heritage often strengthens people and allows them to move successfully into the larger society.

The issue of religious expression in all its forms also raises a variety of intriguing questions. How can a country increasingly populated by diverse and often non-Christian faiths maintain religious tolerance? How might this change in decades ahead? How will the courts and society resolve the issues of religious freedom? This is a particularly important issue in areas such as school prayer, secessionist minorities, creationism, intelligent design, and public religious displays. Some examination of religious ties is fundamental to completing an accurate picture of a person's social identity.

Ethnicity and religion are a basic part of today's social reality and of each individual's identity. The emotions, disputes, and debate over religion and ethnicity in the United States are powerful indeed.

Key Terms

bilingual education 181	English immersion 182	symbolic ethnicity 162
bilingualism 181	ethnicity paradox 203	White privilege 160
blended identity 194	intelligent design 198	
civil religion 188	principle of third-generation	
creationists 198	interest 161	
denomination 185	secessionist minority 199	

Review Questions

1. In what respects are ethnic and religious diversity in the United States related to each other?
2. Is assimilation automatic within any given ethnic group?
3. Apply "Whiteness" to Irish, Italian, and Polish Americans.
4. To what extent has a non-Christian tradition been developing in the United States?
5. How have court rulings affected religious expression?

Critical Thinking

1. When do you see ethnicity becoming more apparent? When does it appear to occur only in response to other people's advancing their own ethnicity? From these situations, how can ethnic identity be both positive and perhaps counterproductive or even destructive?

2. Why do you think we are so often reluctant to show our religion to others? Why might people of certain faiths be more hesitant than others?

3. How does religion reflect conservative and liberal positions on social issues? Consider services for the homeless, the need for child care, the acceptance or rejection of gay men and lesbians, and a woman's right to terminate a pregnancy versus the fetus's right to survive.

Internet Connections—Research Navigator™

Follow the instructions found on page 35 of this text to access the features of Research Navigator™. Once at the Web site, enter your login Name and password. Then, to use the ContentSelect database, enter keywords such as "Mormons," "Amish," and "Whiteness studies," and the research engine will supply relevant and recent scholarly and popular press publications. Use the *New York Times* Search-by-Subject Archive to find recent news articles related to sociology and the Link Library feature to locate relevant Web links organized by the key terms associated with this chapter.

6 The Nation as a Kaleidoscope

CHAPTER OUTLINE

─────────────── ⟨ HIGHLIGHTS ⟩ ───────────────

The nation is likened to a kaleidoscope because the diverse population has not fused into a melting pot, nor is the future composition apt to be as static as a salad bowl. Although nationally, there is considerable, growing diversity, this mosaic varies considerably from one state to another. Racial and ethnic subordinate groups are making progress economically and educationally, but so are Whites. Even relatively successful Asian Americans are undeserving of their model-minority stereotype. That is not the only stereotype widely expressed as one considers the notion that African Americans avoid success in school for fear of being "acting White." We consider whether our face-to-face interaction takes advantage of our diverse society or whether we interpret our social surroundings to conform to more intolerant views of one another.

What metaphor do we use to describe a nation whose racial, ethnic, and religious minorities are now becoming numerical majorities in cities coast-to-coast, as already in the states of California, Hawaii, and Texas (refer to Figure 1.2)? The outpouring of statistical data and personal experience documents the racial and ethnic diversity of the entire nation. And as we see in our compilation of "Top Ten" lists in Table 6.1 (see pp. 208–209), although the mosaic may be different in different regions and different communities, the tapestry of racial and ethnic groups is always close at hand wherever one is in the United States.

Although E Pluribus Unum may be reassuring, it does not describe what a visitor sees along the length of Fifth Avenue in Manhattan or in Monterey Park outside Los Angeles. It is apparent in the increasing numbers of Latinos in the rural river town of Beardstown, Illinois, and the emerging Somali immigrant population in Lewiston, Maine.

For several generations, the melting pot has been used as a convenient description of our culturally diverse nation. The analogy of an alchemist's cauldron was clever, even if a bit jingoistic—in the Middle Ages, the alchemist attempted to change less costly metals into gold and silver.

Melting Pot and Kaleidoscope

The phrase *melting pot* originated as the title of a 1908 play by Israel Zangwill. In this play, a young Russian Jewish immigrant to the United States composes a symphony that portrays a nation that serves as a crucible (or pot) where all ethnic and racial groups dissolve into a new, superior stock.

The belief of the United States as a melting pot became widespread in the first part of the twentieth century, particularly because it suggested that the United States had an almost divinely inspired mission to destroy artificial divisions and create a single humankind. However, the dominant group had indicated its unwillingness to welcome Native Americans, African Americans, Hispanics, Jews, and Asians, among many others, into the melting pot.

Although the metaphor of the melting pot is still used today, observers recognize that it hides as much about a multiethnic United States as it discloses. Therefore, the metaphor of the salad bowl emerged in the 1970s to portray a country ethnically diverse. As we can distinguish the lettuce from the tomatoes from the peppers in a tossed salad, we can see the ethnic restaurants and the persistence of "foreign" language newspapers. The dressing over the ingredients is akin to the shared value system and culture, covering, but not hiding, the different ingredients of the salad.

Yet even the notion of a salad bowl is wilting. Like its melting-pot predecessor, the picture of a salad is static—certainly not what we see in the United States. It also hardly calls to mind the myriad cultural pieces that make up the fabric or mosaic of our diverse nation.

The kaleidoscope offers another familiar, yet more useful, analogy. Patented in 1817 by Scottish scientist Sir David Brewster, the kaleidoscope is both a toy and increasingly a table artifact of upscale living rooms. Users of this optical device are aware that when they turn a set of mirrors, the colors and patterns reflected off pieces of glass, tinsel, or beads seem to be endless. The growing popularity of the phrase "people of color" seems made for the kaleidoscope that is the United States. The changing images correspond to the often-bewildering array of groups found in our country.

How easy is it to describe the image to someone else as we gaze into the eyepiece of a kaleidoscope? It is a challenge similar to that faced by educators who toil with what constitutes the ethnic history of the United States. We can forgive the faux pas by the *Washington Post* writer who described the lack of Hispanic-speaking (rather than Spanish-speaking) police as a factor contributing to the recent hostilities in the capital. Little wonder, given the bewildering ethnic patterns, that Chicago politicians striving to map for the first time a "safe" Hispanic congressional district find themselves scrutinized by Blacks fearful of losing their "safe" districts. We can forgive Marlon Brando for sending an Indian woman to refuse his Oscar, thus protesting Hollywood's portrayal of Native Americans. Was he unaware of Italian Americans' disbelief

Table 6.1 Top Ten Lists

(Largest concentration by percentage by state in 2006)

White Americans (non-Hispanic)

1.	Vermont	95.6
2.	Maine	95.3
3.	West Virginia	94.1
4.	New Hampshire	93.6
5.	Iowa	91.0
6.	North Dakota	90.4
7.	Montana	88.6
8.	Kentucky	88.3
9.	Wyoming	88.0
10.	South Dakota	86.5

Foreign Born

1.	California	27.2
2.	New York	21.6
3.	New Jersey	20.1
4.	Nevada	19.1
5.	Florida	18.9
6.	Hawaii	16.3
7.	Texas	15.9
8.	Arizona	15.1
9.	Massachusetts	14.1
10.	Illinois	12.9

Multiracial (indicate two or more races)

1.	Hawaii	21.5
2.	Alaska	8.1
3.	Oklahoma	6.1
4.	California	3.3
5.	Washington	3.3
6.	Nevada	3.2
7.	New Mexico	3.2
8.	Oregon	3.0
9.	Colorado	2.6
10.	Kansas	2.5

Hispanic or Latino

1.	New Mexico	44.0
2.	California	37.9
3.	Arizona	29.2
4.	Nevada	24.4
5.	Florida	20.1

Table 6.1 Top Ten Lists (*continued*)

6.	Colorado	19.7
7.	New York	16.3
8.	New Jersey	15.6
9.	Utah	11.2
10.	Rhode Island	11.0

African Americans

1.	Mississippi	37.4
2.	Louisiana	31.6
3.	Georgia	29.8
4.	Maryland	28.9
5.	South Carolina	28.6
6.	Alabama	26.3
7.	North Carolina	20.7
8.	Delaware	19.6
9.	Virginia	16.8
10.	Tennessee	15.6

Native Americans (American Indians and Alaska Natives)

1.	Alaska	13.1
2.	New Mexico	9.7
3.	South Dakota	8.6
4.	Oklahoma	6.8
5.	Montana	6.3
6.	North Dakota	5.2
7.	Arizona	4.5
8.	Wyoming	2.2
9.	Oregon	1.8
10.	Washington	1.5

Asian American and Pacific Islanders (including Native Hawaiians)

1.	Hawaii	48.6
2.	California	12.7
3.	New Jersey	7.0
4.	Washington	7.0
5.	New York	6.9
6.	Nevada	6.3
7.	Alaska	5.1
8.	Maryland	5.0
9.	Massachusetts	4.9
10.	Virginia	4.9

Source: Bureau of the Census 2007b. Tables GCT0203, R0202, R0204, R0205, R0207, R0501, and S0201.

when his award-winning performance was in The Godfather? We can understand why the African Americans traumatized by Hurricane Katrina would turn their antagonism from the White power structure that they perceived as ignoring their needs to the Latinos who took advantage of reconstruction projects in New Orleans.

It is difficult to describe the image created by a kaleidoscope because it changes dramatically with little effort. Similarly, in the kaleidoscope of the United States, we find it a challenge to describe the multiracial nature of this republic. Perhaps in viewing the multiethnic, multiracial United States as a kaleidoscope, we may take comfort that the Greek word kalos means "beautiful" (Schaefer 1992).

In order to develop a better understanding of the changing image through the kaleidoscope, we will first try to learn what progress has taken place and why miscommunication among our diverse peoples seems to be the rule rather than the exception.

The Glass Half Empty

A common expression makes reference to a glass half full or half empty of water. If one is thirsty, it is half empty and in need of being replenished. If one is attempting to clear dirty dishes, it is half full. For many people, especially Whites, the progress of subordinate groups or minorities makes it difficult to understand calls for more programs and new reforms and impossible to understand when minority neighborhoods erupt in violence.

In absolute terms, the glass of water has been filling up, but people in the early twenty-first century do not compare themselves with people in the 1960s. For example, Latinos and African Americans regard the appropriate reference group to be Whites today; compared with them, the glass is half empty at best.

In Figure 6.1, we have shown the present picture and recent changes by comparing African Americans and Hispanics with Whites as well as contemporary data for Native Americans (American Indians). We see that the nation's largest minority groups—African Americans and Hispanics—have higher household income, complete more schooling, and enjoy longer life expectancy today than in 1975. White Americans have made similar strides in all three areas. The gap remains and, if one analyzes it closely, has actually increased in some instances. Both Blacks and Latinos in 2005 had just edged out the income level that Whites had exceeded back in 1975. Three decades behind! Also, Black Americans today have barely matched the life expectancy that Whites had a generation earlier. Similarly, many minority Americans remain entrenched in poverty: nearly one out of four Hispanics and African Americans.

Little has changed since 1975. We have chosen 1975 because that was a year for which we have comparable data for Latinos, Whites, and African

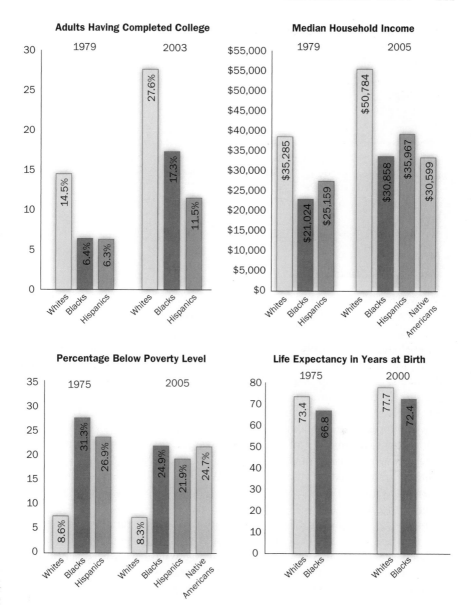

Figure 6.1 Changes in Schooling, Income, and Life Expectancy

Note: Native American data are for 2000. Education data include people 25 and over. Hispanic education 1975 data estimated by author from data for 1970 and 1980. White data are for non-Hispanic (except in education).

Sources: Bureau of the Census 1988, p. 167, 2005a, p. 44; DeNavas-Walt et al. 2006, pp. 17–20; Ogunwole 2006.

Ask Yourself

Are single images deceiving or do they help us understand social reality? Images of successful people like comedian George Lopez lead us to think racial and ethnic groups have truly "arrived." But what about the image of a barrio in urban America?

Americans. However, the patterns would be no different if we considered 1950, 1960, or 1970.

These data provide only the broadest overview. Detailed analyses do not yield a brighter picture. For example, about 1 in 9 Whites were without health insurance in 2005 compared to 1 of 5 African Americans and 1 of 3 Latinos. Similarly, 3.9 percent of all doctorates were awarded to African Americans in 1981. By 2002, the proportion had increased only to 5.4 percent. The United States continues to rely on overseas students to fill the places on the educational ladder. The number of doctorates awarded to nonresident aliens (i.e., immigrants who gained entry for schooling with no other ties to U.S. citizens) was three times that of Blacks, Asian Americans, Latinos, and American Indians *combined* (Bureau of the Census 2005a; DeNavas-Walt et al. 2006; Hoffer et al. 2001).

Stereotypes are not dead, even if color-blind racism renders them to be expressed less often in public and even in private. However, two generalizations persist widely—model minority and acting White. We will next consider the notions that Asian Americans are a model minority and that African American youth avoid success in fear of being viewed as "acting White."

The "Model Minority" Image Explored

"Asian Americans are a success! They achieve! They succeed! There are no protests, no demands. They just do it!" This is the general image that people in the United States so often hold of Asian Americans as a group. They constitute

a **model or ideal minority** because, although they have experienced prejudice and discrimination, they seem to have succeeded economically, socially,
and educationally without resorting to political or violent confrontations with
Whites. Some observers point to the existence of a model minority as a reaffir-
mation that anyone can get ahead in the United States. Proponents of the
model minority view declare that because Asian Americans have achieved success, they have ceased to be subordinate and are no longer disadvantaged.
This is only a variation of blaming the victim; with Asian Americans, it is "prais-
ing the victim." An examination of aspects of their socioeconomic status will
allow a more thorough exploration of this view (Chang and Demyan 2007;
Fong 2002; Hurh and Kim 1989; Thrupkaew 2002).

Asian Americans, as a group, have impressive school enrollment rates in
comparison to the total population. In 2004, 48.2 percent of Asian Americans
25 years old or older held bachelor's degrees, compared with 29.7 percent of
the non-Hispanic White population. These rates vary among Asian American
groups, with Asian Indians, Korean Americans, and Chinese Americans having
higher levels of educational achievement than others (Bureau of the Census
2007a).

This encouraging picture does have some qualifications, however, which
call into question the optimistic model minority view. According to a study of
California's state university system, although Asian Americans often are viewed
as successful overachievers, they have unrecognized and overlooked needs
and experience discomfort and harassment on campus. As a group, they also
lack Asian faculty and staff members to whom they can turn for support. They
confront many identity issues and have to do a "cultural balancing act" along
with all the usual pressures faced by college students. The report noted that an
"alarming number" of Asian American students appear to be experiencing
intense stress and alienation, problems that have often been "exacerbated by
racial harassment" (Ohnuma 1991; Zhou 2004).

Even the positive stereotype of Asian American students as "academic stars"
or "whiz kids" can be burdensome to the people so labeled. Asian Americans
who do only modestly well in school may face criticism from their parents or
teachers for their failure to conform to the "whiz kid" image. Some Asian
American youths disengage from school when faced with these expectations
or receive little support for their interest in vocational pursuits or athletics
(Kibria 2002).

That Asian Americans as a group work in the same occupations as Whites
suggests that they have been successful, and many have. However, the pattern
shows some differences. Asian immigrants, like other minorities and immigrants
before them, are found disproportionately in the low-paying service occupations. At the same time, they are also concentrated at the top in professional
and managerial positions. Yet as we will see, they rarely reach the very top.
They hit the glass ceiling (as described in Chapter 3) or, as some others say, try

SECRET ASIAN MAN by Tak Toyoshima

Discussions of race and ethnicity often leave out Asian Americans, yet Asian Americans too are subject to stereotypes today such as the model-minority image. (United Media/United Feature Syndicate, Inc).

to "climb a broken ladder," before they reach management. In 2002, only 2 percent of 11,500 people who serve on the boards of the nation's 1,000 largest corporations were Asian American (Strauss 2002).

The absence of Asian Americans as top executives also indicates that their success is not complete. Asian Americans have done well in small businesses and modest agricultural ventures. Although self-employed and managing their own businesses, Asian Americans have had very modest-sized operations. Because of the long hours of work, the income from such a business may be below prevailing wage standards, so even when they are business owners, they may still constitute cheap labor, although they also get the profits. Chinese restaurants, Korean American cleaning businesses and fruit and vegetable stores and motels, gasoline stations, and newspaper vending businesses operated by Asian Indians fall into this category.

Another misleading sign of the apparent success of Asian Americans is their high incomes as a group. Like other elements of the image, however, this deserves closer inspection. Asian American family income approaches parity with that of Whites because of their greater achievement than Whites in formal schooling. If we look at specific educational levels, Whites earn more than their Asian counterparts of the same age. Asian Americans' average earnings increased by at least $2,300 for each additional year of schooling, whereas Whites gained almost $3,000. Asian Americans as a group have significantly more formal schooling but, actually, have lower household family income. We should note that, to some degree, some Asian Americans' education is from

From Kawasaki to Chicago

Miku Ishii

I was born a citizen of Japan in an area named Kawasaki, which is basically the suburbs of Tokyo. My parents raised me in a small apartment in Kawasaki until I was six years old. From then, my father's company decided to transfer him to the U.S. and my mother, my father and my brother all moved to Illinois. Japanese is my native language and as I came to America, I was forced to learn English. It took me 4 years in bilingual school to fully be able to speak English and get sent off to the "regular" school where there were no foreigners like me. Since we moved to the Northwest suburbs of Chicago, I grew up with mostly Caucasian kids and a mediocre percentage of Asians. There were hardly any African American people in the town of Schaumburg. In elementary school, I was mistreated so badly at my "regular" school that I hardly spoke and was incredibly shy.

The very first time I had experienced the excruciating pain of pure racism was when I was only in the second grade. A Caucasian girl with big bright blue eyes and short bouncy blonde hair had a habit of picking at me constantly. She said it was because of my slanted slim slits of an eye. It was because of my dark jet-black pigtails that hung thick as horses tail around my face. One afternoon during recess, I climbed up a dome that she also happened to be on. As she saw me coming near, she jumped back down on the ground and ran to the teacher. The next thing I knew, my teacher was punishing me, saying that I should not be pushing this grinning blonde haired blue-eyed girl. At the time, I was only a beginner in bilingual class so I was barely able to say anything but "Where is the bathroom?" and "I don't know." I tried to explain to the teacher. But all that came out were words in Japanese. Of course they looked at me wide eyed, as I tried to speak broken English with Japanese. Finally, the teacher, who could not understand me to hear my self-defense, banned me from going out to recess for a week. I was furious and embarrassed and felt ashamed of my race.

Even the bus ride to school and back could not be near peaceful for me. The back of the bus was where all the cool white kids sat. When I would try to sit in the back because there were no other seats, those kids would call me Chinese or chink and make that obnoxious sound which clearly mocked the language. Some days they threw chewed gum at me. Not because I did anything to them. But because I was a chink and they wanted to see how crazy I would react. I would always just ignore it and stay quiet. I wanted to make it seem like it did not bother me, but inside, it was breaking my heart. Heck, I was not even Chinese but I was always called that in such disdainful manner. Going to school became something I feared. I remember I felt so miserable and ashamed to death for being born "Chinese." All I wanted was to be white.

I stand here today still remembering those days very vividly. In all essence, those experiences have molded me into person that I am today. I like to think that I am very open-minded and I love diversity. I love to learn about other cultures and I have a very ethnic variety of friends. I would say relative to others, my multicultural experience has been rich because of the fact that I am an immigrant, a minority. And as I have expressed before, for many years when I first came to the United States, I have experienced so much hate and prejudice for just being born my race. I am still a citizen of Japan to this day and I go back to Kawasaki about every 2 years. I feel that I have grown up in two different worlds. The experiences that I have undergone have made me accept people at face value. A lot of times for me, I forget about color because I never judge by race but I am also not oblivious or blind to the fact that racism does exist. I think, as sad as it sounds, that it is an evil that will never go away.

Source: Ishii, M. 2006.

overseas and, therefore, may be devalued by U.S. employers. Yet in the end, educational attainment does pay off as much if you are of Asian descent as it does for White non-Hispanics (Wu 2002; Zeng and Xie 2004; Zhou and Kamo 1994).

There are striking contrasts among Asian Americans. Nevertheless, for every Asian American family with an annual income of $75,000 or more, another earns less than $10,000 a year. In New York City's Chinatown neighborhood, about one-quarter of all families live below the poverty level. In San Diego, dropout rates were close to 60 percent among Southeast Asians in 1997. Even successful Asian Americans continue to face obstacles because of their racial heritage. According to a study of three major public hospitals in Los Angeles, Asian Americans account for 34 percent of all physicians and nurses but fill only 11 percent of management positions at these hospitals (Dunn 1994; Reeves and Bennett 2003; Sengupta 1997).

At first, one might be puzzled to see criticism of a positive generalization such as "model minority." Why should the stereotype of adjusting without problems be a disservice to Asian Americans? The answer is that this incorrect view helps to exclude Asian Americans from social programs and conceals unemployment and other social ills. When representatives of Asian groups do seek assistance for those in need, those who have accepted the model minority stereotype resent them. If a minority group is viewed as successful, it is unlikely that its members will be included in programs designed to alleviate the problems they encounter as minorities. The positive stereotype reaffirms the United States system of mobility. New immigrants as well as established subordinate groups ought to achieve more merely by working within the system. At the same time, viewed from the conflict perspective outlined in Chapter 1, this becomes yet another instance of "blaming the victim"; if Asian Americans have succeeded, Blacks and Latinos must be responsible for their own low status (Committee of 100 2001; Ryan 1976).

For young Asian Americans, life in the United States often is a struggle for one's identity when their heritage is so devalued by those in positions of influence. In Listen to Our Voices, we follow the trek of a Japanese-born young woman coming of age in the Midwest, which underscores the path that most Asian Americans take far from the model minority stereotype. Sometimes identity means finding a role in White America; other times, it involves finding a place among Asian Americans collectively, the panethnicity we spoke of in Chapter 1, and then locating oneself within one's own racial or ethnic community. Now we turn to the issue of identity and quite a different stereotype.

Acting White, Acting Black, or Neither

A common view advanced by some educators is that the reason African Americans, especially males, do not succeed in school is that they do not want to be caught "**acting White.**" That is, they avoid at all costs taking school seriously and do not accept the authority of teachers and administrators. Whatever the accuracy of such a generalization, acting White clearly shifts the responsibility of low school attainment from the school to the individual and, therefore, can be seen as yet another example of blaming the victim. Acting White is also associated with speaking proper English or cultural preferences like listening to rock music rather than prefering Hip Hop (Feguson 2007; Fordham and Ogbu 1986; Fryer 2006; Ogbu 2004; Ogbu with Davis 2003).

"Acting White" sparks strong emotions. In 2004, comedian Bill Cosby sparked the latest round of debates on the subject in a NAACP-sponsored speech he made to mark the fiftieth anniversary of the Brown decision. He criticized Black families for tolerating their children not taking school seriously. Social scientists and pundits quickly weighed in not only to deal with the issue but also to question the appropriateness of a Black person criticizing other Blacks in public.

To what extent do Blacks not want to act White in the context of high achievers? Many scholars have noted that individuals' efforts to avoid looking like they want an education has a long history and is hardly exclusive to any one race. Students of all colors may hold back for fear of being accused of as "too hard-working."

Back in the 1950s, one heard disparaging references to "teacher's pet" and "brown nosing." Does popularity come to high school debaters and National Honor Society students or to cheerleaders and athletes? Academic-oriented classmates are often viewed as social misfits, nerds, and geeks and are seen as socially inept even if their skill building will later make them more economically independent and often more socially desirable. For minority children, including African Americans, to take school seriously means they must overcome their White classmates' same desire to be cool and not a nerd. In addition, Black youth must also come to embrace a curriculum and respect teachers who are much less likely to look or sound like them (Chang and Demyan 2007; Feguson 2007; Tyson et al. 2005).

The "acting White" thesis overemphasizes personal responsibility rather than structural features such as quality of schools, curriculum, and teachers. Therefore, it locates the source of Black miseducation—and by implication, the remedy—in the African American household. As scholar Michael Dyson (2005) observes, "When you think the problems are personal, you think the solutions are the same." If we could only get African American parents to encourage their children to work a little harder and act better (i.e., White), everything would be fine. As Dyson notes, "It's hard to argue against any of these things in the abstract; in principle such suggestions sound just fine."

Of course, not all Whites "act White." To equate "acting White" with high academic achievement has little empirical or cultural support. Although more Whites between ages 18 and 19 are in school, the differences are hardly dramatic—64.4 percent of Whites compared to 61.9 percent of Blacks. Studies comparing attitudes and performance show that Black students have the same attitudes—good and bad—about achievement as their White counterparts. Too often we tend to view White slackers who give a hard time to the advanced placement kids as "normal," but when low-performing African Americans do the same thing, it becomes a systemic pathology undermining everything good about schools. The primary stumbling block is not acting White or acting Black but being presented with similar educational opportunities (Bureau of the Census 2005a, 144; Tough 2004; Tyson et al. 2005).

Persistence of Inequality

Progress has occurred. Indignities and injustices have been eliminated allowing us to focus on the remaining barriers to equity. But why do the gaps in income, living wages, education, and even life expectancy persist? Especially perplexing is, is this glass half full or half empty, given the numerous civil rights laws, study commissions, favorable court decisions and efforts by nonprofits, faith-based organizations, and private sectors.

In trying to comprehend the persistence of inequality among racial and ethnic groups, sociologists and other social scientists have found it useful to think in terms of the role played by social and cultural capital. Popularized by the French sociologist Pierre Bourdieu, these concepts refer to assets that are not necessarily economic but do impact economic capital for one's family and future. Less cultural and social capital may be passed on from one generation to the next especially when prejudice and discrimination make it difficult to overcome deficits. Racial and ethnic minorities reproduce disadvantage, while Whites are more likely to reproduce privilege (Bourdieu 1983; Bourdieu and Passeron 1990).

Cultural capital refers to noneconomic forces such as family background, past investments in education that are then reflected in knowledge about the arts and language. It is not necessarily book knowledge but the kind of education

Racial and ethnic minorities may not have the cultural and social capital of privileged Whites, but they treasure their rich heritage. Education on reservations stresses American Indian and tribal culture more than in the past. Pictured is a classroom on the Crow Reservation in Montana.

valued by the elites. African Americans and Native Americans have in the past faced significant restrictions in receiving quality education. Immigrants have faced challenges due to English not being spoken at home. Muslim immigrants face an immediate challenge in functioning in a culture that advantages a different form of spirituality and lifestyle. The general historical pattern has been for immigrants, especially those who came in large numbers and settled in ethnic enclaves, to take two or three generations to reach educational parity. Knowledge of hip-hop and familiarity with Polish cuisine is culture, but it is not the culture that is valued and prestigious. Society privileges or values some lifestyles over others. This is not good, but it is social reality. Differentiating between pirogis will not get you to the top of corporate America as fast as will differentiating among wines. This is, of course, not unique to the United States. Someone settling in Japan would have to deal with cultural capital that includes knowledge of Noh Theatre and tea ceremonies. In most countries, you are much better off following the run-up to the World Cup rather than the contenders for the next Super Bowl (DiMaggio 2005).

Social capital refers to the collective benefit of durable social networks and their patterns of reciprocal trust. Much has been written about the strength of family and friendship networks among all racial and ethnic minorities. Family reunions are major events. Family history and storytelling is rich and full. Kinfolk are not merely acquaintances but truly living assets upon which one depends or, at the very least, feels comfortable to call upon repeatedly. Networks outside the family are critical to coping in a society that often seems to be

❓ Ask Yourself

How common do you think it is for any student for his or her interest in school, or even to underperform, to be cool? The "acting White" stereotype is alive and well despite the academic success of so many African Americans. Pictured here is Howard University, founded in 1867 in Washington DC, which continues to serve as a pivotal institution in the education of African Americans.

determined to keep anyone who looks like you down. But given past as well as current discrimination and prejudice, these social networks may help you become a construction worker, but they are less likely to get you into a board room. Residential and school segregation make developing social capital more difficult. Immigrant professionals find their skills or advanced degrees are devalued, and they are shut out of networks of the educated and influential. Working-class Latino and Black workers have begun to develop informal social ties with their White coworkers and neighbors. Professional immigrants, in time, become accepted as equals, but racial and ethnic minority communities continue to resist institutional marginalization (Coleman 1988; Cranford 2005).

As the ranks of the powerful and important have been reached by all racial and ethnic groups, social capital is more widely shared, but this process has proven to be slower than advocates of social equality would wish. Perhaps accelerating it will be the tendency for successful minority members to be more likely to network with up and coming members of their own community while Whites are more likely to be more comfortable, even complacent, with the next generation making it on their own. We are increasingly appreciative of the importance of aspirations and motivation that is often much more present among people with poor or immigrant backgrounds than those born of affluence. We know that bilingualism is an asset not a detriment. Children who have translated for their parents develop "real-world" skills at a much earlier age than their monolingual English counterparts (Bauder 2003; Monkman et al. 2005; Portes 1998; Yosso 2005).

Considering cultural and social capital does leave room for measured optimism. Racial and ethnic groups have shared their cultural capital whether it be the music we dance to or the food we eat. As the barriers to privilege weaken and eventually fall, people of all colors will be able to advance. The particular strength that African Americans, tribal people, Latinos, Asian Americans, and arriving immigrants bring to the table is that they also have the ability to resist and to refuse to accept second-class status. The role that cultural and social capital play also points to the need to embrace strategies of intervention that will increasingly acknowledge the skills and talents found in a pluralistic society.

Talking Past One Another

African Americans, Italian Americans, Korean Americans, Puerto Ricans, Native Americans, Mexican Americans, and many others live in the United States and interact daily, sometimes face-to-face and constantly through the media. But communication does not mean we listen to, much less understand, one another. Sometimes, we assume that, as we become a nation educated, we will set aside our prejudices. Yet, in recent years, our college campuses have been the scenes of tension, insults, and even violence. Fletcher Blanchard, Teri Lilly, and Leigh Ann Vaughn (1991) conducted an experiment at Smith College and found that even overheard statements can influence expressions of opinion on the issue of racism.

The researchers asked a student who said she was conducting an opinion poll for a class to approach seventy-two White students as each was walking across the campus. Each time she did so, she also stopped a second White student—actually a confederate working with the researchers—and asked her to participate in the survey as well. Both students were asked how Smith College should respond to anonymous racist notes actually sent to four African American students in 1989. However, the confederate was always instructed to answer first. In some cases, she condemned the notes; in others, she justified them. Blanchard and his colleagues (1991) concluded that "hearing at least one other person express strongly antiracist opinions produced dramatically more strongly antiracist public reactions to racism than hearing others express equivocal opinions or opinions more accepting of racism" (pp. 102–103). However, a second experiment demonstrated that when the confederate expressed sentiments justifying racism, the subjects were much less likely to express antiracist opinions

than were those who heard no one else offer opinions. In this experiment, social control (through the process of conformity) influenced people's attitudes and the expression of those attitudes.

Why is there so much disagreement and tension? There is a growing realization that people do not mean the same thing when they are addressing problems of race, ethnicity, gender, or religion. A husband regularly does the dishes and feels he is an equal partner in doing the housework, not recognizing that the care of his infant daughter is left totally to his wife. A manager is delighted that he has been able to hire a Puerto Rican salesperson but makes no effort to see that the new employee will adjust to an all-White, non-Hispanic staff.

Ask Yourself

People of different races, religions, and ethnic backgrounds talk to each other, but do we talk past one another?

We talk, but do we talk past one another? Surveys regularly show that different ethnic and racial groups have different perceptions, whether on immigration policies, racial profiling, or whether discrimination occurs in the labor force. Sociologist Robert Blauner (1989, 1992) contends that Blacks and Whites see racism differently. Minorities see racism as central to society, as ever present, whereas Whites regard it as a peripheral concern and a national concern only when accompanied by violence or involving a celebrity. African Americans and other minorities consider racist acts in a broader context: "It is racist if my college fails to have Blacks significantly present as advisers, teachers, and administrators." Whites would generally accept a racism charge if there had been an explicit denial of a job to an appropriately qualified minority member. Furthermore, Whites would apply the label racist only to the person or the few people who were actually responsible for the act. Members of minority groups would be more willing to call most of the college's members racist for allowing racist practices to persist. For many Whites, the word racism is a red flag, and they are reluctant to give it the wide use typically employed by minorities, that is, those who have been oppressed by racism (Lichtenberg, 1992).

People today evoke a color-blind racism and see little evidence of intolerance except when confronted by a horrendous hate crime. Others contend that racism is couched often in a "backstage" manner through discussions of immigration, affirmative action, antipoverty programs, and profiling for national security (Dirks, 2008).

Is one view correct—the broader minority perspective or the more limited White outlook? No, but both are a part of the social reality in which we all live. We need to recognize both interpretations.

As we saw when we considered Whiteness in Chapter 5, the need to confront racism, however perceived, is not to make Whites guilty and absolve Blacks, Asians, Hispanics, and Native Americans of any responsibility for their present plight. Rather, to understand racism, past and present, is to understand how its impact has shaped both a single person's behavior and that of the entire society (Bonilla-Silva and Baiocchi 2001; Duke, 1992).

Conclusion

As the United States promotes racial, ethnic, and religious diversity, it strives also to impose universal criteria on employers, educators, and realtors so that subordinate racial and ethnic groups can participate fully in the larger society. In some instances, to bring about equality of results—not just equality of opportunity—programs have been developed to give competitive advantages to women and minority men. Only more recently have similar strides been made on behalf of people with disabilities. These latest answers to social inequality have provoked much controversy over how to achieve the admirable goal of a multiracial, multiethnic society, undifferentiated in opportunity and rewards.

Relations between racial, ethnic, or religious groups take two broad forms, as situations characterized by either consensus or conflict. Consensus prevails where assimilation or fusion of groups has been completed. Consensus also prevails in a pluralistic society in the sense that members have agreed to respect differences between groups. By eliminating the contending group, extermination and expulsion also lead to a consensus society. In the study of intergroup relations, it is often easy to ignore conflict where there is a high degree of consensus because it is assumed that an orderly society has no problems. In some instances, however, this assumption is misleading. Through long periods of history, misery inflicted on a racial, ethnic, or religious group was judged to be appropriate, if not actually divinely inspired.

In recent history, harmonious relations between all racial, ethnic, and religious groups have been widely accepted as a worthy goal. The struggle against oppression and inequality is not new. It dates back at least to the revolutions in England, France, and the American colonies in the seventeenth and eighteenth centuries. The twentieth century was unique in the extension of equality to the less-privileged classes, many of whose members are racial and ethnic minorities. Conflict along racial and ethnic lines is especially bitter now because it evokes memories of slavery, colonial oppression, and overt discrimination. Today's African Americans are much more aware of slavery than contemporary poor people are of seventeenth century debtors' prison.

Unquestionably, the struggle for justice among racial and ethnic groups has not completely met its goals. Many people are still committed to repression, although they may see it only as the benign neglect of those less privileged. Such repression leads to the dehumanization of both the subordinated individual and the oppressor. Growth in equal rights movements and self-determination for Third World countries largely populated by non-White people has moved the world onto a course that seems irreversible. The old ethnic battle lines now renewed in Iran,

Kenya, Sudan, and Chechnya in Russia have only added to the tensions.

Self-determination, whether for groups or individuals, often is impossible in societies as they are currently structured. Bringing about social equality, therefore, will entail significant changes in existing institutions. Because such changes are not likely to come about with everyone's willing cooperation, the social costs will be high. However, if there is a trend in racial and ethnic relations in the world today, it is the growing belief that the social costs, however high, must be paid to achieve self-determination.

It is naive to foresee a world of societies in which one person equals one vote and all are accepted without regard to race, ethnicity, religion, gender, age, disability status, or sexual orientation. It is equally unlikely to expect to see a society, let alone a world, that is without a privileged class or prestigious jobholders. Contact between different peoples, as we have seen numerous times, precedes conflict. Contact also may initiate mutual understanding and appreciation.

Assimilation, even when strictly followed, does not necessarily bring with it acceptance as an equal, nor does it even mean that one will be tolerated. Segregation persists. Efforts toward pluralism can be identified, but we can also easily see the counter efforts, whether they are the legal efforts to make English the official language or acts of intimidation by Klansmen, skinheads, and others. However, the sheer changing population of the United States guarantees that we will learn, work, and play in a more diverse society.

The task of making this kaleidoscope image of diverse cultures, languages, colors, and religions into a picture of harmony remains a challenge. But the all too frequent outbursts of hostility and documented discrimination leave us no alternative but to continue to try. We can applaud success and even take time to congratulate ourselves, but we must also review the unfinished agenda.

Key Terms

acting White   217
cultural capital   218

model or ideal minority   213
social capital   219

Review Questions

1. What contributes to the changing image of diversity in the United States?
2. Pose views of some issue facing contemporary society that takes the position of "half full" and then "half empty."
3. Why is it harmful to be viewed as a model minority?
4. Is one view of racism the correct one?
5. Why are White Americans less likely to be concerned with social and cultural capital?

Critical Thinking Questions

1. Considering the stereotypes that persist, how does it affect both the people who are stereotyped as well as those who express them?
2. Consider conversations you have with people very different than yourself. Why do you feel those people are very different? To what degree did you talk to them or past them? To what degree do they talk to you or past you?
3. How have places you worked, even part-time, been different from those of your parents or grandparents in terms of diversity of the workforce? What explains these changes?

Internet Connections—Research Navigator™

Follow the instructions given in "Internet Connections—Research Navigator" in Chapter 1 of this text to access the features of Research Navigator™. Once at the Web site, enter your login name and password. Then, to use the ContentSelect database, enter keywords such as "model minority" and "inequality," and the research engine will supply relevant and recent scholarly and popular press publications. Use the *New York Times* Search-by-Subject Archive to find recent news articles related to sociology, and the Link Library feature to locate relevant Web links organized by the key terms associated with this chapter.

Internet Resource Directory

The following is a sample of the thousands of Web sites that offer information on race, ethnicity, religion, and other related topics. They have been grouped by broad areas as most sites touch on a number of areas and subjects. Web sites have been selected that have stable URLs and are in English (or multilingual, including English). Most of these Web sites, in turn, have links to other useful information.

GENERAL

All of Us Are Related, Each of Us Is Unique (Syracuse University)
http://allrelated.syr.edu/

Death Penalty Information Center
http://www.deathpenaltyinfo.org

Equal Employment Opportunity Commission
http://www.eeoc.gov

Ethnic Media: New America Media
http://news.newamericamedia.org/news

Facing History and Ourselves Foundation
http://facinghistory.org

FBI Uniform Crime Reports Data on Hate Crimes
http://www.fbi.gov/ucr/ucr.htm

Hate Crimes Laws
http://www.adl.org/99hatecrime/intro.asp

Hurricane Katrina: U.S. Department of Health and Human Services
http://www.hhs.gov/disasters/emergency/naturaldisasters/hurricanes/katrina/index.html

Lutheran Immigration and Refugee Service
http://www.lirs.org

Minorities in Medical School (Association of American Medical Colleges)
http://www.aamc.org/students/minorities

National Conference for Community and Justice
  http://nccj.org

Partners Against Hate
  http://partnersagainsthate.org

The Prejudice Institute
  http://www.prejudiceinstitute.org

Project Implicit (Attitudes Test)
  http://www.projectimplicit.net

Race. Are We So Different? (American Anthropological Association)
  http://www.understandingrace.org/home.htm

Race Traitor (Constructing Whiteness)
  http://www.racetraitor.org

Refugees and Immigrants: Lutheran Immigration and Refugee Service
  http://www.lirs.org/

Refugees and Immigrants: U.S. Committee for Refugees and Immigrants
  http://www.refugeesusa.org/

Simon Wiesenthal Center
  http://www.wiesenthal.com

Southern Poverty Law Center (Tolerance Education)
  http://www.splcenter.org and www.tolerance.org

U.S. Census Bureau
  http://www.census.gov and specifically www.census.gov/pubinfo/www/hotlinks.html

U.S. Census Bureau Revisions to the Standards for the Classification of Federal Data on Race and Ethnicity (Office of Management and Budget)
  http://www.census.gov/population/www/socdemo/race/Ombdir15.html

U.S. Citizenship and Immigration Services
  http://www.uscis.gov

U.S. Commission on Civil Rights
  http://www.usccr.gov

U.S. Commission on Immigration Reform
  http://www.utexas.edu/lbj/uscir/

AFRICAN AMERICANS

African American History and Culture (The Smithsonian)
  http://nmahc.si.edu

African American Research (National Archives)
  http://www.archives.gov/genealogy/african-american/index.html

Black Collegian Online
  http://www.black-collegian.com/

MelaNET (The UnCut Black Experience)
  http://www.melanet.com/

Official Kwanzaa Web Site
  http://www.officialkwanzaawebsite.org

Rainbow/PUSH Coalition
  http://www.rainbowpush.org

Southern Christian Leadership Conference (SCLC) Web Site
  http://www.sclcnational.org

ASIAN AMERICANS AND PACIFIC ISLANDERS

Asian American Network
  http://www.asianamerican.net/

Asian American Justice Center
  http://www.napalc.org

Asian American Studies, Yale University Guide to
  http://www.library.yale.edu/rsc/asian-american/

Asians/Pacific Islanders
  http://www.nea.org/mco/asians.html

Chinese Immigration Records
  http://www.archives.gov/genealogy/heritage/chinese-immigration.html

Densho: The Japanese American Legacy Project
  http://www.densho.org/

The Fred Korematsu Story "Of Civil Wrongs and Rights" (by Eric Paul Fornier)
  http://www.pbs.org/pov/pov2001/ofcivilwrongsandrights/index.html

Hmong Home Page
  http://www.stolaf.edu/people/cdr/hmong/

Internment Archives
  http://www.internmentarchives.com

Japanese American Citizens League
  http://www.jacl.org

Japanese American Historical Society
  http://www.njahs.org

Japanese American National Museum
  http://www.janm.org

Japanese American Records (National Archives)
  http://www.archives.gov/genealogy/heritage/Japanese-americans.html

Little India (Magazine Web Site)
  http://www.littleindia.com/

Little Saigon Net
  http://www.littlesaigon.com/

Nation of Hawaii
  http://hawaii-nation.org/

National Japanese American Memorial Foundation
  http://www.njamf.com

Southeast Asia Resource Action Center
 http://www.searac.org/

U.S. Census Bureau: Public Information Office
 http://www.census.gov/pubinfo/www/NEWapiML1.html

HISPANICS AND LATINOS

Afro Cubans as well as Cuba and the Caribbean
 http://www.afrocubaweb.com/

Hispanic American Records
 http://www.archives.gov/genealogy/heritage/hispanic-americans.html

International Boundaries Research Unit
 http://www.dur.ac.uk/ibru/

Julian Samora Research Institute (Michigan State University)
 http://www.jsri.msu.edu/

Latin American National Information Center
 http://lanic.utexas.edu

Mexican American Studies and Research Center (University of Arizona)
 http://masrc.arizona.edu/

Mexican Migration Project
 http://mmp.opr.princeton.edu/

Mexico–U.S. Binational Migration Study Report
 http://www.utexas.edu/lbj/uscir/binational.html

National Council of La Raza:
 http://www.nclr.org

Nijmegen Centre for Border Research
 http://www.ru.nl/ncbr

Pew Hispanic Center
 http://pewhispanic.org/

Puerto Ricans and the American Dream
 http://prdream.com/

Puerto Rican Legal Defense and Education Fund
 http://www.prldef.org

JEWS AND JUDAISM

American Jewish Committee
 http://www.ajc.org

Anti-Defamation League
 http://www.adl.org

Hebrew Immigrant Aid Society (HIAS)
 http://www.hias.org/

Jewish American History Research

http://www.archives.gov/genealogy/heritage/jewish-american.html

Jewish Culture

http://myjewishlearning.com

Judaism and Jewish Resources

http://shamash.org

MUSLIM AND ARAB AMERICANS

American-Arab Anti-Discrimination Committee

http://www.adc.org

American Muslim Perspective

http://ampolitics.ghazali.net/

Arab American Institute

http://www.aaiusa.org/

Muslim Students Association

http://msa-natl.org

NATIVE AMERICANS

American Indian Higher Education Consortium (AIHEC) Virtual Library

http://www.aihecvl.org/

Bureau of Indian Affairs

http://www.doi.gov/bureau-indian-affairs.html

National Congress of American Indians

http://www.ncai.org

National Indian Youth Council

http://www.niyc-alb.org

Native American Records

http://www.archives.gov/genealogy/heritage/native-american/index.html

Native Web

http://www.nativeweb.org

Smithsonian National Museum of the American Indian

http://www.nmai.si.edu

ETHNIC GROUPS AND OTHER SUBORDINATE GROUPS

Administration on Aging

http://www.aoa.dhhs.gov

Anti-Violence Project (New York City Gay and Lesbian Anti-Violence Project)

http://avp.org/

Catholics for a Free Choice

http://www.cath4choice.org

Disability Law Center (Massachusetts)
http://dlc-ma.org/

Disability Social History Project
http://www.disabilityhistory.org

Ellis Island Immigration Museum
http://www.ellisisland.com/

Ethnicity in Twentieth-Century America (Thomas J. Archdeacon at University of Wisconsin)
http://history.wisc.edu/archdeacon/404tja

German Americans (German Embassy Site)
http://www.germany-info.org/

Human Rights Web
http://www.hrweb.org

Interracial Voice (People of Mixed Racial Background)
http://www.webcom.com/~intvoice

Irish Americans: American Irish Historical Society
http://www.aihs.org

National Gay and Lesbian Task Force
http://www.ngltf.org

National Women's Law Center
http://nwlc.org

Norwegian-American Historical Association
http://www.stolaf.edu/naha

Norwegian Americans: Sons of Norway
http://www.sofn.com

Norwegian Americans: Vesterheim Norwegian-American Museum
http://www.vesterheim.org

Polish American Association
http://www.polish.org

Polish Americans: American Institute of Polish Culture
http://www.ampolinstitute.org

Swedish-American Museum
http://www.samac.org

Society and Culture: Disabilities (Yahoo)
http://www.yahoo.com/Society_and_Culture/Disabilities/

Violence Against Women Office
http://www.ovw.usdoj.gov

THE AUTHOR

Richard T. Schaefer
schaeferrt@aol.com
www.schaefersociology.net

Glossary

Parenthetical numbers refer to the pages on which the term is introduced.

absolute deprivation The minimum level of subsistence below which families or individuals should not be expected to exist. (87)

acting White Taking school seriously and accepting the authority of teachers and administrators. (217)

affirmative action Positive efforts to recruit subordinate group members, including women, for jobs, promotions, and educational opportunities. (108)

Afrocentric perspective An emphasis on the customs of African cultures and how they have pervaded the history, culture, and behavior of Blacks in the United States and around the world. (42)

amalgamation The process by which a dominant group and a subordinate group combine through intermarriage to form a new group. (30)

assimilation The process by which a subordinate individual or group takes on the characteristics of the dominant group. (31)

asylees Foreigners who have already entered the United States and now seek protection because of persecution or a well-founded fear of persecution. (151)

authoritarian personality Adherence to conventional values, uncritical acceptance of authority, and concern with power and toughness. (57)

bilingual education A program designed to allow students to learn academic concepts in their native language while they learn a second language. (181)

bilingualism The use of two or more languages in places of work or education and the treatment of each language as legitimate. (181)

biological race The mistaken notion of a genetically isolated human group. (13)

blaming the victim Portraying the problems of racial and ethnic minorities as their fault rather than recognizing society's responsibilities. (21)

blended identity Self-image and worldview that is a combination of religious faith, cultural background based on nationality, and current residency. (194)

Bogardus scale Technique to measure social distance toward different racial and ethnic groups. (74)

brain drain Immigration to the United States of skilled workers, professionals, and technicians who are desperately needed by their home countries. (134)

chain immigration Immigrants sponsor several other immigrants who upon their arrival may sponsor still more. (123)

civil religion The religious dimension in American life that merges the state with sacred beliefs. (188)

class As defined by Max Weber, people who share similar levels of wealth. (17)

colonialism A foreign power's maintenance of political, social, economic, and cultural dominance over people for an extended period. (24)

color-blind racism The use of race-neutral principles to defend the racially unequal status quo. (64)

conflict perspective A sociological approach that assumes that the social structure is best understood in terms of conflict or tension between competing groups. (20)

contact hypothesis An interactionist perspective stating that intergroup contact between people of equal status in noncompetitive circumstances will reduce prejudice. (76)

creationists People who support a literal interpretation of the biblical book of Genesis on the origins of the universe and argue that evolution should not be presented as established scientific thought. (198)

cultural capital Noneconomic forces such as family background and past investments in education that are then reflected in knowledge about the arts and language. (218)

denomination A large, organized religion not officially linked with the state or government. (185)

discrimination The denial of opportunities and equal rights to individuals and groups because of prejudice or for other arbitrary reasons. (52)

dual labor market Division of the economy into two areas of employment, the secondary one of which is populated primarily by minorities working at menial jobs. (95)

dysfunction An element of society that may disrupt a social system or decrease its stability. (20)

emigration Leaving a country to settle in another. (23)

English immersion Teaching in English by teachers who know the students' native language but use it only when students do not understand the lessons. (182)

environmental justice Efforts to ensure that hazardous substances are controlled so that all communities receive protection regardless of race or socioeconomic circumstances. (106)

ethnic cleansing Forced deportation of people accompanied by systematic violence. (27)

ethnic group A group set apart from others because of its national origin or distinctive cultural patterns. (9)

ethnicity paradox The maintenance of one's ethnic ties in a way that can assist with assimilation in larger society. (203)

ethnocentrism The tendency to assume that one's culture and way of life are superior to all others. (49)

ethnophaulism Ethnic or racial slurs, including derisive nicknames. (52)

exploitation theory A Marxist theory that views racial subordination in the United States as a manifestation of the class system inherent in capitalism. (58)

functionalist perspective A sociological approach emphasizing how parts of a society are structured to maintain its stability. (19)

fusion A minority and a majority group combining to form a new group. (30)

genocide The deliberate, systematic killing of an entire people or nation. (27)

glass ceiling The barrier that blocks the promotion of a qualified worker because of gender or minority membership. (114)

glass escalator The male advantage experienced in occupations dominated by women. (116)

glass wall A barrier to moving laterally in a business to positions that are more likely to lead to upward mobility. (116)

globalization Worldwide integration of government policies, cultures, social movements, and financial markets through trade, movements of people, and the exchange of ideas. (24)

hate crime Criminal offense committed because of the offender's bias against a race, religion, ethnic or national origin group, or sexual orientation group. (50)

ideal minority See model minority. (213)

immigration Coming into a new country as a permanent resident. (23)

income Salaries, wages, and other money received. (105)

informal economy Transfers of money, goods, or services that are not reported to the government. Common in inner-city neighborhoods and poverty-stricken rural areas. (94)

institutional discrimination A denial of opportunities and equal rights to individuals or groups resulting from the normal operations of a society. (92)

intelligence quotient (IQ) The ratio of a person's mental age (as computed by an IQ test) to his or her chronological age, multiplied by 100. (13)

intelligent design View that life is so complex that must have been created by a higher intelligence. (198)

internal colonialism The treatment of subordinate peoples as colonial subjects by those in power. (26)

irregular or underground economy See informal economy. (94)

labeling theory A sociological approach introduced by Howard Becker that attempts to explain why certain people are viewed as deviants and others engaging in the same behavior are not. (21)

marginality The status of being between two cultures at the same time, such as the status of Jewish immigrants in the United States. (38)

matrix of domination Cumulative impact of oppression because of race, gender, and class as well as sexual orientation, religion, disability status, and age. (39)

melting pot Diverse racial or ethnic groups or both, forming a new creation, a new cultural entity. (31)

migradollars (or remittances) The money that immigrant workers send back to families in their native societies. (146)

migration A general term that describes any transfer of population. (23)

minority group A subordinate group whose members have significantly less control or power over their own lives than do the members of a dominant or majority group. (6)

mixed-status family Families where one or more is a citizen and the one or more is a non-citizen. (136)

model or ideal minority A group that, despite past prejudice and discrimination, succeeds economically, socially, and educationally without resorting to political or violent confrontations with Whites. (213)

nativism Beliefs and policies favoring native-born citizens over immigrants. (126)

naturalization Conferring of citizenship on a person after birth. (142)

normative approach The view that prejudice is influenced by societal norms and situations that encourage or discourage the tolerance of minorities. (58)

panethnicity The development of solidarity between ethnic subgroups, as reflected in the terms Hispanic or Asian American. (36)

pluralism Mutual respect between the various groups in a society for one another's cultures, allowing minorities to express their own culture without experiencing prejudice or hostility. (33)

prejudice A negative attitude toward an entire category of people, such as a racial or ethnic minority. (52)

principle of third-generation interest Marcus Hansen's contention that ethnic interest and awareness increase in the third generation, among the grandchildren of immigrants. (161)

racial formation A sociohistorical process by which racial categories are created, inhibited, transformed, and destroyed. (16)

racial group A group that is socially set apart because of obvious physical differences. (8)

racial profiling Any arbitrary police-initiated action based on race, ethnicity, or natural origin rather than a person's behavior. (63)

racism A doctrine that one race is superior. (16)

redlining The pattern of discrimination against people trying to buy homes in minority and racially changing neighborhoods. (103)

refugees People living outside their country of citizenship for fear of political or religious persecution. (150)

relative deprivation The conscious experience of a negative discrepancy between legitimate expectations and present actualities. (87)

remittances (or migradollars) The monies that immigrants return to their country of origin. (146)

resegregation Physical separation of racial and ethnic groups reappearing after a period of relative integration. (29)

reverse discrimination Actions that cause better-qualified White men to be passed over for women and minority men. (112)

scapegoating theory Prejudiced people believing they are society's victims. (56)

secessionist minority Groups, such as the Amish, that reject both assimilation and promote coexistence and pluralism. (199)

segregation The physical separation of two groups, often imposed on a subordinate group by the dominant group. (28)

self-fulfilling prophecy The tendency to respond to and act on the basis of stereotypes, a predisposition that can lead one to validate false definitions. (22)

sinophobes People with a fear of anything associated with China. (128)

social capital Collective benefits of durable social networks and their patterns of reciprocal trust. (219)

social distance Tendency to approach or withdraw from a racial group. (74)

sociology The systematic study of social behavior and human groups. (17)

stereotypes Unreliable, exaggerated generalizations about all members of a group that do not take individual differences into account. (21)

stratification A structured ranking of entire groups of people that perpetuates unequal rewards and power in a society. (17)

symbolic ethnicity Herbert Gans's term that describes emphasis on ethnic food and ethnically associated political issues rather than deeper ties to one's heritage. (162)

total discrimination The combination of current discrimination with past discrimination created by poor schools and menial jobs. (90)

transnationals Immigrants who sustain multiple social relationships linking their societies of origin and settlement. (149)

wealth An inclusive term encompassing all of a person's material assets, including land and other types of property. (105)

White privilege Rights or immunities granted as a particular benefit or favor for being White. (160)

world systems theory A view of the global economic system as divided between nations that control wealth and those that provide natural resources and labor. (25)

xenophobia The fear or hatred of strangers or foreigners. (126)

References

ABDO, GENEIVE. 2004. A Muslim Rap Finds Voice. *Chicago Tribune* June 30, 1, 19.

ADELMAN, ROBERT M., AND JAMES CLARKE GOCKER. 2007. Racial Residential Segregation in Urban America. *Sociology Compass* 1 (1): 402–423.

ADORNO, T. W., ELSE FRENKEL-BRUNSWIK, DANIEL J. LEVINSON, AND R. NEVITT SANFORD. 1950. *The Authoritarian Personality.* New York: Wiley.

ALBA, RICHARD, AND DALIA ABDEL-HADY. 2005. Galileo's Children: Italian Americans' Difficult Entry into the Intellectual Elite. *Sociological Quarterly* 46: 3–18.

ALLPORT, GORDON W. 1979. *The Nature of Prejudice.* 25th anniversary ed. Reading, MA: Addison-Wesley.

ALONSO-ZALDIVAR, RICARDO, AND JENNIFER OLDHAN. 2002. New Airport Screener Jobs Going Mostly to Whites. *Los Angeles Times,* September 24, A18.

ALVAREZ, SANDY. 2008. Haitian and Cuban Immigration: A Comparison. In vol. 1 of *Encyclopedia of Race, Ethnicity, and Society,* ed. Richard T. Schaefer, 576–578. Thousand Oaks, CA: Sage.

AMERICAN COMMUNITY SURVEY. 2006. American Community Survey 2005. Released August, 2006, http://www.census.gov.

ANSELL, ANY E. 2008. Color Blindness. In vol. 1 of *Encyclopedia of Race, Ethnicity, and Society,* ed. Richard T. Schaefer, 320–322. Thousand Oaks, CA: Sage.

APPLEBOME, PETER. 1996. 70 Years after Scopes Trial, Creation Debate Lives. *New York Times* March 10, 1, 22.

ASANTE, MOLEFI KETE. 2007. *An Afrocentric Manifesto: Toward an African Renaissance.* Cambridge, UK: Polity.

———. 2008. Afrocentricity. In vol. 1 of *Encyclopedia of Race, Ethnicity, and Society,* ed. Richard T. Schaefer, 41–42. Thousand Oaks, CA: Sage.

BADGETT, M. V. LEE, AND HEIDI I. HARTMANN. 1995. The Effectiveness of Equal Employment Opportunity Policies. In *Economic Perspectives in Affirmative Action,* ed. Margaret C. Simms, 55–83. Washington, DC: Joint Center for Political and Economic Studies.

BALTZELL, E. DIGBY. 1964. *The Protestant Establishment: Aristocracy and Caste in America.* New York: Vintage Books.

BAMSHAD, MICHAEL J., AND STEVE E. OLSON. 2003. Does Race Exist? *Scientific American,* December, 78–85.

BANTON, MICHAEL. 2007. Max Weber on "Ethnic Communities": A Critique. *Nations and Nationalism* 13 (1): 19–35.

BARRINGER, FELICITY. 2004. Bitter Division for Sierra Club on Immigration *New York Times,* March 14, A1, A16.

BASH, HARRY M. 2001. If I'm So White, Why Ain't I Right? Some Methodological Misgivings on Taking Identity Ascriptions at Face Value. Paper presented at the annual meeting of the Midwest Sociological Society, St. Louis.

BAUDER, HARALD. 2003. Brain Abuse, or the Devaluation of Immigrant Labour in Canada. *Antipode* 35 (September): 699–717.

BA-YUNUS, ILYAS, AND KASSIM KONE. 2004. Muslim Americans: A Demographic Report. In *Muslims' Place in the American Public Square,* eds. Zahid H. Bukhari et al., 299–322. Walnut Creek, CA: Atamira Press.

BEAN, FRANK D., AND G. STEVENS. 2003. *America's Newcomers and the Dynamics of Diversity.* New York: Russell Sage Foundation.

BEAN, FRANK D., JENNIFER LEE, JEANNE BATALOVA, AND MARK LEACH. 2004. *Immigration and Fading Color Lines in America.* New York: Russell Sage Foundation.

BEISEL, NICOLA, AND TAMARA KAY. 2004. Abortion: Race and Gender in Nineteenth Century America. *American Sociological Review* 69 (August): 498–518.

BELL, DERRICK. 1994. The Freedom of Employment Act. *The Nation* 258 (May 23): 708, 710–714.

BELL, WENDELL. 1991. Colonialism and Internal Colonialism. In *The Encyclopedic Dictionary of Sociology,* ed. Richard Lachmann. pp. 52–53. 4th ed. Guilford, CT: Dushkin Publishing Group.

BELLAH, ROBERT. 1967. Civil Religion in America. *Daedalus* 96 (Winter): 1–21.

BELT, DON. 2002. The World of Islam. *National Geographic* (January): 76–85.

BENNETT, BRIAN. 2008. Coming to America. *Time* 171 (February 4).

BENNETT, PHILLIP. 1993. Ethnic Labels Fail to Keep Up with Reality. *The Cincinnati Enquirer* (November 18): A10.

BEST, JOEL. 2001. Social Progress and Social Problems: Toward a Sociology of Gloom. *Sociological Quarterly* 42 (1): 1–12.

BILLSON, JANET MANCINI. 1988. No Owner of Soil: The Concept of Marginality Revisited on Its Sixtieth Birthday. *International Review of Modern Sociology* 18 (Autumn): 183–204.

BLACKWELL, JUDITH C., MURRAY E. G. SMITH, AND JOHN S. SORENSON. 2003. *Culture of Prejudice: Arguments in Critical Social Science.* Toronto: Broadview Press.

BLANCHARD, FLETCHER A., LILLY, TERI, AND VAUGHN, LEIGH ANN. 1991. Reducing the Expression of Racial Prejudice. *Psychological Science* 2 (March): 101–105.

BLAUNER, ROBERT. 1969. Internal Colonialism and Ghetto Revolt. *Social Problems* 16 (Spring): 393–408.

———. 1972. *Racial Oppression in America.* New York: Harper & Row.

———. 1989. *Black Lives, White Lives: Three Decades of Race Relations in America.* Berkeley: University of California Press.

———. 1992. The Two Languages of Race. *The American Prospect* (Summer): 55–64.

BLOOM, LEONARD. 1971. *The Social Psychology of Race Relations.* Cambridge, MA: Schenkman Publishing Co., Inc.

BOCIAN, DEBBIE GRUENSTEIN, KEITH S. ERNST, AND WEI LI. 2006. *Unfair Lending: The Effect of Race and Ethnicity on the Price of Subprime Mortgages.* Oakland, CA: Center for Responsible Lending.

BOGARDUS, EMORY. 1968. Comparing Racial Distance in Ethiopia, South Africa, and the United States. *Sociology and Social Research* 52 (January): 149–156.

BOHMER, SUSANNE, AND KAYLEEN V. OKA. 2007. Teaching Affirmative Action: An Opportunity to Apply, Segregate, and Reinforce Sociological Concepts. *Teaching Sociology* 35 (October): 334–349.

BONACICH, EDNA. 1972. A Theory of Ethnic Antagonism: The Split Labor Market. *American Sociological Review* 37 (October): 547–559.

———. 1976. Advanced Capitalism and Black/White Race Relations in the United States: A Split Labor Market Interpretation. *American Sociological Review* 41 (February): 34–51.

BONILLA-SILVA, EDUARDO. 1996. Rethinking Racism: Toward a Structural Interpretation. *American Sociological Review* 62 (June): 465–480.

———. 2002. The Linguistics of Color Blind Racism: How to Talk Nasty about Blacks without Sounding Racist. *Critical Sociology* 28 (1–2): 41–64.

———. 2004. From Bi-racial to Tri-racial: Towards a New System of Racial Stratification in the USA. *Ethnic and Racial Studies* 27 (November): 931–950.

———. 2006. *Racism without Racists.* 2nd ed. Lanham, MD: Rowman and Littlefield.

BONILLA-SILVA, EDUARDO, AND GIANPAOLO BAIOCCHI. 2001. Anything but Racism: How Sociologists Limit the Significance of Racism. *Race and Society* 4: 117–131.

BONILLA-SILVA, EDUARDO, AND DAVID G. EMBRICK. 2007. "Every Place Has a Ghetto . . .": The Significance of Whites' Social and Residential Segregation. *Symbolic Interaction* 30 (3): 323–345.

BORDT, REBECCA L. 2005. Using a Research Article to Facilitate a Deep Structure Understanding of Discrimination. *Teaching Sociology* 33 (October): 403–410.

BORJAS, GEORGE J., JEFFERY GROGGER, AND GORDON H. HANSON. 2006. Immigration and African-American Employment Opportunities: The Response of Wages, Employment, and Incarceration to Labor Supply Shocks. Working Paper 12518. Cambridge, MA: National Bureau of Economic Research.

BORK, ROBERT H. 1995. What to Do about the First Amendment. *Commentary* 99 (February): 23–29.

BOURDIEU, PIERRE. 1983. The Forms of Capital. In *Handbook of Theory and Research for the Sociology of Education,* ed. J. G. Richardson, 241–258. Westport, CT: Greenwood.

BOURDIEU, PIERRE, AND JEAN-CLAUDE PASSERON. 1990. *Reproduction in Education, Society and Culture.* 2nd ed. London: Sage (Originally published as *La Reproduction* 1970).

BOWLES, SCOTT. 2000. Bans on Racial Profiling Gain Steam. *USA Today* 2 (June): 3A.

BOWMAN, TOM. 1998. Evangelicals Allege Bias in U.S. Navy, Marine Chaplain Corps. *Baltimore Sun* 23 (August): A12.

BOWSER, BENJAMIN, AND RAYMOND G. HUNT, EDS. 1996. *Impacts of Racism on White Americans.* Beverly Hills, CA: Sage Publications.

BREWINGTON, KELLY. 2008. Broken Families. *Baltimore Sun* 26 (January).

BRIGGS, XAVIER DE SOUZA. 2007. "Some of My Best Friends Are . . .": Interracial Friendships, Class, and Segregation in America. *City and Community* 6 (4): 263–290.

BRIMMER, ANDREW. 1995. The Economic Cost of Discrimination against Black Americans. In *Economic Perspectives in Affirmative Action,* ed. Margaret C. Simms, 9–29. Washington, DC: Joint Center for Political and Economic Studies.

BRODIE, MOLLYANN, ANNIE STEFFENSON, JAMIE VALDEZ, REBECCA LEVIN, AND ROBERTO SURO. 2002. *2002 National Survey of Latinos.* Menlo Park, CA: Henry J. Kaiser Foundation and Pew Hispanic Center.

BROOKS-GUNN, JEANNE, PAMELA K. KLEBANOV, AND GREG J. DUNCAN. 1996. Ethnic Differences in Children's Intelligence Test Scores: Role of Economic Deprivation, Home Environment, and Maternal Characteristics. *Child Development* 67 (April): 396–408.

BROWN, PATRICIA LEIGH. 2003. For the Muslim Prom Queen, There Are No Kings Allowed. *New York Times* 9 (June): A1, A24.

BROWNE, IRENE, ED. 2001. *Latinas and African American Women at Work: Race, Gender, and Economic Inequality.* New York: Russell Sage Foundation.

BROWNSTEIN, ANDREW. 2001. A Battle over a Name in the Land of the Sioux. *Chronicle of Higher Education* 47 (February 23): A46–A49.

BRULLIARD, KARIN. 2006. A Proper Goodbye: Funeral Homes Learn Immigrants' Traditions. *Washington Post National Weekly Edition,* May 7, 31.

BRUNSMA, DAVID L., ED. 2006. *Mixed Messages: Multiracial Identities in the "Color-Blind" Era.* Boulder, CO: Lynn Rienner.

BUDIG, MICHELLE J. 2002. Male Advantage and the Gender Composition of Jobs: Who Rides the Glass Escalator? *Social Problems* 49 (2): 258–277.

BUKOWCYK, JOHN J. 1996. *Polish Americans and Their History: Community, Culture and Politics.* Pittsburgh: University of Pittsburgh Press.

BUREAU OF THE CENSUS. 1988. *Statistical Abstract of the United States, 1988.* Washington, DC: U.S. Government Printing Office.

———. 2001. *Census 2000 Phc-T.6., Population by Race and Hispanic or Latino Origin in the United States,* http://www.census.gov (accessed February 5, 2001).

———. 2003. *Statistical Abstract of the United States, 2003.* Washington, DC: U.S. Government Printing Office.

———. 2004. *U.S. Interim Projections by Age, Sex, Race, and Hispanic Origin.* Released March 18, 2004, http://www.census.gov/ipc/www/usinterimproj.

———. 2005a. *Statistical Abstract of the United States, 2004–2005.* Washington, DC: U.S. Government Printing Office.

———. 2005b. *Texas Becomes Nation's Newest "Majority-Minority" States, Census Bureau Announces. CBO5-118.* Washington, DC: U.S. Government Printing Office.

———. 2005c. "Foreign-Born Population of the United States Current Population Survey—March 2004 Detailed Tables (PPl-176)", http://www.census.gov/population/www/socdemo/foreign/ppl-176.html (accessed May 21, 2008).

———. 2007a. *Statistical Abstract of the United States, 2006.* Washington, DC: U.S. Government Printing Office.

———. 2007b. *American Community Survey 2006,* http://factfinder.census.gov.

———. 2007c. *The American Community—Asians: 2004.* Report ACS-05. Washington, DC: U.S. Government Printing Office.

———. 2008a. *Statistical Abstract of the United States, 2007.* Washington, DC: U.S. Government Printing Office.

———. 2008b. Irish-American Heritage Month (March) and St. Patrick's Day (March 17) 2008, http://www.census.gov/ (accessed January 2, 2008).

BUREAU OF JUSTICE STATISTICS. 2004. *First Release from State Prisons 2001.* Washington, DC: Bureau of Justice Statistics.

CAMAROTA, STEVEN A. 2007a. *Immigrants in the United States, 2007: A Profile of America's Foreign-Born Population.* Washington, DC: Center for Immigrant Statistics.

———. 2007b. *100 Million More. Projecting the Impact of Immigration on the U.S. Population, 2007 to 2060.* Washington, DC: Center for Immigrant Statistics.

CAPPS, RANDY, KU LEIGHTON, AND MICHAEL FIX. 2002. *How Are Immigrants Faring after Welfare Reform? Preliminary Evidence from Los Angeles and New York City.* Washington, DC: Urban Institute.

CARBERRY, MAEGAN. 2006. "Multiculti Chic." *Red Eye* (Chicago), February 16.

CARD, DAVID, JOHN DiNARDO, AND EUGENA ESTES. 1998. The More Things Change: Immigrants and the Children of Immigrants in the 1940s, the 1970s, and the 1990s. Paper presented at the Joint Center for Poverty Research, Northwestern University of Chicago, April 9.

CARRELL, MICHAEL R., NORBERT F. ELBERT, AND ROBERT D. HATFIELD. 2000. *Human Resource Management: Strategies for Managing a Diverse and Global Workforce.* 6th ed. Orlando, FL: Dryden Press.

CARRIER, JIM. 2000. *Ten Ways to Fight Hate.* 2nd ed. Montgomery, AL: Tolerance.org.

CARROLL, JOSEPH. 2006. Public National Anthem Should Be Sung in English. *The Gallup Poll* May 3.

CARVAJAL, DOREEN. 1995. Diversity Pays Off in a Babel of Yellow Pages. *New York Times* December 3, 1, 23.

CATALYST. 2001. Women Satisfied with Current Job in Financial Industry but Barriers Still Exist. Press Release July 25, 2001, http://www.catalystwomen.org (accessed January 31, 2002).

CHANG, DORIS F., AND AMY DEMYAN. 2007. Teachers' Stereotypes of Asian, Black and White Students. *School Psychology Quarterly* 22 (2): 91–114.

CHICAGO TRIBUNE. 2006. Newark is No. 1 in U.S. Ordinations. May 26, 12.

CHIROT, DANIEL, AND JENNIFER EDWARDS. 2003. Making Sense of the Senseless: Understanding Genocide. *Contexts* 2 (Spring): 12–19.

CHU, JEFF, AND NADIA MUSTAFA. 2006. Between Two Worlds. *Time,* January 16.

CITIZENSHIP AND IMMIGRATION SERVICES (CIS). 2008. Typical Questions, http://www.uscis.gov/files/nativedocuments/Flashcard_questions.pdf (accessed February 13, 2008).

CITRIN, JACK, AMY LERMAN, MICHAEL MURAKAMI, AND KATHRYN PEARSON. 2007. Testing Huntington: Is Hispanic Immigration a Threat to American Identity. *Perspectives on Politics* 5 (March): 31–48.

CLARK, KENNETH B., AND MAMIE P. CLARK. 1947. Racial Identification and Preferences in Negro Children. In *Readings in Social Psychology,* eds. Theodore M. Newcomb and Eugene L. Hartley, 169–178. New York: Holt, Rinehart & Winston.

CLEMMITT, MARCIA. 2005. Intelligent Design. *CQ Researcher* 95 (July 29): 637–660.

COGNARD-BLACK, ANDREW J. 2004. Will They Stay, or Will They Go? Sex—Atypical among Token Men Who Teach. *Sociological Quarterly* 45 (1): 113–139.

COLBURN, DAVID R., CHARLES E. YOUNG, AND VICTOR M. YELLEN. 2008. Admissions and Public Higher Education in California, Texas, and Florida: The Post-Affirmative Action Era. *Interactions: UCLA Journal of Education and Information Studies* 4 (1): 2, http://repositories.cdib.org/gseis/interactions/vol4/issl/art2 (accessed April 20, 2008).

COLEMAN, JAMES S. 1988. Social Capital in the Creation of Human Capital. *American Journal of Sociology* 94 (Supplement): S95–S120.

COLLINS, PATRICIA HILL. 2000. *Black Feminist Thought: Knowledge, Consciousness, and the Politics of Empowerment.* 2nd ed. New York: Routledge.

COLLURA, HEATHER. 2007. Roommate Concerns Fed by Facebook. *USA Today* (August 8): 6D.

COMMISSION ON CIVIL RIGHTS. 1976. *Fulfilling the Letter and Spirit of the Law: Desegregation of the Nation's Public Schools.* Washington, DC: U.S. Government Printing Office.

———. 1981. *Affirmative Action in the 1980s: Dismantling the Process of Discrimination.* Washington, DC: U.S. Government Printing Office.

COMMITTEE OF 100. 2001. *American Attitudes Towards Chinese Americans and Asian Immigrants.* New York: Committee of 100.

CONYERS, JR., JAMES L. 2004. The Evolution of Africology: An Afrocentric Appraisal. *Journal of Black Studies* 34 (May): 640–652.

COOPER, MARY H. 2004. Voting Rights. *CQ Researcher* 14 (October 29): 901–924.

COOPERMAN, ALAN. 2005. One Way to Pray? *Washington Post National Weekly Edition* 22 (September 5): 10–11.

CORNACCHIA, EUGENE J., AND DALE C. NELSON. 1992. Historical Differences in the Political Experiences of American Blacks and White Ethnics: Revisiting an Unresolved Controversy. *Ethnic and Racial Studies* (January 15): 102–124.

CORRELL, JOSHUA, BERNADETTE PARK, CHARLES M. JUDD, AND BERND WITTENBRINK. 2007a. The Influence of Stereotypes on Decisions to Shoot. *European Journal of Social Psychology* 37: 1102–1117.

CORRELL, JOSHUA, BERNADETTE PARK, CHARLES M. JUDD, BERND WITTENBRINK, MELODY S. SADLER, AND TRACIE KEESEE. 2007b. Across the Thin Blue Line: Police Officers and Racial Bias in the Decision to Shoot. *Journal of Personality and Social Psychology* 92 (6): 1006–1023.

COSE, ELLIS. 1993. *The Rage of a Privileged Class.* New York: HarperCollins.

COX, OLIVER C. 1942. The Modern Caste School of Social Relations. *Social Forces* 21 (December): 218–226.

CRANFORD, CYNTHIA J. 2005. Networks of Exploitation: Immigrant Labor and the Restructuring of the Los Angeles Janitorial Industry. *Social Problems* 52 (3): 379–397.

DAHLBURG, JOHN-THOR. 2001. A New World for Haitians. *Los Angeles Times,* September 4, A1, A9.

DART, BOB. 1998. Preserving America: Lancaster County, PA. *Atlanta Journal and Constitution* (June 28).

DAVIS, JAMES A., TOM W. SMITH, AND PETER V. MARSDEN. 2007. *General Social Surveys, 1972–2006: Cumulative Codebook.* Chicago: NORC.

DE ANDA, ROBERTO M. 2004. *Chicanas and Chicanos in Contemporary Society.* 2nd ed. Lanham, MD: Rowman and Littlefield & Bacon.

DE LA GARZA, RODOLFO O., LOUIS DESIPIO, F. CHRIS GARCIA, JOHN GARCIA, AND ANGELO FALCON. 1992. *Latino Voices: Mexican, Puerto Rican, and Cuban Perspectives on American Politics.* Boulder, CO: Westview Press.

DEL OLMO, FRANK. 2003. Slow Motion Carnage at the Border. *Los Angeles Times* (May 18): M5.

DEMIRJILAN, KARORN. 2007. Iraqi Arrivals up in U.S., but Still Lag Goals. *Chicago Tribune,* November 12, 1, 18.

DENAVAS-WALT, CARMEN, BERNADETTE D. PROCTOR, AND CHERYL HILL LEE. 2006. *Income, Poverty, and Health Insurance Coverage in the United States: 2005.* Current Population Reports, 60–231. Washington, DC: U.S. Government Printing Office.

DENAVAS-WALT, CARMEN, BERNADETTE D. PROCTOR, AND JESSICA SMITH. 2007. *Income, Poverty, and Health Insurance Coverage in the United States: 2006.* Current Population Reports, 60–233. Washington, DC: U.S. Government Printing Office.

Department of Justice. 2001. Report to the Congress of the United States: A Review of Restrictions on Persons of Italian Ancestry During World War II, http://www.house.gov/judiciary/Italians.pdf (accessed February 1, 2002).

———. 2007. Hate Crime Statistics, 2006, http://www.fbi.gov/ucr/ucr.htm.

———. 2008. Hate Crime – Overview, http://www.fbi.gov (accessed January 28, 2008).

Department of State. 2008. Dual Nationality, http://travel.state.gov/travel/cis_pa_tw/cis/cis_1753.html# (accessed February 6, 2008).

DEUTSCHER, IRWIN, FRED P. PESTELLO, AND H. FRANCES PESTELLO. 1993. *Sentiments and Acts.* New York: Aldine de Gruyter.

DIAMOND, JARED. 2003. Globalization, Then. *Los Angeles Times,* September 14, M1, M3.

DICKSON, LISA M. 2006. Book Review: Italians Then, Mexicans Now. *Industrial and Labor Relations Review* 60 (2): 293–295.

DIRKS, DANIELLE. 2008. Racetalk. In vol. 3 of *Encyclopedia of Race, Ethnicity, and Society,* ed. Richard T. Schaefer, 1100–1102. Thousand Oaks, CA: Sage.

DIMAGGIO, PAUL. 2005. Cultural Capital. In *Encyclopaedia of Social Theory,* ed. George Ritzer, 167–170. Thousand Oaks, CA: Sage Publications.

DITOMASO, NANCY, CORINNE POST, AND ROCHELLE PARKS-YANCY. 2007. Workforce Diversity and Inequality: Power,

238   REFERENCES

Status, and Numbers. *Annual Review of Sociology* 33: 473–501.

DOLAN, MAURA. 2000. State Justices Deal New Set Back to Affirmative Action. *Los Angeles Times,* December 1.

DOLAN, SEAN, AND SANDRA STOTSKY. 1997. *The Polish Americans.* New York: Chelsea House.

DOVIDIO, JOHN F. 2001. On the Nature of Contemporary Prejudice: The Third Wave. *Journal of Social Issues* 57 (4): 829–849.

DU BOIS, W. E. B. 1903. *The Souls of Black Folks: Essays and Sketches.* Reprint, New York: Facade Publications, 1961.

———. 1969a [1900]. *An ABC of Color.* New York: International Publications.

DUDLEY, CARL S., AND DAVID A. ROOZEN. 2001. *Faith Communities Today.* Hartford, CT: Hartford Seminary.

DUKE, LYNNE. 1992. You See Color-Blindness, I See Discrimination. *Washington Post National Weekly Edition* 9 (June 15): 33.

DUNN, ASHLEY. 1994. Southeast Asians Highly Dependent on Welfare in U.S. *New York Times* (May 19): A1, A20.

DUSZAK, THOMAS. 1997. Lattimer Massacre Centennial Commemoration. *Polish American Journal* August, http://www.polamjournal.com/Library/APHistory/Lattimer/lattimer.html (accessed June 4, 2008).

DYSON, MICHAEL ERIC. 2005. *Is Bill Cosby right?* New York: Basic Civitas, Perseus Books.

ECHAVESTE, MARIA. 2005. Target Employees. *American Prospect* (November): A10–A11.

ECKSTROM, KEVIN. 2001. New, Diverse Take Spot on Catholic Altars. *Chicago Tribune* (August 31): 8.

Economic Mobility Project. 2007a. *Economic Mobility of Black and White Families.* Washington, DC: Pew Charitable Trust.

———. 2007b. *Economic Mobility of Immigrants in the United States.* Washington, DC: Pew Charitable Trust.

Economist. 2004a. An Amish Exception, February 7, 33.

———. 2004b. Who's Winning the Fight?, July 30, 38.

EL NASSER, HAYA. 1997. Varied Heritage Claimed and Extolled by Millions. *USA Today* (May 8): 1A, 2A.

ELY, ROBIN J., DEBRA E. MEYERSON, AND MARTIN N. DAVIDSON. 2006. Rethinking Political Correctness. *Harvard Business Review* 84 (September): 79–87.

EPSTEIN, CYNTHIA FUCHS. 1999. The Major Myth of the Women's Movement. *Dissent* (Fall): 83–111.

ERDMANS, MARY PATRICE. 1998. *Opposite Poles: Immigrants and Ethnics in Polish Chicago, 1976–1990.* University Park: Pennsylvania State University.

———. 2006. New Chicago Polonia: Urban and Suburban. In *The New Chicago,* eds. John Koval et al., 115–127. Philadelphia: Temple University Press.

ESPIRITU, YEN LE. 1992. *Asian American Panethnicity: Bridging Institutions and Identities.* Philadelphia, PA: Temple University Press.

FAILOA, ANTHONY. 2007. Hispanics Bring Catholicism to Its Feet. *Washington Post National Weekly Edition* 24 (May 21): 35.

FALLOWS, MARJORIE R. 1979. *Irish Americans: Identity and Assimilation.* England Cliffs, NJ: Prentice-Hall.

FARKAS, STEVE. 2003. *What Immigrants Say about Life in the United States.* Washington, DC: Migration Policy Institute.

FEAGIN, JOE R., AND KARYN D. MCKINNEY. 2003. *The Many Costs of Racism.* Lanham, MD: Rowan and Littlefield.

FEAGIN, JOE R., AND EILEEN O'BRIEN. 2003. *White Men on Race, Power, Privilege, and the Shaping of Cultural Consciousness.* Boston, MA: Beacon Press.

FEAGIN, JOE R., HERNÁN VERA, AND PINAR BATUR. 2000. *White Racism.* 2nd ed. New York: Routledge.

FEGUSON, RONALD. 2007. Parenting Practices, Teenage Lifestyles, and Academic Achievement among African-American Children. *Focus* 25 (Spring–Summer): 18–26.

FERBER, ABBY L. 2007. Whiteness Studies and the Erasure of Gender. *Sociology Compass* 1 (1): 256–282.

———. 2008. Privilege. In vol. 3 of *Encyclopedia of Race, Ethnicity, and Society,* ed. Richard T. Schaefer, pp. 1073–1074. Thousand Oaks, CA: Sage.

FERNANDEZ, MANNY, AND KAREEM FAHIM. 2006. 5 on Plane Are Detained at Newark, but Later Freed. *New York Times,* May 5, 29.

FINE, GARY. 2008. Robber's Cave. In vol. 3 of *Encyclopedia of Race, Ethnicity, and Society,* ed. Richard T. Schaefer, pp. 1163–1164. Thousand Oaks, CA: Sage.

FIX, MICHAEL E., AND JEFFERY S. PASSEL. 2001. *The Integration of Immigrant Families in the United States.* Washington, DC: The Urban Institute.

FIX, MICHAEL E., AND WENDY ZIMMERMAN. 1999. *All under One Roof: Mixed Status Families in an Era of Reform.* Washington, DC: Urban Institute.

FOERSTRER, AMY. 2004. Race, Identity, and Belonging: "Blackness" and the Struggle for Solidarity in a Multiethnic Labor Union. *Social Problems* 51 (3): 386–409.

FONG, STANLEY L. M. 2002. *The Contemporary Asian American Experience: Beyond the Model Minority.* 2nd ed. Upper Saddle River, NJ: Prentice Hall.

FORDHAM, SIGNITHIA, AND JOHN U. OGBU. 1986. Black Students' School Success: Coping with the Burden of "Acting White." *Urban Review* 18 (3): 176–206.

FOX, STEPHEN. 1990. *The Unknown Internment.* Boston, MA: Twayne.

FREEDMAN, SAMUEL G. 2004. Latino Parents Decry Bilingual Programs. *New York Times,* July 14, A21.

FRYER, RONALD G. 2006. Acting White. *Education Next* (Winter): 53–59.

FULLER, CHEVON. 1998. Service Redlining. *Civil Rights Journal* 3 (Fall): 33–36.

GALLAGHER, MARI. 2005. *Chain Reaction: Income, Race, and Access to Chicago's Major Player Grocers.* Chicago: Metro Chicago Information Center.

GALLUP. 2008. *Immigration,* www.gallup.com (accessed February 6, 2008).

GANS, HERBERT J. 1979. Symbolic Ethnicity: The Future of Ethnic Groups and Cultures in America. *Ethnic and Racial Studies* 2 (January): 1–20.

GERTH, H. H., AND C. WRIGHT MILLS. 1958. *From Max Weber: Essays in Sociology.* New York: Galaxy Books.

GIBSON, CAMPBELL, AND KAY JUNG. 2006. Historical Census Statistics on the Foreign-Born Population of the United States: 1850 to 2000. Working Paper No. 81. Washington, DC: Bureau of the Census.

GIRARDELLI, DAVIDE. 2004. Commodified Identities: The Myth of Italian Food in the United States. *Journal of Communication Inquiry* 28 (October): 307–324.

GLEASON, PHILIP. 1980. American Identity and Americanization. In *Harvard Encyclopedia of American Ethnic Groups,* ed. Stephen Therstromm, 31–58. Cambridge: Belknap Press of Harvard University Press.

GOERING, JOHN M. 1971. The Emergence of Ethnic Interests: A Case of Serendipity. *Social Forces* 48 (March): 379–384.

GOMPERS, SAMUEL, AND HERMAN GUSTADT. 1908. *Meat vs. Rice: American Manhood against Asiatic Coolieism: Which Shall Survive?* San Francisco: Asiatic Exclusion League.

GOODSTEIN, LAURIE. 2005. Issuing Rebuke: Judge Rejects Teaching of Intelligent Design. *New York Times,* December 21, A1, A21.

GORDON, MILTON M. 1964. *Assimilation in American Life: The Role of Race, Religion, and National Origins.* New York: Oxford University Press.

GRAY-LITTLE, BERNADETTE, AND HAFDAHL, ADAM R. 2000. Factors Influencing Racial Comparisons of Self-Esteem: A Qualitative Review. *Psychological Bulletin* 126 (1): 26–54.

GREATER NEW ORLEANS FAIR HOUSING ACTION CENTER. 2007. *For Rent, Unless You're Black.* New Orleans: Greater New Orleans Fair Housing Action Center.

GREELEY, ANDREW M. 1981. *The Irish Americans: The Rise to Money and Power.* New York: Harper & Row.

GREENHOUSE, LINDA. 1996. Case on Government Interface in Religion Tied to Separation of Powers. *New York Times,* October 16, C23.

———. 2003. Justices Back Affirmative Action by 5–4, but Wider Vote Bans a Racial Point System. *New York Times,* June 24, A1, A25.

———. 2007. Justices Ruling Limits Lawsuits on Pay Disparity. *New York Times,* May 30, A1, A18.

GRIECO, ELIZABETH M., AND RACHEL C. CASSIDY. 2001. *Overview of Race and Hispanic Origin.* Current Population Reports Ser. CENBR/01-1. Washington, DC: U.S. Government Printing Office.

GUGLIELMO, JENNIFER, AND SALERNO SALVATORE, EDS. 2003. *Are Italians White?* New York: Routledge.

HAMM, JILL V., B. BRADFORD BROWN, AND DANIEL J. HECK. 2005. Bridging the Ethnic Divide: Students and School Characteristics in African American, Asian-Descent, Latino,

and White Adolescents' Cross-Ethnic Friend Nominations. *Journal of Research on Adolescence* 15 (1): 21–46.

HAGENBAUGH, BARBARA. 2006. Sending Money Back Has Vital Role. *USA Today* (April 11): 2B.

HAKIMZADEH, SHIRIN, AND D'VERA COHN. 2007. *English Usage among Hispanics in the United States.* Washington, DC: Pew Hispanic Center.

HAMILTON, SCOTT. 2008. Tilghman's Career Hangs in Balance. *Golfweek* (January 10): 6, 8.

HANDLIN, OSCAR. 1951. *The Uprooted: The Epic Story of the Great Migrations that Made the American People.* New York: Grossett and Dunlap.

HANSEN, MARCUS LEE. 1952. The Third Generation in America. *Commentary* (November 14): 493–500.

HARLOW, CAROLINE WOLF. 2005. Hate Crime Reported by Victims and Police. Bureau of Justice Statistics Special Report, November, http://www.ojp.usdoj.gov/bjs/pub/pdf/hcrvp.pdf (accessed May 8, 2008).

HASSRICK, ELIZABETH MCGHEE. 2007. The Transnational Production of White Ethnic Symbolic Identities. Paper presented at the Annual Meeting of the American Sociological Association.

HECHINGER, FRED M. 1987. Bilingual Programs. *New York Times* (April 7): C10.

HENNESSY-FISKE, MOLLY. 2006. The Town that Didn't Look Away. *Los Angeles Times,* July 23.

HERRNSTEIN, RICHARD J., AND CHARLES MURRAY. 1994. *The Bell Curve: Intelligence and Class Structure in American Life.* New York: Free Press.

HILL, HERBERT. 1967. The Racial Practices of Organized Labor: The Age of Gompers and after. In *Employment, Race, and Poverty,* eds. Arthur M. Ross and Herbert Hill, 365–402. New York: Harcourt, Brace & World.

HIRSLEY, MICHAEL. 1991. Religious Display Needs Firm Count. *Chicago Tribune,* December 20, Section 2, 10.

HOCHSCHILD, JENNIFER L. 1995. *Facing up to the American Dream: Race, Class, and the Soul of the Nation.* Princeton, NJ: Rutgers University Press.

HOFFER, THOMAS B., ET AL. 2001. *Doctorate Recipients from United States Universities: Summary Report 2000.* Chicago, IL: National Opinion Research Center.

HONDAGNEU-SOTELO, PIERETTE, ED. 2003. *Gender and U.S. Immigration: Contemporary Trends.* Berkeley: University of California Press.

HOOKS, BELL. 1984. *Feminist Theory: From Margin to Center.* Boston, MA: South End Press.

HUGHLETT, MIKE. 2006. Judge: Craigslist Not Liable for Ad Content. *Chicago Tribune,* November 16, Section 3, 1.

HUNTINGTON, SAMUEL P. 1993. The Clash of Civilizations? *Foreign Affairs* 73, no. 3 (Summer): 22–49.

———. 1996. *The Clash of Civilizations and the Remaking of World Order.* New York: Simon & Schuster.

HURH, WON MOO, AND KWANG CHUNG KIM. 1989. The "Success" Image of Asian Americans: Its Validity, and Its

Practical and Theoretical Implications. *Ethnic and Racial Studies* (October 12): 512–538.

IGNATIEV, NOEL. 1994. Treason to Whiteness Is Loyalty to Humanity. Interview with Noel Ignatiev. *Utne Reader* (November–December): 83–86.

———. 1995. *How the Irish became White.* New York: Routledge.

Institute for Social Policy and Understanding. 2004. *The USA Patriot Act: Impact on the Arab and Muslim American Community.* Clinton Township, MI: ISPU.

International Fund for Agricultural Development. 2007. *Sending Money Home: Worldwide Remittance Flows to Developing and Transition Countries.* Rome, Italy: IFAD.

ISHII, MIKU. 2006. Multicultural Autobiography. Unpublished Paper. Chicago, IL: DePaul University.

JAROSZYŃSKA-KIRCHMANN. 2004. *The Exile Mission: The Polish Political Diaspora and Polish Americans, 1939–1956.* Athens: Ohio University Press.

JEFFERYS, KELLY. 2007. *Refugees of Asylees: 2006.* Washington, DC: Office of Immigration Statistics.

JOHNSON, KEVIN. 1992. German Ancestry Is Strong beneath Milwaukee Surface. *USA Today,* August 4, 9A.

———. 2004. *Immigration and Civil Rights.* Philadelphia, PA: Temple University Press.

JOHNSTON, TIM. 2008. "Australia to Apologize to Aborigines for Past Mistreatment." *New York Times,* January 31.

JONES, NICHOLAS, AND AMY SYMENS SMITH. 2001. *The Two or More Races Population: 2000. Series C2KBR/01-6.* Washington, DC: U.S. Government Printing Office.

KAGAN, JEROME. 1971. The Magical Aura of the IQ. *Saturday Review of Literature* 4 (December 4): 92–93.

KANEYA, RUI. 2004. Native Tongue. *The Chicago Reporter* (November 7): 6–7.

KAO, GRACE. 2006. Where Are the Asian and Hispanic Victims of Katrina? *DuBois Review* 3 (1): 223–231.

KAO, GRACE, AND KARA JOYNER. 2004. Do Race and Ethnicity Matter Among Friends? *Sociological Quarterly* 45(3): 557–573.

KAO, GRACE, AND ELIZABETH VAQUERA. 2006. The Salience of Racial and Ethnic Identification in Friendship Choice among Hispanic Adolescents. *Hispanic Journal of Behavioral Sciences* 28 (February): 23–47.

KATZ, MICHAEL B., MARK J. STERN, AND JAMIE J. FADER. 2007. The Mexican Immigration Debate. *Social Science History* 3 (Summer): 157–189.

KIBRIA, NAZLI. 2002. Becoming Asian American: Second-Generation Chinese and Korean American Identities. Baltimore: Johns Hopkins Press.

KILSON, MARTIN. 1995. Affirmative Action. *Dissent* 42 (Fall): 469–470.

KING, MEREDITH L. 2007. *Immigrants in the U.S. Health Care System.* Washington, DC: Center for American Progress.

KING, PETER. 2004. Their Spiritual Thirst Found a Desert Spring. *Los Angeles Times,* August 4, A1, A16, A17.

KINLOCH, GRAHAM C. 1974. *The Dynamics of Race Relations: A Sociological Analysis.* New York: McGraw-Hill.

KIVISTO, PETER. 2008. *Third Generation Principle.* In vol. 3 of *Encyclopedia of Race, Ethnicity, and Society,* ed. Richard T. Schaefer, pp. 1302–1304. Thousand Oaks, CA: Sage.

KLEIN, JENNIFER. 2008. Iraqi Americans. In vol. 2 of *Encyclopedia of Race, Ethnicity, and Society,* ed. Richard T. Schaefer, pp. 754–755. Thousand Oaks, CA: Sage.

KOCH, WENDY. 2006. Push for "Official" English Heats up. *USA Today,* October 9, 1A.

KOCHHAR, RAKESH. 2006. *Growth in the Foreign-Born Workforce and Employment of the Native Born.* Washington, DC: Pew Hispanic Center.

KRAYBILL, DONALD B. 2001. *The Riddle of Amish Culture.* Rev. ed. Baltimore: Johns Hopkins University Press.

———, ED. 2003. *The Amish and the State.* 2nd ed. Baltimore: John Hopkins University Press.

KRAYBILL, DONALD B. 2008. Amish. In vol. 1 of *Encyclopedia of Race, Ethnicity, and Society,* ed. Richard T. Schaefer, pp. 68–71. Thousand Oaks, CA: Sage.

KRAYBILL, DONALD B., AND STEVEN M. NOLT. 1995. *Amish Enterprises: From Plows to Profits.* Baltimore: Johns Hopkins Press.

KROEGER, BROOKE. 2004. When a Dissertation Makes a Difference, www.racematters.org/devahpager.htm (accessed January 15, 2005).

KUPPER, JR., WILLIAM P. 2008. We're Sorry, http://www.golfweek.com (accessed January 21, 2008).

LAL, BARBARA BALLIS. 1995. Symbolic Interaction Theories. *American Behavioral Scientist* 38 (January): 421–441.

LANDALE, NANCY S., NIMFA B. OGENA, AND BRIDGET K. GORMAN. 2000. Migration and Infant Death: Assimilation or Selective Migration among Puerto Ricans? *American Sociological Review* 65 (December): 888–909.

LAPIERE, RICHARD T. 1934. Attitudes vs. Actions. *Social Forces* (October 13): 230–237.

———. 1969. Comment of Irwin Deutscher's Looking Backward. *American Sociologist* 4 (February): 41–42.

LARA, MARIELENA, CRISTINA GRAMBOA, M. IYA KAHRAMANIAN, LEO S. MORALES, AND DAVID E. HAYES BAUTISTA. 2005. Acculturation and Latino Health in the United States: A Review of the Literature and Its Sociopolitical Context. In *Annual Review of Public Health 2005,* 367–397. Palo Alto, CA: Annual Reviews Inc.

LEAVITT, PAUL. 2002. Bush Calls Agent Kicked off Flight "Honorable Fellow." *USA Today.* January 8.

LEE, J. J., AND MARION R. CASEY. 2006. *Making the Irish American.* New York: New York University Press.

LEE, JENNIFER, AND FRANK D. BEAN. 2007. Redrawing the Color Line. *City and Community* 6 (March): 49–62.

LEEHOTZ, ROBERT. 1995. Is Concept of Race a Relic? *Los Angeles Times,* April 15, A1, A14.

LEINWAND, DONNA. 2004. Muslims See New Opposition to Building Mosques since 9/11. *USA Today,* March 9, A1, A2.

LEONARD, KAREN ISAKSEN. 2003. *Muslims in the United States: The State of Research*. New York: Russell Sage Foundation.

LEVITT, PEGGY, AND B. NADYA JAWORSKY. 2007. Transnational Migration Studies: Past Developments and Future Trends. *Annual Review of Sociology* 33:129–156.

LEWIN, TAMAR. 2006. Campaign to End Race Preferences Splits Michigan. *New York Times,* October 31, A1, A19.

LEWIS, AMANDA E. 2004. "What Group?" Studying Whites and Whiteness in the Era of "Color-Blindness." *Sociological Theory* 22 (December): 623–646.

LEWIS, GREGORY. 2007. Love Sees No Color. *Sun Sentinel* (June 16): 1A, 17A.

Lewis Mumford Center. 2001. *Ethnic Diversity Grows, Neighborhood Integration Is at a Standstill*. Albany, NY: Lewis Mumford Center.

LEWONTIN, RICHARD. 2005. The Fallacy of Racial Medicine. *Genewatch* 18 (July–August): 5–7, 17.

LICHTBLAU, ERIC. 2005. Profiling Report Leads to a Clash and a Demotion. *New York Times,* August 24, A1, A9.

LICHTENBERG, JUDITH. 1992. Racism in the Head, Racism in the World. *Report from the Institute for Philosophy and Public Policy* 12 (Spring–Summer): 3–5.

LINDNER, EILEEN, ED. 2008. *Yearbook of American and Canadian Churches 2008*. Nashville, TN: Abingdon Press.

LINDSLEY, SHERYL L. 1998. Organizational Interventions to Prejudice. In *Communicating Prejudice,* ed. Michael L. Hecht, 302–310. Thousand Oaks, CA: Sage Publications.

LODDER, LEEANN, SCOTT McFARLAND, AND DIANA WHITE. 2003. *Racial Preference and Suburban Employment Opportunities*. Chicago, IL: Chicago Urban League.

LOEWEN, JAMES W. 2005. *Sundown Towns: A Hidden Dimension of American Racism*. New York: The New Press.

———— AND RICHARD T. SCHAEFER. 2008. Sundown Towns. In vol. 3, *Encyclopedia of Race, Ethnicity and Society,* ed. Richard T. Schaefer, pp. 1282–1285. Thousand Oaks, CA: Sage.

LOGAN, JOHN R. 2001a. *The New Latinos: Who They Are, Where They Are*. Albany: Lewis Mumford Center for Comparative Urban and Regional Research, State University of New York at Albany.

————. 2001b. *The New Ethnic Enclaves in America Suburbs*. Albany, NY: Lewis Mumford Center for Comparative Urban and Regional Research, State University of New York at Albany.

LOGAN, JOHN R., BRIAN J. STULTS, AND REYNOLDS FARLEY. 2004. Segregation of Minorities in the Metropolis: Two Decades of Change. *Demography* 41 (February): 1–22.

LOGAN, JOHN R., ALBA RICHARD D., AND WERQUAN ZHANG. 2002. Immigrant Enclaves and Ethnic Communities in New York and Los Angeles. *American Sociological Review* 67 (April): 299–322.

LOGAN, RAYFORD W. 1954. *The Negro in American Life and Thought: The Nadir, 1877–1901*. New York: Dial Press.

LOPATA, HELENA ZNANIECKI. 1994. *Polish Americans*. 2nd ed. New Brunswick, NJ: Transaction Books.

LOPEZ, DAVID, AND YEN ESPIRITU. 1990. Panethnicity in the United States: A Theoretical Framework. *Ethnic and Racial Studies* (April 13): 198–224.

LOPEZ, JULIE AMPARANO. 1992. Women Face Glass Walls as Well as Ceilings. *Wall Street Journal,* March 3.

LOPEZ, STEVE. 2007. Fires in Malibu ignite rage on the web. *Los Angeles Times,* October 22.

LOWENSTEIN, ROGER. 2006. What Is She Really Doing to American Jobs and Wages? *New York Times Magazine* (July 9): 36–43ff.

LUCONI, STEFANO. 2001. *From Peasant to White Ethnics: The Italian Experience in Philadelphia*. Albany: State University Press of New York.

MACK, RAYMOND W. 1996. Whose Affirmative Action? *Society* 33 (March–April): 41–43.

MacLEAN, VICKY M., AND JOYCE E. WILLIAMS. 2008. Shifting Paradigms: Sociological Presentations of Race. *American Behavioral Scientist* 51 (January): 599–624.

MANING, ANITA. 1997. Troubled Waters: Environmental Racism Suit Makes Waves. *USA Today,* July 31, A1.

MANNING, ROBERT D. 1995. Multiculturalism in the United States: Clashing Concepts, Changing Demographics, and Competing Cultures. *International Journal of Group Tensions* (Summer): 117–168.

MARSHALL, PATRICK. 2001. Religion in Schools. *CQ Research* 11 (July 12): 1–24.

MARUBBIO, M. ELISE. 2006. *Killing the Indian Maiden: Images of Native American Women in Film*. Lexington: University Press of Kentucky.

MARX, KARL, AND FREDERICK ENGELS. 1955. *Selected Works in Two Volumes*. Moscow: Foreign Languages Publishing House.

MASON, HEATHER. 2003. *Does Bilingual Education Translate to Success?* http://www.gallup.com (accessed July 8, 2003).

MASSEY, DOUGLAS. 2004. Segregation and Stratification: A Biosocial Perspective. *Dubois Review* 1 (1): 7–25.

MASSEY, DOUGLAS, AND NANCY A. DENTON. 1993. *American Apartheid: Segregation and the Making of the Underclass*. Cambridge, MA: Harvard University Press.

MASSEY, DOUGLAS, AND MARGARITA MOONEY. 2007. The Effects of America's Three Affirmative Action Programs on Academic Performance. *Social Problems* 54 (1): 99–117.

MAURO, TONY. 1995. Ruling Helps Communities Set Guidelines. *USA Today,* December 21, A1, A2.

MAYER, EGON. 2001. *American Religious Identification Survey*. New York: The Graduate Center of the City University of New York.

McGHEE, BERNARD. 2006. Young Resigns from Wal-Mart Committee Amid Criticism of Remarks. *Chicago Tribune,* August 19, 3.

McINTOSH, PEGGY. 1988. *White Privilege: Unpacking the Invisible Knapsack*. Wellesley, MA: Wellesley College Center for Research on Women.

McKinney, K. D. 2003. I Feel "Whiteness" When I Hear People Blaming Whites: Whiteness as Cultural Victimization. *Race and Society* 6:39–55.

McNamara, Mary. 2006. Friends Tell of Complicated Man. *Chicago Tribune,* August 4, 8.

Meagher, Timothy J. 2005. *The Columbia Guide to Irish American History.* New York: Columbia University Press.

Merton, Robert K. 1949. Discrimination and the American Creed. In *Discrimination and National Welfare,* ed. Robert M. MacIver, 99–126. New York: Harper & Row.

———. 1976. *Sociological Ambivalence and Other Essays.* New York: Free Press.

Miller, Norman. 2002. Personalization and the Promise of Contact Theory. *Journal of Social Issues* 58 (Summer): 387–410.

Mocha, Frank, ed. 1998. *American "Polonia" and Poland.* New York: Columbia University Press.

Mock, Brentin. 2008. Immigrant Backlash: Hate Crimes against Latinos Flourish, http://www.splcenter.org (accessed January 28, 2008).

Monkman, Karen, Margaret Ronald, and Florence Délimon Thérámène. 2005. Social and Cultural Capital in an Urban Latino School Community. *Urban Education* 40 (January): 4–33.

Montagu, Ashley. 1972. *Statement on Race.* New York: Oxford University Press.

Mosisa, Abraham T. 2006. Foreign-Born Workforce, 2004: A Visual Essay. *Monthly Labor Review* 129 (July): 48–56.

Mostofi, Nilou. 2003. Who We Are: The Perplexity of Iranian-American Identity. *Sociological Quarterly* 44 (Fall): 681–703.

Moulder, Frances V. 1996. Teaching about Race and Ethnicity: A Message of Despair, or a Message of Hope? Paper presented at the annual meeting of the American Sociological Association, New York.

Mouw, Ted, and Barbara Entwisle. 2006. Residential Segregation and Interracial Friendship in Schools. *American Journal of Sociology* 112 (September): 394–441.

Mullen, Fitzhugh. 2005. The Metrics of the Physician Brain Drain. *New England Journal of Medicine* 353 (October 27): 1810–1818.

Murphy, Dean, and Neela Banerjee. 2005. Catholics in U.S. Keep Faith but Live with Contradictions. *New York Times,* April 11, A1, A16.

Myers, Dowell, John Pitkin, and Julie Park. 2004. *California's Immigrants Turn the Corner. Urban Initiative Policy Relief.* Los Angeles: University of Southern California.

Myrdal, Gunnar. 1944. *An American Dilemma: The Negro Problem and Modern Democracy.* New York: Harper & Row.

Naimark, Norman M. 2004. Ethnic Cleaning, History of. In *International Encyclopedia of Social and Behavioral Sciences,* eds. N. J. Smelser and P. B. Baltes, 4799–4802. New York: Elsevier.

Nash, Manning. 1962. Race and the Ideology of Race. *Current Anthropology* 3 (June): 285–288.

National Conference of Christians and Jews (NCCJ). 1994. *Taking America's Pulse.* New York: NCCJ.

National Italian American Foundation. 2006. Stop Ethnic Bashing. *New York Times,* January, http://www.niaf.org/news/index.asp?id=422 (accessed June 4, 2008).

Navarro, Mireya. 1998. With a Vote for "None of the Above," Puerto Ricans Endorse Island's Status Quo. *New York Times,* December 14, A12.

NCAA (National Collegiate Athletic Association). 2005. *NCAA Executive Committee Issues Guidelines for Use of Native American Mascots at Championship Events.* August 5, 2005, http://www.ncaa.org (accessed February 1, 2006).

New America Media. 2007. *Deep Decisions, Shared Destiny.* San Francisco, CA: New America Media.

Newman, Maria. 2007. Jena, La. *New York Times,* September 24.

Newman, William M. 1973. *American Pluralism: A Study of Minority Groups and Social Theory.* New York: Harper & Row.

Newport, Frank. 2007. Questions and Answers "about Americans' Religion," www.gallup.com (accessed February 7, 2008).

New York Times. 1917a. Illiteracy Is Not All Alike. February 8, 12.

———. 1917b. The Immigration Bill Veto. January 31, 210.

———. 1991. For 2, an Answer to Years of Doubt on Use of Peyote in Religious Rite. July 9, A14.

———. 2005a. U.S. Panel Backs Nuclear Dump on Indian Reservation in Utah. September 10, A10.

———. 2005b. Warnings Raised about Exodus of Philippine Doctors and Nurses. November 27, 13.

Niebuhr, Gustav. 1998. Southern Baptists Declare Wife Should "Submit" to Her Husband. *New York Times.*

Office of Immigration Statistics. 2006. *2004 Yearbook of Immigration Statistics.* Washington, DC: U.S. Government Printing Office.

———. 2007. *2006 Yearbook of Immigration Statistics.* Washington, DC: U.S. Department of Homeland Security.

Ogbu, John U. 2004. Collective Identity and the Burden of "Acting White" in Black History, Community, and Education. *Urban Review* 36 (March): 1–35.

Ogbu, John U. with Astrid Davis. 2003. *Black American Students in an Affluent Suburb: A Study of Academic Disengagement.* Mahwah, NJ: Lawrence Erlbaum Associates.

Ogunwole, Stella V. 2006. *We the People: American Indians and Alaska Natives in the United States. Censr-28.* Washington, DC: U.S. Government Printing Office.

Ohnuma, Keiko. 1991. Study Finds Asians Unhappy at CSU. *AsianWeek* 12 (August 8): 5.

Oliver, Melvin L., and Thomas M. Shapiro. 2006. *Black Wealth/White Wealth.* 10th anniversary ed. New York: Routledge.

OMI, MICHAEL, AND HOWARD WINANT. 1994. *Racial Forma-tion in the United States*. 2nd ed. New York: Routledge.

O'NEILL, MAGGIE. 2008. Authoritarian Personality. In vol. 1 of *Encyclopedia of Race, Ethnicity, and Society*, ed. Richard T. Schaefer, pp. 119–121. Thousand Oaks, CA: Sage.

ORFIELD, GARY. 2007. The Supreme Court and the Resegre-gation of America's Schools. *Focus* (September–October): 1, 15–16.

ORFIELD, GARY, AND CHUNGMEI LEE. 2007. *Historic Reversals, Accelerating Resegregation, and the Need for New Integra-tion Strategies*. Los Angeles: Civil Rights Project, UCLA.

ORFIELD, GARY, AND HOLLY J. LIEBOWITZ, EDS. 1999. *Religion, Race, and Justice in a Changing America*. New York: The Twentieth Century Fund.

PAGE, SCOTT E. 2007. *The Difference: How the Power of Diversity Creates Better Groups, Firms, Schools, and Soci-eties*. Princeton, NJ: Princeton University Press.

PAGER, DEVAH. 2003. The Mark of a Criminal. *American Journal of Sociology* 108: 937–975.

PAGER, DEVAH. 2007a. *Marked: Race, Crime, and Finding Work in an Era of Mass Incarceration*. Chicago: University of Chicago Press.

———. 2007b. The Use of Field Experiments for Studies of Employment Discrimination: Contributions, Critiques, and Directions for the Future. *Annals* 609 (January): 104–133.

PAGER, DEVAH, AND LINCOLN QUILLIAN. 2005. Walking the Talk? What Employers Say Versus What They Do. *American Sociological Review* 70 (3): 355–380.

PAGER, DEVAH, AND BRUCE WESTERN. 2006. Race at Work: Real-ities of Race and Criminal Record in the NYC Job Market. Report prepared for the 50th Anniversary of the New York City Museum on Human Rights, http://www.princeton.edu/~pager/race_at_work.pdf (accessed June 3, 2008).

PAIK, NANCY. 2001. *One Nation: Islam in America,* http://www.channelonenews.com/special/islam/media.html (accessed March 15, 2001).

PARK, ROBERT E. 1928. Human Migration and the Marginal Man. *American Journal of Sociology* 33 (May): 881–893.

———. 1950. Race and Culture: Essays in the Sociology of Contemporary Man. New York: Free Press.

PARK, ROBERT E., AND ERNEST W. BURGESS. 1921. *Introduction to the Science of Sociology*. Chicago: University of Chicago Press.

PARRILLO, VINCENT. 2008. Italian Americans. In vol. 2 of *Encyclopedia of Race, Ethnicity, and Society,* ed. Richard T. Schaefer, pp. 766–771. Thousand Oaks, CA: Sage.

PASSEL, JEFFERY S. 2005. *Unauthorized Migrants: Numbers and Characteristics*. Washington, DC: Pew Hispanic Center.

———. 2006. *The Size and Characteristics of the Unautho-rized Migrant Population in the Us: Estimates Based on the March 2005 Current Population Survey*. Washington, DC: Pew Hispanic Center.

PASSEL, JEFFERY S., AND D'VERA COHN. 2008. *U.S. Population Projections: 2005–2050*. Washington, DC: Pew Research Center.

PASTOR, JR., MANUEL, RACHEL MORELLO-FROSCH, AND JAMES L. SAAD. 2005. The Air Is Always Cleaner on the Other Side: Race, Space, and Ambient Air Toxics Exposure in Cali-fornia. *Journal of Urban Affairs* 27 (2): 127–148.

PEAR, ROBERT. 2007. '86 Law Looms over Immigration Fight. *New York Times,* June 12, A15.

PEARSON, BRYAN. 2006. Brain Drain Human Resource Crisis. *The Africa Report* (October): 95–98.

PEASE, JOHN, AND LEE MARTIN. 1997. Want Ads and Jobs for the Poor: A Glaring Mismatch. *Sociological Forum* 12 (4): 545–564.

PEDDER, SOPHIE. 1991. Social Isolation and the Labour Market: Black Americans in Chicago. Paper presented at the Chicago Urban Poverty and Family Life Conference, Chicago.

PELLOW, DAVID NAGUIB, AND ROBERT J. BRULLE. 2007. Poison-ing the Planet: The Struggle for Environmental Justice. *Contexts* 6 (Winter): 37–41.

PERLMANN, JOEL. 2005. *Italians Then, Mexicans Now: Immi-grant Origins and Second-Generation Progress, 1890–2000*. New York: Russell Sage Foundation.

PERRY, BARBARA, ED. 2003. *Hate and Bias Crime: A Reader.* New York: Routledge.

Pew Forum on Religion and Public Life. 2008. *U.S. Reli-gious Landscape Survey*. Washington, DC: Pew Forum on Religion and Public Life.

PINCUS, FRED L. 2003. *Reverse Discrimination: Dismantling the Myth*. Boulder, CO: Lynne Rienner.

———. 2008. *Reverse Discrimination*. In vol. 3 of *Encyclopedia of Race, Ethnicity, and Society,* ed. Richard T. Schaefer, pp. 1159–1161. Thousand Oaks, CA: Sage.

POLZIN, THERESITA. 1973. *The Polish Americans: Whence and Whither*. Pulaski, WI: Franciscan Publishers.

PORTER, EDUARDO. 2005. Illegal Immigrants Are Bolstering Social Security with Billions. *New York Times,* April 5, A1, C6.

PORTES, ALEJANDRO. 1998. Social Capital: Its Origins and Applications in Modern Society. In *Annual Review of Soci-ology 1998*, 1–24. Palo Alto, CA: Annual Review.

———. 2006. Paths of Assimilation in the Second Genera-tion. *Sociological Forum* 21 (September): 499–503.

PORTES, ALEJANDRO, AND RUBÉN G. RUMBAUT. 2006. *Immigrant America*. 3rd ed. Berkeley and Los Angeles, CA: University of California Press.

POWELL-HOPSON, DARLENE, AND HOPSON, DEREK. 1988. Impli-cations of Doll Color Preferences among Black Preschool Children and White Preschool Children. *Journal of Black Psychology* 14 (February): 57–63.

PRESTON, JULIA. 2007a. Judge Voids Ordinance on Illegal Immigrants. *New York Times,* July 27.

———. 2007b. Polls Surveys Ethnic Views among Chief Minorities. *New York Times,* December 13.

PUBLIC BROADCASTING SYSTEM. 1998. *Weekend Edition: National Public Radio with Eric Westervelt and Scott Simon.* May 30.

PURDY, MATTHEW. 2001. Ignoring and Then Embracing the Truth about Racial Profiling. *New York Times,* March 11.

QUILLIAN, LINCOLN. 2006. New Approaches to Understanding Racial Prejudice and Discrimination. In *Annual Reviews of Sociology 2006*, ed. Karen S. Cook, 299–328. Palo Alto CA: Annual Reviews Inc.

RAYBON, PATRICIA. 1989. A Case for "Severe Bias." *Newsweek* 114 (October 2): 11.

READ, JEN'NAN GHAZAL, AND MICHAEL O. EMERSON. 2005. Racial Context, Black Immigration and the U.S. Black/White Health Disparity. *Social Forces* (September): 181–199.

REEVES, TERRANCE, AND CLAUDETTE BENNETT. 2003. *The Asian and Pacific Islander Population in the United States: March 2002.* Current Population Reports. Ser. P20. No. 540. Washington, DC: U.S. Government Printing Office.

RESKIN, BARBARA F. 1998. *The Realities of Affirmative Action in Employment.* Washington, DC: American Sociological Association.

RICH, MEGHAN ASHLIN. 2008. Resegregation. In vol. 3 of *Encyclopedia of Race, Ethnicity, and Society,* ed. Richard T. Schaefer, 1152–1153. Thousand Oaks, CA: Sage.

RICHMOND, ANTHONY H. 2002. Globalization: Implications for Immigrants and Refugees. *Ethnic and Racial Studies* 25 (September): 707–727.

RIDGEWAY, GREG. 2007. *Analysis of Racial Disparities in the New York Police Department's Stop, Question, and Frisk Pictures.* Santa Monica, CA: Rand.

ROBELEN, ERIK W. 2007. "Moment-of-Silence" Generates Loud Debate in Illinois. *Education Week* (October 24).

ROCKSTAR GAMES. 2008. Grand Theft Auto IV, www.rockstargames.com/IV/ (accessed January 28, 2008).

ROEDIGER, DAVID R. 1994. *Towards the Abolition of Whiteness: Essays on Race, Politics, and Working Class History (Haymarket).* New York: Verso Books.

———. 2006. Whiteness and Its Complications. *Chronicle of Higher Education* 52 (July 14): B6–B8.

ROOF, WADE CLARK. 2007. Introduction. *The Annals* 612 (July): 6–12.

ROSE, ARNOLD. 1951. *The Roots of Prejudice.* Paris: UNESCO.

RUSK, DAVID. 2001. *The "Segregation Tax": The Cost of Racial Segregation to Black Homeowners.* Washington, DC: Brookings Institution.

RYAN, WILLIAM. 1976. *Blaming the Victim.* Rev. ed. New York: Random House.

SAAD, LYDIA. 1998. America Divided over Status of Puerto Rico. *Gallup Poll Monthly* 390 (March): 278.

———. 2006a. Anti-Muslim Sentiments Fairly Commonplace. *The Gallup Poll* (August 10).

———. 2006b. "Grin and Bear It" Is Motto for Most Air Travelers, http://www.gallup.com/poll (accessed January 28, 2008).

SASSLER, SHARON L. 2006. School Participation among Immigrant Youths: The Case of Segmented Assimilation in the Early 20th Century. *Sociology of Education* 79 (January): 1–24.

SAULNY, SUSAN. 2007. After Darfur, Starting Anew in the Midwest. *New York Times,* April 2, A1, A20.

SCHAEFER, RICHARD T. 1976. *The Extent and Content of Racial Prejudice in Great Britain.* San Francisco, CA: R & E Research Associates.

———. 1986. Racial Prejudice in a Capitalist State: What Has Happened to the American Creed? *Phylon* 47 (September): 192–198.

———. 1992. People of Color: The "Kaleidoscope" May Be a Better Way to Describe America Than "the Melting Pot." *Peoria Journal Star* (January 19): A7.

———. 1996. Education and Prejudice: Unraveling the Relationship. *Sociological Quarterly* 37 (January): 1–16.

———. 2008. Nativism. In vol. 2 of *Encyclopedia of Race, Ethnicity, and Society,* ed. Richard T. Schaefer, pp. 969–970. Thousand Oaks, CA: Sage.

SCHAEFER, RICHARD T., AND WILLIAM ZELLNER. 2008. *Extraordinary Groups.* 8th ed. New York: Worth.

SCHMIDT, PETER. 2007. 5 More States May Curtail Affirmative Action. *Chronicle of Higher Education* 54 (October 19): A1, A19–A20.

SCHWARTZ, ALEX. 2001. *The State of Minority Access to Home Mortgage Lending: A Profile of the New York Metropolitan Area.* Washington, DC: Brooking Institution Center on Urban and Metropolitan Policy.

SCOTT, JANNY. 2003. Debating White Private Clubs Are Acceptable and Private. *New York Times,* December 8, Section 7, 5.

SENGUPTA, SOMINI. 1997. Asians' Advances Academically Are Found to Obscure a Need. *New York Times,* November 9, 17.

SENTENCING PROJECT. 2008. Felony Disenfranchisement, http://www.sentencingproject.org/IssueAreaHome.aspx?IssueID=4 (accessed January 30, 2008).

SHAFFER, AMANDA, AND ROBERT GOTTLIEB. 2007. Filling in "Food Deserts." *Los Angeles Times,* November 5, A17.

SHANKLIN, EUGENIA. 1994. *Anthropology and Race.* Belmont, CA: Wadsworth.

SHERIF, MUSAFER, AND CAROLYN SHERIF. 1969. *Social Psychology.* New York: Harper & Row.

SHESKIN, IRA M., AND ARNOLD DASHEFSKY. 2006. Jewish Population of the United States, 2006. In *American Jewish Year Book 2006,* eds. David Singer and Lawrence Grossman, 131–200. New York: American Jewish Committee.

SHIN, HYON S., AND ROSALIND BRUNO. 2003. *Language Use and English-Speaking Ability: 2000.* C2KBR-29. Washington, DC: U.S. Government Printing Office.

SIGELMAN, LEE, AND STEVEN A. TUCH. 1997. Metastereotypes: Blacks' Perception of Whites' Stereotypes of Blacks. *Public Opinion Quarterly* 61 (Spring): 87–101.

SIMANSKI, JOHN. 2007. *Naturalizations in the United States: 2006.* Washington, DC: Office of Immigration Statistics.

SIMMONS, ANN M. 2007. New Orleans' Blacks See Rental Block. *Los Angeles Times,* April 25, A16.

SIMON, STEPHANIE. 2004. Muslim Call to Prayer Stirs a Midwest Town. *Los Angeles Times,* May 8, A17.

SIMPSON, JACQUELINE C. 1995. Pluralism: The Evolution of a Nebulous Concept. *American Behavioral Scientist* 38 (January): 459–477.

SKULL VALLEY GOSHUTES. 2006. Home Page, www.skullvalleygoshutes.org.

SLAVIN, ROBERT E., AND ALAN CHEUNG. 2003. *Effective Reading Programs for English Language Learners.* Baltimore: Center for Research on the Education of Students Placed at Risk, Johns Hopkins University.

SMITH, TOM W. 1999. Measuring Inter-Racial Friendships: Experimental Comparisons. GSS Methodogical Report No. 91. Chicago: NORC.

———. 2001. *Religious Diversity in America: The Emergence of Muslims, Buddhists, Hindus, and Others.* New York: American Jewish Committee.

———. 2006. *Taking America's Pulse Iii. Intergroup Relations in Contemporary America.* Chicago, IL: National Opinion Research Center, University of Chicago.

Society for Human Resource Management. 2002. Diversity Aspects Covered in Corporate America. *New York Times Magazine* (August 15): 100.

SOLTERO, SONIA WHITE. 2004. *Dual Language: Teaching and Learning in Two Languages.* Boston, MA: Allyn & Bacon.

———. 2008. *Bilingual Education.* In vol. 1 of *Encyclopedia of Race, Ethnicity, and Society* edited by Richard T. Schaefer, 142–146. Thousand Oaks, CA: Sage.

SONG, TAE-HYON. 1991. *Social Contact and Ethnic Distance between Koreans and the U.S. Whites in the United States.* M.A. thesis, Western Illinois University, Macomb.

SOUTHERN, DAVID W. 1987. *Gunnar Myrdal and Black-White Relations.* Baton Rouge: Louisiana State University.

Southern Poverty Law Center. 2006b. Intelligence Project: Top Hate Watch Headlines, http://www.splcenter.org (accessed February 12, 2006).

STARK, RODNEY, AND GLOCK, CHARLES. 1968. *American Piety: The Nature of Religious Commitment.* Berkeley: University of California Press.

STEINBERG, STEPHEN. 2005. Immigration, African Americans, and Race Discourse. *New Politics* (Winter): 10.

STEINHAUER, JENNIFER. 2006. An Unwelcome Light on Club Where Legends Teed off. *New York Times,* September 23, A8.

STONE, EMILY. 2006. Hearing the Call—In Polish. *Chicago Tribune,* October 13, 15.

STONEQUIST, EVERETT V. 1937. *The Marginal Man: A Study in Personality and Culture Conflict.* New York: Scribner's.

STRAUSS, GARY. 2002. Good Old Boys' Network Still Rules Corporate Boards. *USA Today,* November 1, B1, B2.

STRETESKY, PAUL, AND MICHAEL LYNCH. 2002. Environmental Hazards and School Segregation in Hillsborough County, Florida, 1987–1999. *Sociological Quarterly* 43:553–573.

SULLIVAN, KEITH. 2005. Desperate Moves. *Washington Post National Weekly Edition.* (March 14): 9–10.

SUM, ANDREW, PAUL HARRINGTON, AND ISHWAR KHATIWDA. 2006. *The Impact of New Immigrants on Young Native-Born Workers, 2000–2005.* Washington, DC: Center for Immigration Studies.

SUMNER, WILLIAM G. 1906. *Folkways.* New York: Ginn.

TAFOYA, SONYA M., HANS JOHNSON, AND LAURA E. HILL. 2004. *Who Chooses to Choose Two?* New York: Russell Sage Foundation and Population Reference Bureau.

TAKAKI, RONALD. 1989. *Strangers from a Different Shore: A History of Asian Americans.* Boston, MA: Little, Brown.

TAYLOR, STUART, JR. 1987. High Court Backs Basing Promotion on a Racial Quota. *New York Times,* February 26, 1, 14.

———. 1988. Justices Back New York Law Ending Sex Bias by Big Clubs. *New York Times,* June 21, A1, A18.

TERBA, HARALLAMB. 2004. My Name Is Harallamb Terba. In *An Immigrant Class: Oral Histories from Chicago's Newest Immigrants,* ed. Jeff Libman, 184–195. Chicago: Flying Kite.

THOMAS, WILLIAM ISAAC. 1923. *The Unadjusted Girl.* Boston, MA: Little, Brown.

THOMAS, WILLIAM ISAAC, AND FLORIAN ZNANIECKI. 1996. *The Polish Peasant in Europe and America,* ed. Eli Zaretsky. 5 vols. Urbana: University of Illinois Press.

THREADCRAFT, SHATEMA A. 2008. Welfare Queen. In vol. 3 of *Encyclopedia of Race, Ethnicity, and Society,* ed. Richard T. Schaefer, pp. 1384–1386. Thousand Oaks, CA: Sage.

THRUPKAEW, NOY. 2002. The Myth of the Model Minority. *The American Prospect* 13 (April 8): 38–47.

Time. 1974. Are You a Jew? 104 (September 2): 56, 59.

TOUGH, PAUL. 2004. The "Acting White" Myth. *New York Times,* December 12.

TRUJILLO-PAGAN, NICOLE. 2006. Hazardous Constructions of Latino Immigrants in the Construction Industry: The Case of a Post-Katrina New Orleans. Paper presented at the annual meeting of the American Sociological Association, Montreal, Quebec, August 10.

TUMULTY, KAREN. 2006. Should They Stay or Should They Go? *Time* (April 10): 28–41.

TURE, KWAME, AND CHARLES HAMILTON. 1992. *Black Power: The Politics of Liberation.* New York: Vintage Books.

TURNER, MARGERY AUSTIN, FRED FREIBURG, ERIN GODFREY, CLARK HERBIG, DIANE K. LEVY, AND ROBIN R. SMITH. 2002. *All Other Things Being Equal: A Paired Testing Study of Mortgage Lending Institutions.* Washington, DC: Urban Institute.

TYSON, KAROLYN, WILLIAM DARITY, JR., AND DOMINI R. CASTELLINO. 2005. It's not "a Black Thing": Understanding the Burden of Acting White and Other Dilemmas of High Achievement. *American Sociological Review* 70 (August): 582–605.

UMBERGER, MARY. 2006. Mortgage Law under Fire. *Chicago Tribune,* August 18, 1, 8.

U.S. Committee for Refugees. 2003. *World Refugee Survey 2003.* Washington, DC: U.S. Committee for Refugees.

U.S. English. 2008. Welcome to U.S. English, Inc., www.us-english.org/inc (accessed February 9, 2008).

USDANSKY, MARGARET L. 1992. Old Ethnic Influences Still Play in Cities. *USA Today,* August 4, 9A.

VALDEZ, ZULEMA. 2006. Segmented Assimilation among Mexicans in the Southwest. *Sociological Quarterly* 47 (3): 397–424.

VERHOVEK, SAM HOWE. 1997. Racial Tensions in Suit Slowing Drive for "Environmental Justice." *New York Times,* September 7, 1, 16.

WAGLEY, CHARLES, AND MARVIN HARRIS. 1958. *Minorities in the New World: Six Case Studies.* New York: Columbia University Press.

WALLERSTEIN, IMMANUEL. 1974. *The Modern World System.* New York: Academic Press.

WARNER, W. LLOYD, AND LEO SROLE. 1945. *The Social Systems of American Ethnic Groups.* New Haven, CT: Yale University Press.

WATERS, MARY. 1990. *Ethnic Options. Choosing Identities in America.* Berkeley: University of California Press.

WEBER, MAX [1913–1922]. 1947. *The Theory of Social and Economic Organization,* tr. Henderson and T. Parsons. New York: Free Press.

WEINBERG, DANIEL H. 2007. Earnings by Gender: Evidence from Census 2000. *Monthly Labor Review* (July–August): 26–34.

WESSEL, DAVID. 2001. Hidden Costs of Brain Drain. *Wall Street Journal,* March 1, 1.

WHITE, JACK E. 1997. I'm Just Who I Am. *Time* 149 (May 5): 32–34, 36.

WICKHAM, DEWAYNE. 1993. Subtle Racism Thrives. *USA Today,* October 25, 2A.

WIEHLE, ASHLEY. 2008. "Prayer" Stays in School Law Title. *Chicago Tribune,* February 15, 3.

WILGOREN, JODI. 2001. On Campus and on Knees, Facing Mecca. *New York Times,* February 15, A1, A26.

WILLIAMS, KIM M. 2005. Multiculturalism and the Civil Rights Future. *Daedalus* 134 (1): 53–60.

WILLIAMS, PATRICIA J. 1997. *Of Race and Risk. The Nation Digital Edition,* http://www.thenation.com (accessed December 12, 1997).

WILLIAMS, TIMOTHY, AND NINA BERNSTEIN. 2007. After Uproar Toys 'R' Us Steers Ruling on Baby Prize. *New York Times,* January 7, 23.

WINANT, HOWARD. 1994. *Racial Conditions: Politics, Theory, Comparisons.* Minneapolis: University of Minnesota Press.

———. 2004. *The New Politics of Race: Globalism, Difference, Justice.* Minneapolis: University of Minnesota Press.

———. 2006. Race and Racism: Towards a Global Future. *Ethnic and Racial Studies* 29 (September): 986–1003.

WINSEMAN, ALBERT L. 2004. *U.S. Churches Looking for a Few White Men,* www.gallup.com (accessed July 27, 2004).

WINTER, S. ALAN. 2008. *Symbolic Ethnicity.* In vol. 3 of *Encyclopedia of Race, Ethnicity, and Society,* ed. Richard T. Schaefer, pp. 1288–1290. Thousand Oaks, CA: Sage.

WITHROW, BRIAN L. 2006. *Racial Profiling: From Rhetoric to Reason.* Upper Saddle River, NJ: Prentice Hall.

WITT, BERNARD. 2007. What Is a Hate Crime? *Chicago Tribune,* June 10, 1, 18.

WORKING, RUSSELL. 2007. Illegal Abroad, Hate Web Sites Thrive Here. *Chicago Tribune,* November 13, A1, A15.

WRONG, DENNIS H. 1972. How Important Is Social Class? *Dissent* 19 (Winter): 278–285.

WU, FRANK M. 2002. *Yellow: Race in America beyond Black and White.* New York: Basic Books.

WYMAN, MARK. 1993. *Round-Trip to America. The Immigrants Return to Europe, 1830–1930.* Ithaca, NY: Cornell University Press.

YANCEY, GEORGE. 2003. *Who Is White? Latinos, Asians, and the New Black–Nonblack Divide.* Boulder, CO: Lynne Rienner.

YINGER, JOHN. 1995. *Closed Doors, Opportunities Lost: The Continuing Costs of Housing Discrimination.* New York: Russell Sage Foundation.

YOSSO, TARA J. 2005. Whose Culture Has Capital? A Critical Race Theory Discussion of Community Cultural Wealth. *Race Ethnicity and Education* 8 (March): 69–91.

YOUNG, JEFFREY R. 2003. Researchers Change Racial Bias on the SAT. *Chronicle of Higher Education* (October 10): A34–A35.

YOUNGE, GARY. 2004. Election Trail. *Guardian Weekly* ((Manchester, England), November 4, 8.

ZANGWILL, ISRAEL. 1909. *The Melting Pot.* New York: Macmillan.

ZENG, ZHEN, AND YU XIE. 2004. Asian-Americans' Earnings Disadvantage Reexamined: The Role of Place of Education. *American Journal of Sociology* 109 (March): 1075–1108.

ZIA, HELEN. 2000. *Asian American Dreams: The Emergence of an American People.* New York: Farrar, Straus & Giroux.

ZHOU, MIN. 2004. Are Asian Americans Becoming "White?" *Contexts* 3 (Winter): 29–37.

ZHOU, MIN, AND YOSHINORI KAMO. 1994. An Analysis of Earnings Patterns for Chinese, Japanese, and Non-Hispanic White Males in the United States. *Sociological Quarterly* 35 (4): 581–602.

Photo Credits

Author Index

Subject Index